• Bartholomew •

GLASGOW

Streetfinder

COLOUR STREET ATLAS

Bartholomew

A Division of HarperCollins*Publishers*

Glasgow Colour Atlas
Contents

Legend

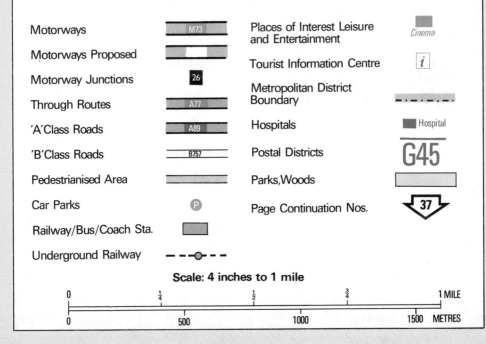

Motorways	M73	Places of Interest Leisure and Entertainment — Cinema
Motorways Proposed		Tourist Information Centre — i
Motorway Junctions	26	Metropolitan District Boundary
Through Routes	A77	Hospitals — Hospital
'A'Class Roads	A89	Postal Districts — G45
'B'Class Roads	B757	
Pedestrianised Area		Parks,Woods
Car Parks	P	Page Continuation Nos. — 37
Railway/Bus/Coach Sta.		
Underground Railway		

Scale: 4 inches to 1 mile

0   ¼   ½   ¾   1 MILE

0   500   1000   1500   METRES

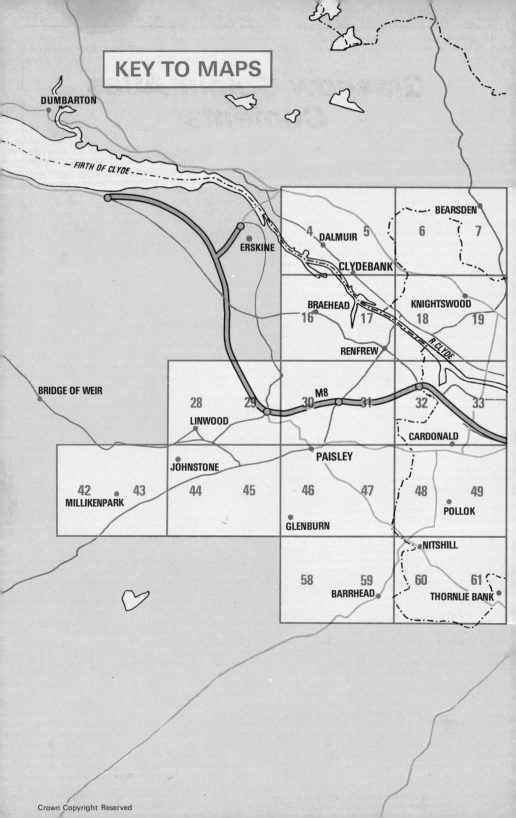

KEY TO MAPS

DUMBARTON

FIRTH OF CLYDE

ERSKINE

BEARSDEN

4 DALMUIR 5 6 7

CLYDEBANK

BRAEHEAD 16 17 KNIGHTSWOOD 18 19

RENFREW

R. CLYDE

BRIDGE OF WEIR

28 29 30 M8 31 32 33

LINWOOD

CARDONALD

JOHNSTONE PAISLEY

42 43 44 45 46 47 48 49
MILLIKENPARK POLLOK

GLENBURN

NITSHILL

58 59 60 61
BARRHEAD THORNLIE BANK

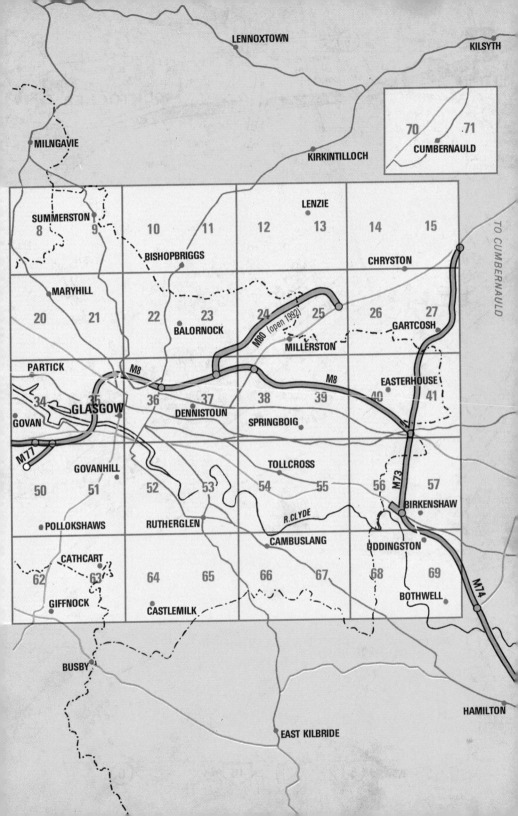

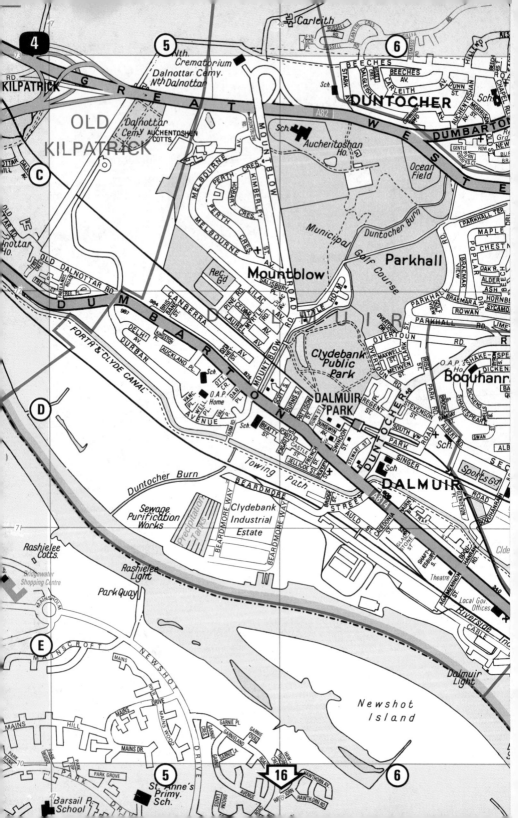

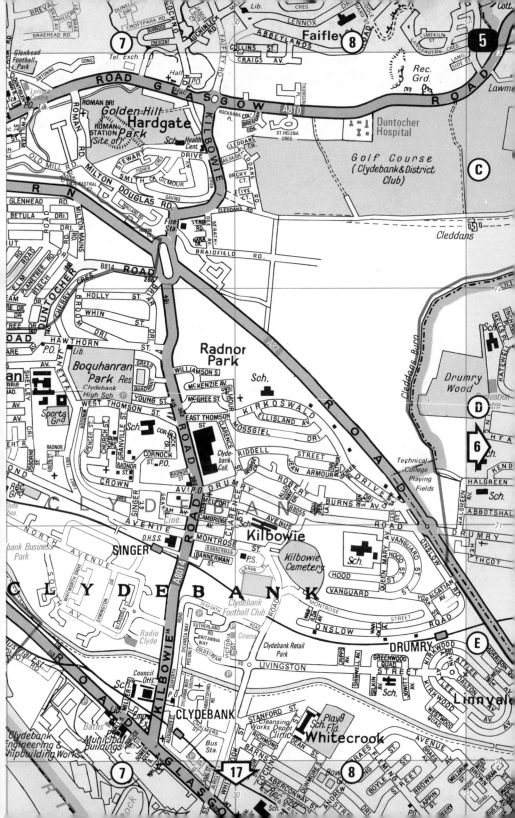

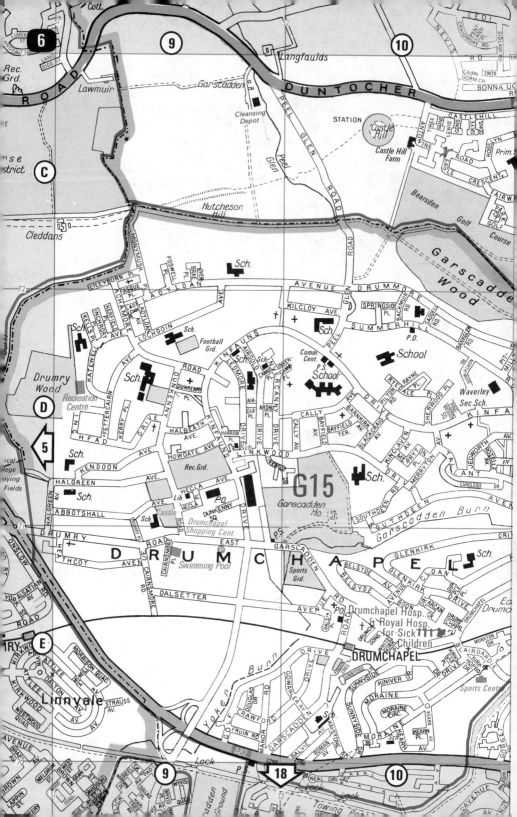

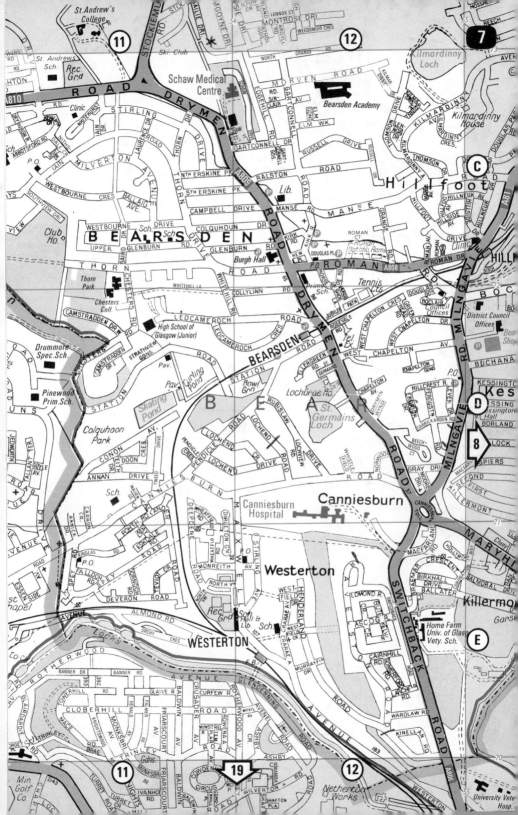

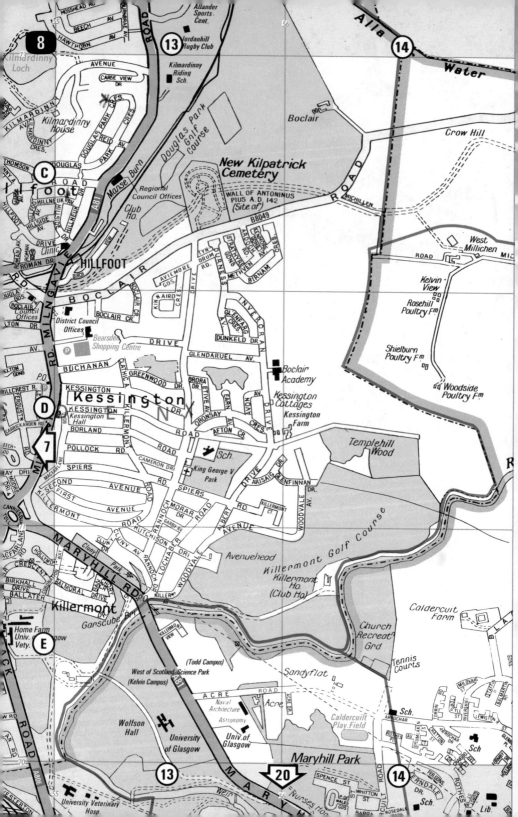

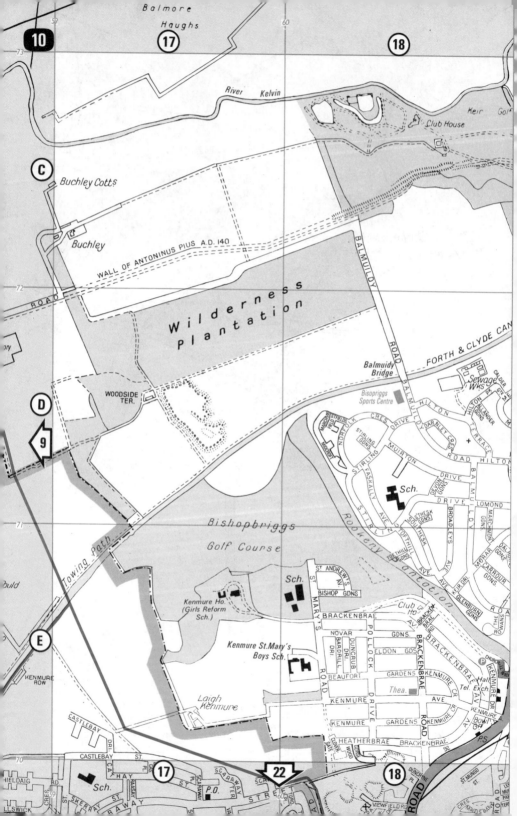

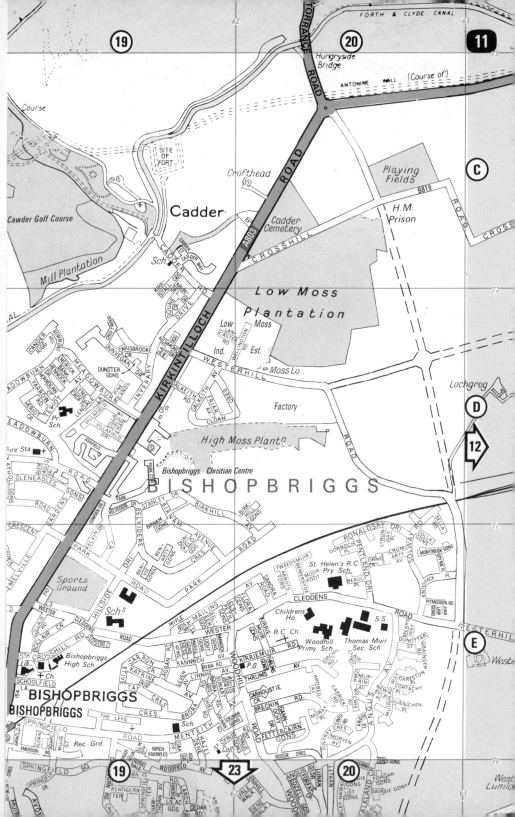

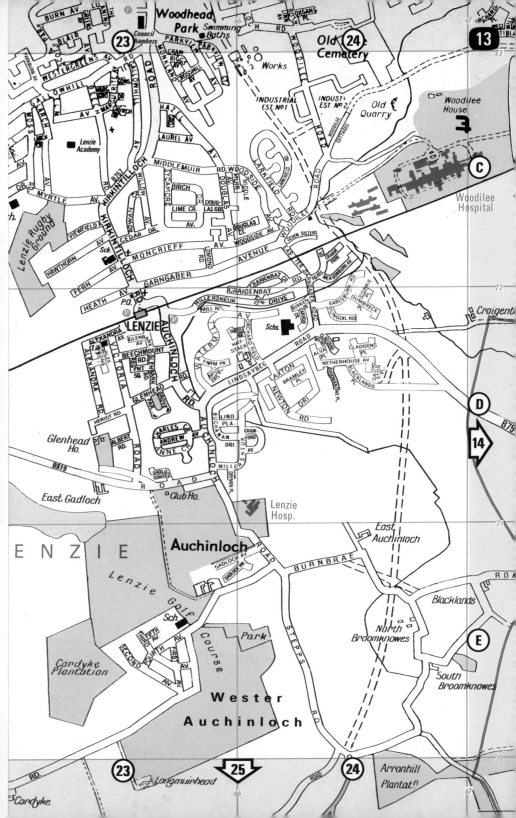

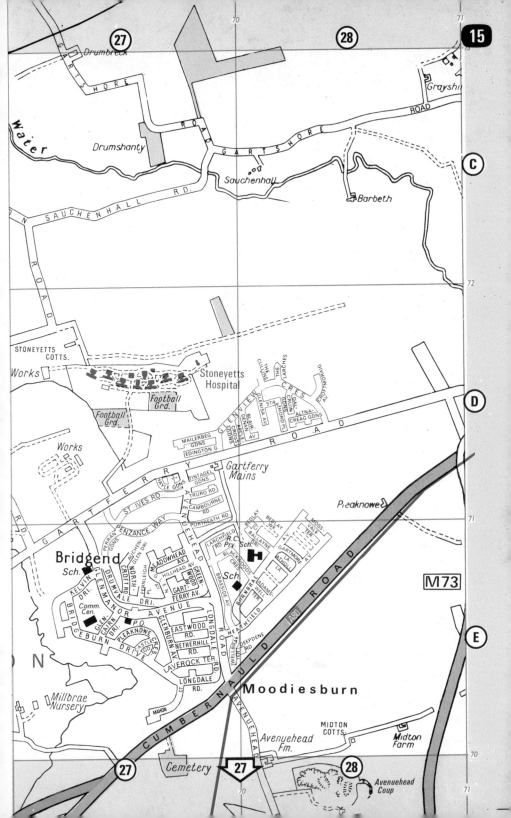

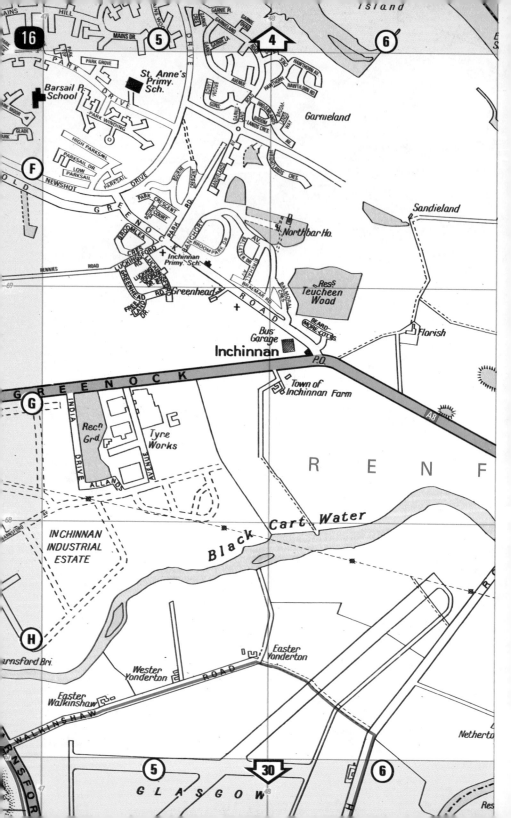

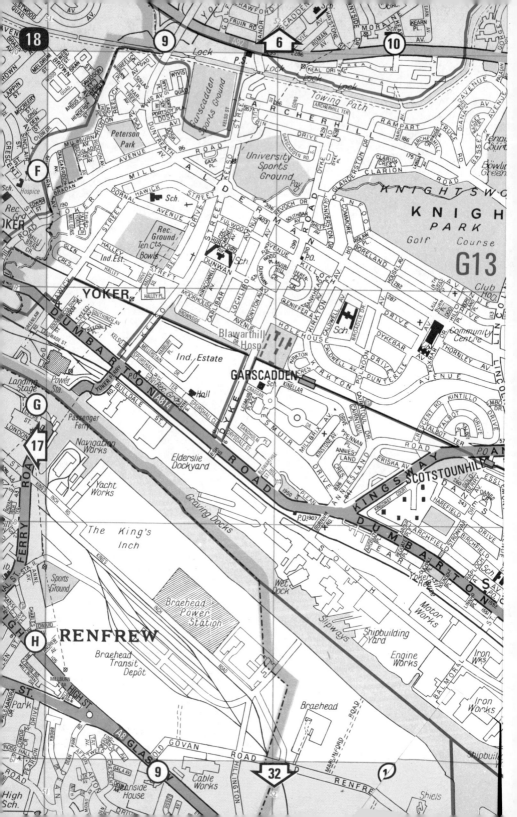

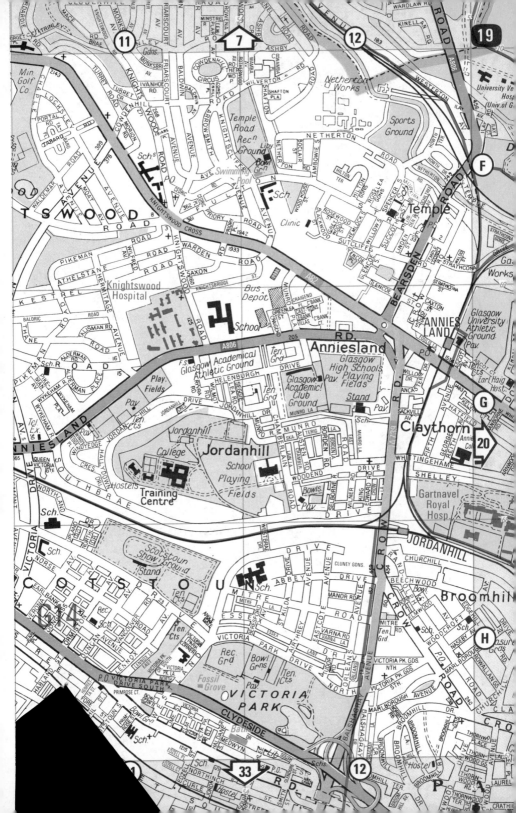

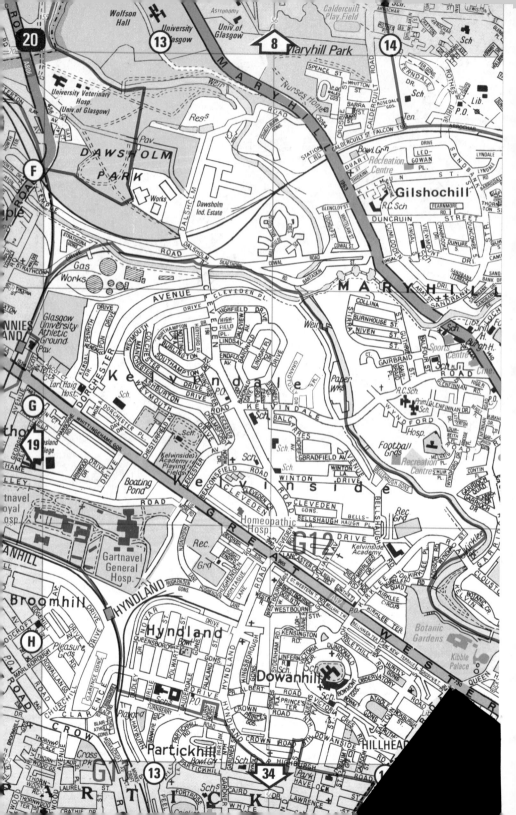

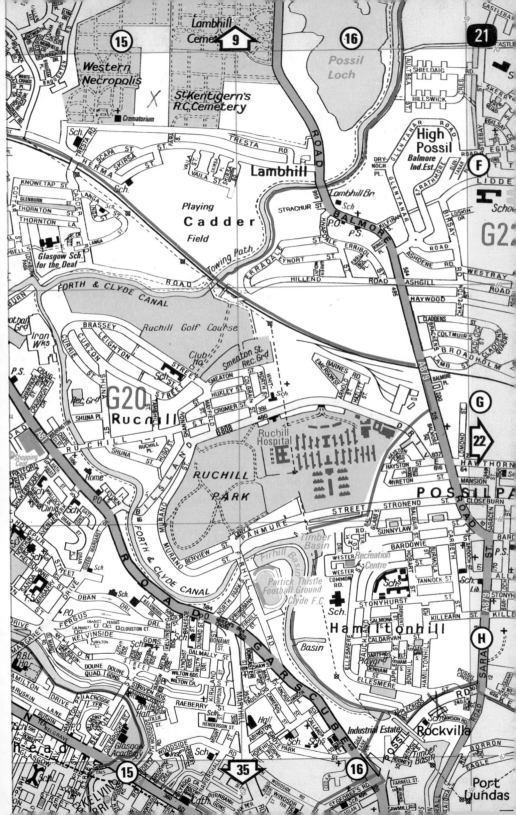

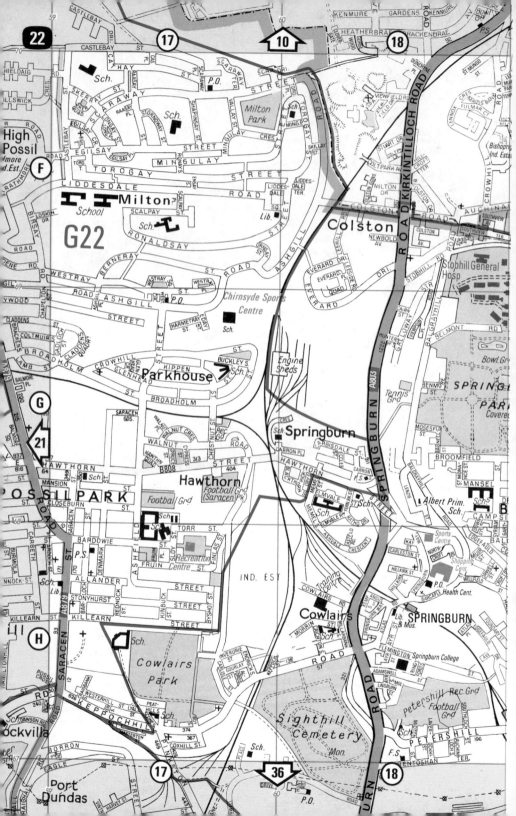

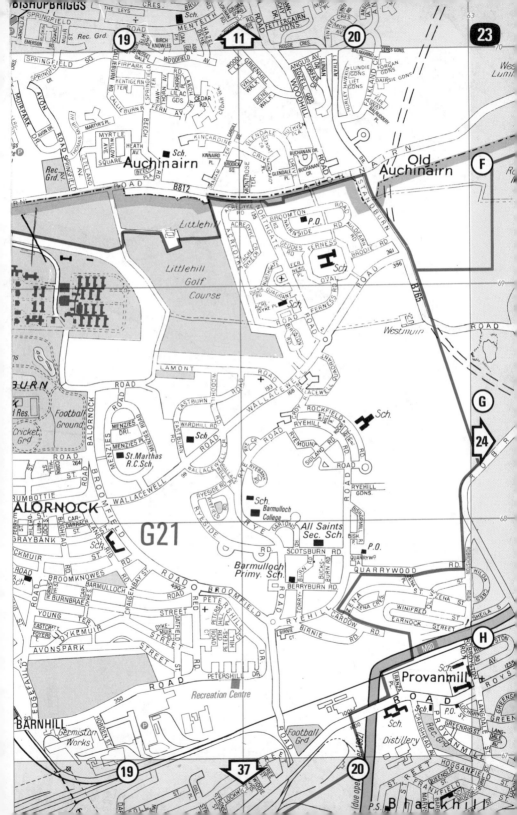

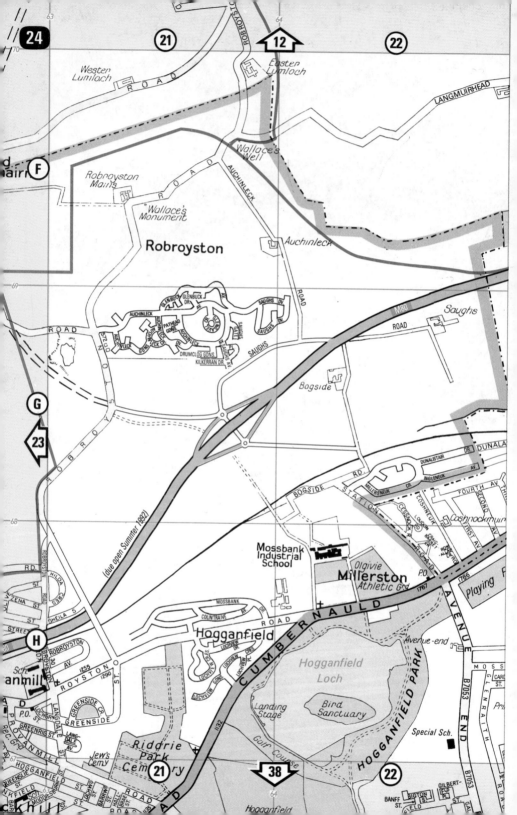

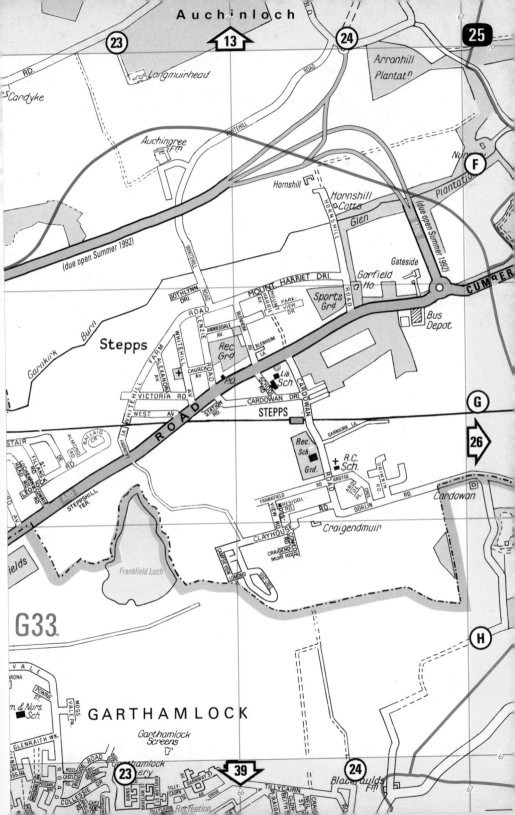

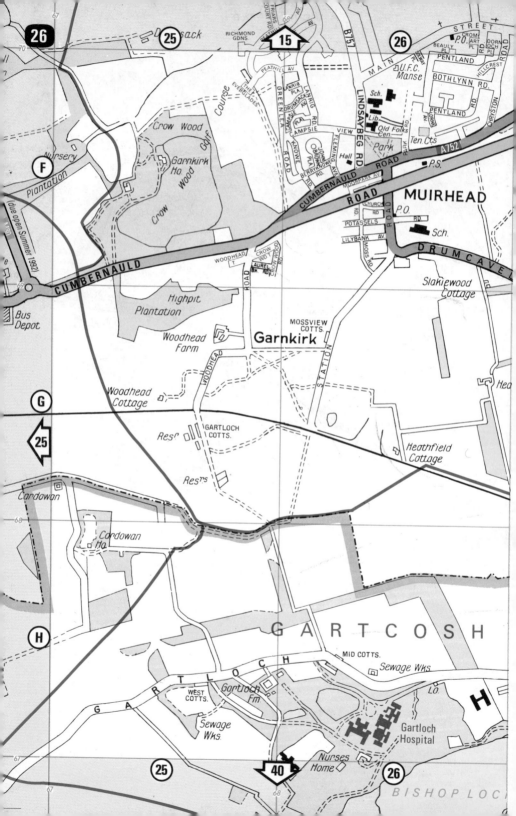

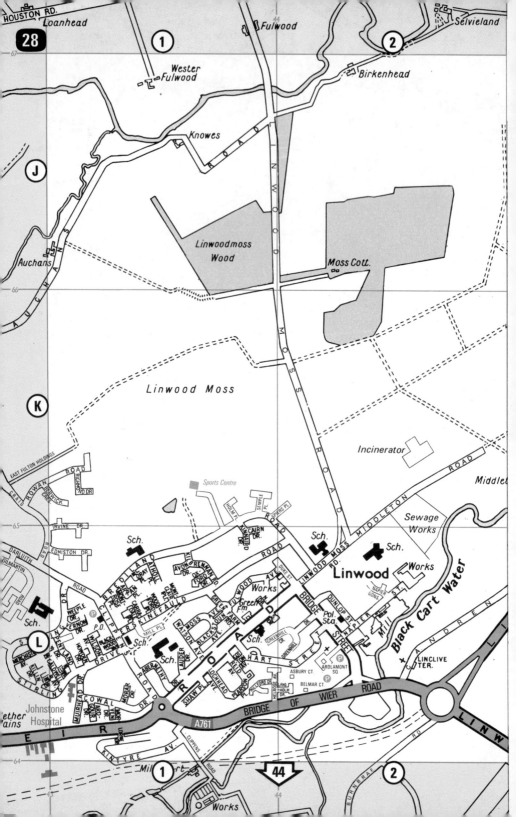

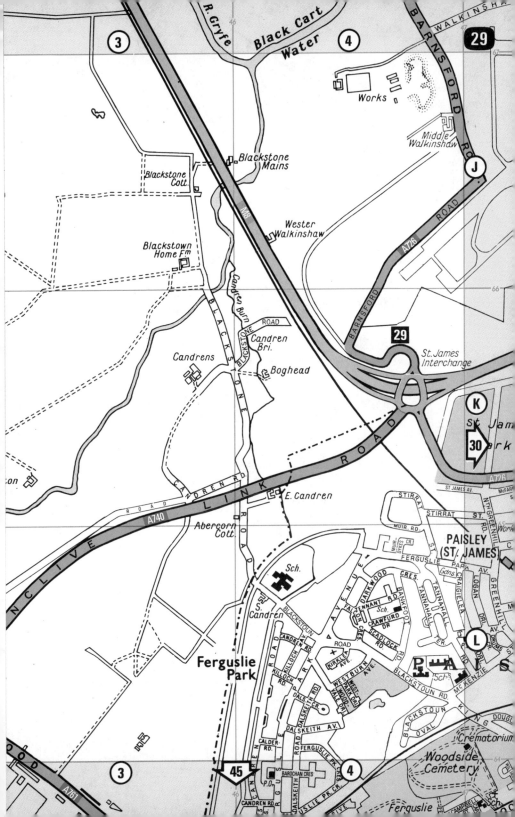

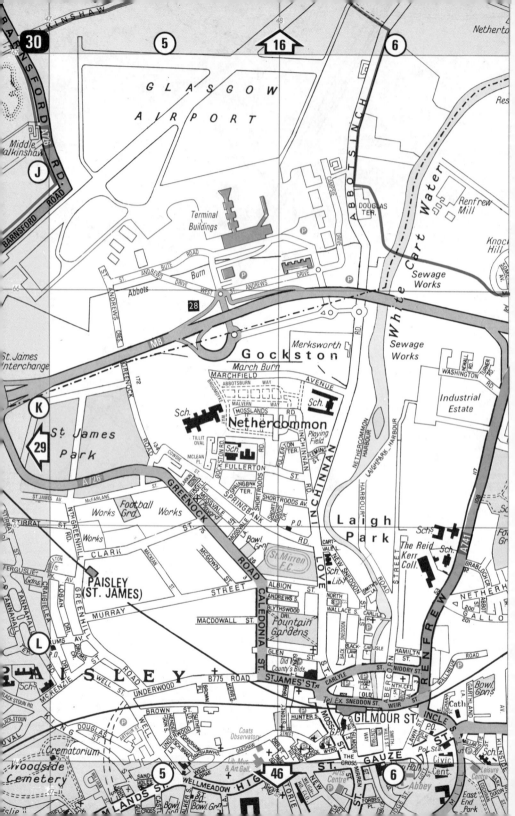

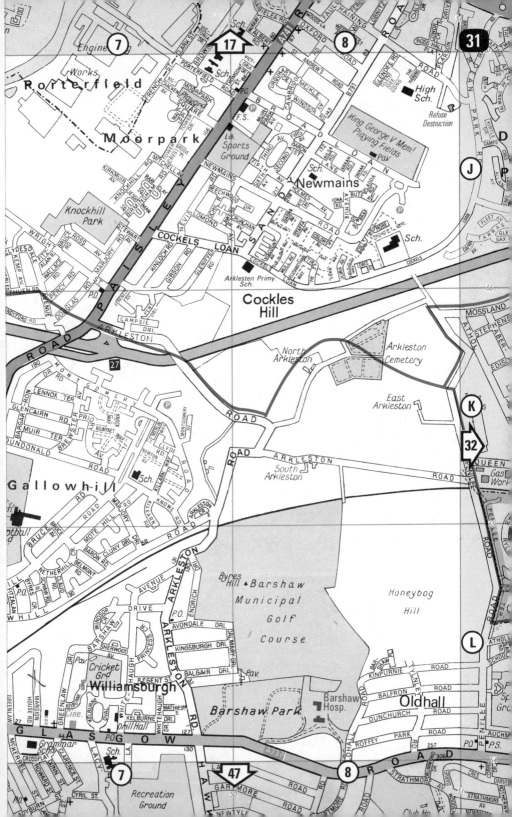

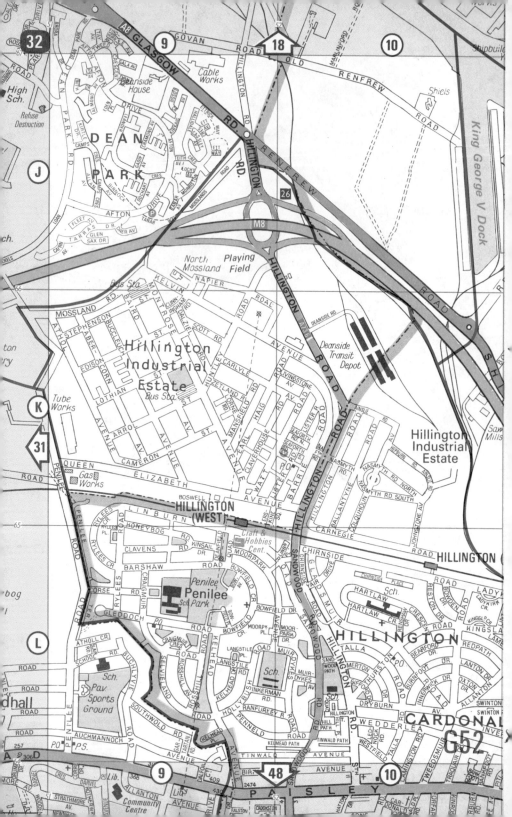

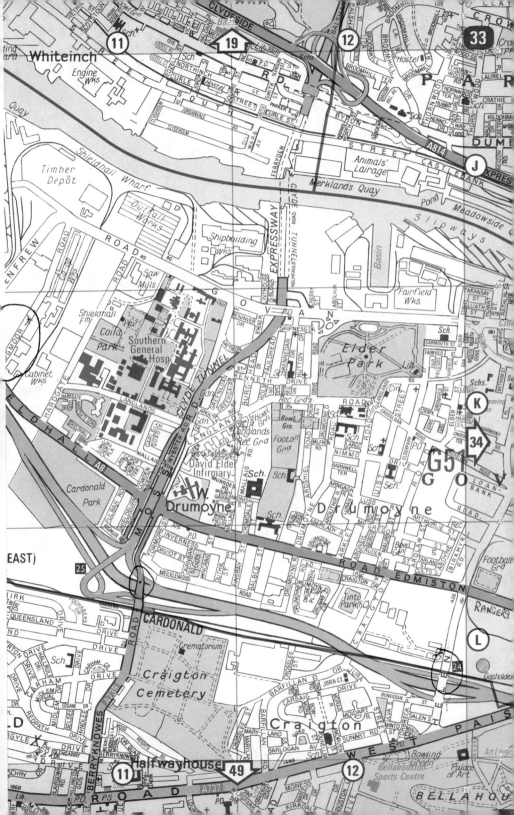

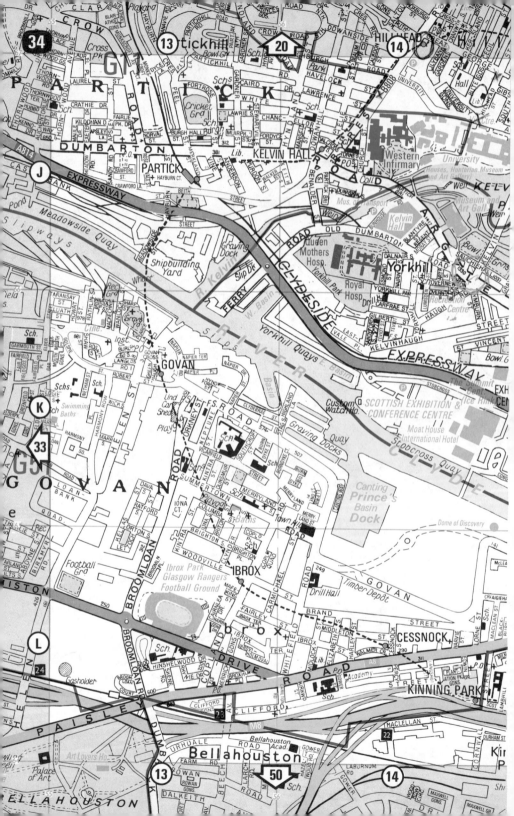

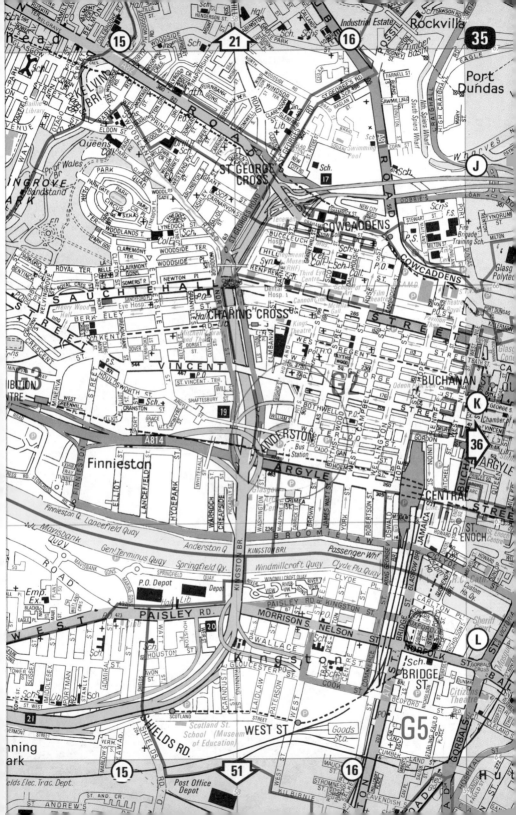

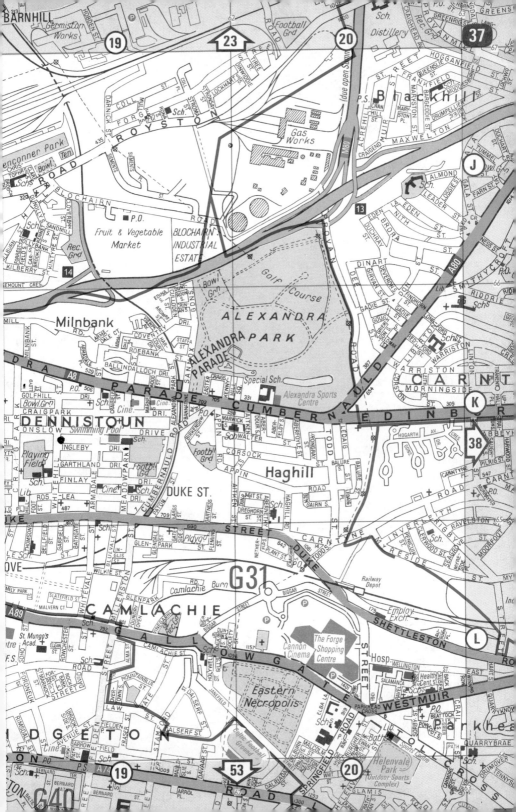

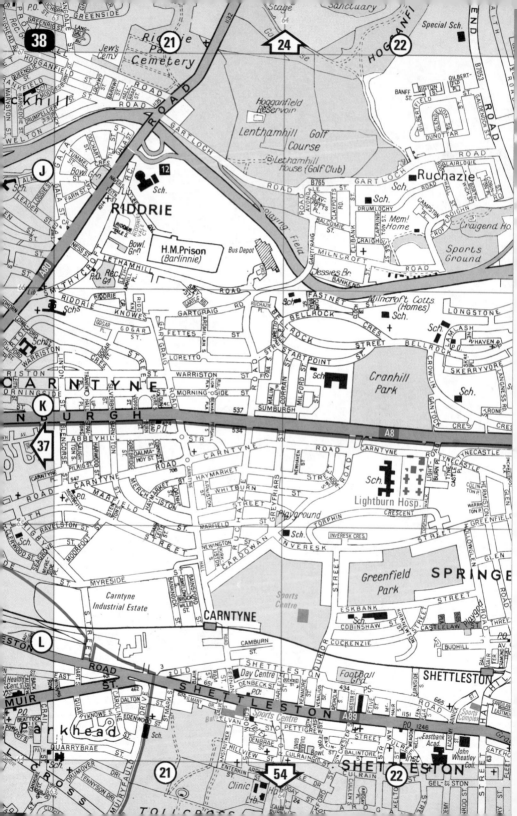

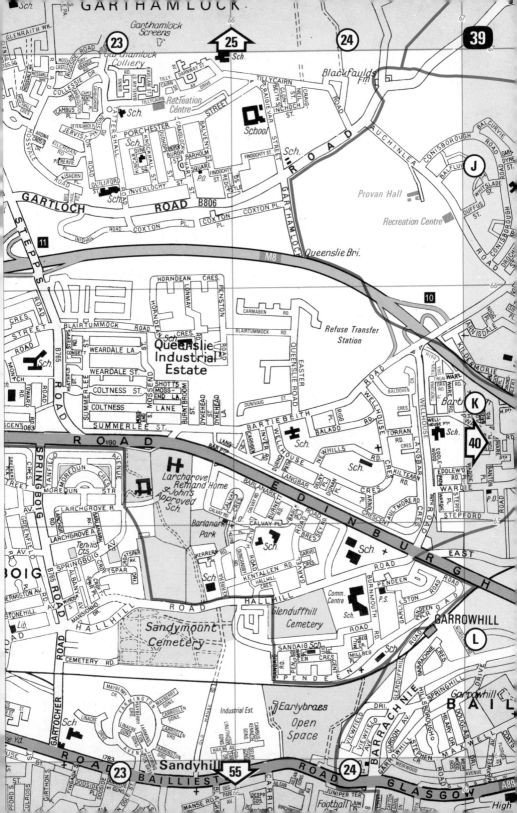

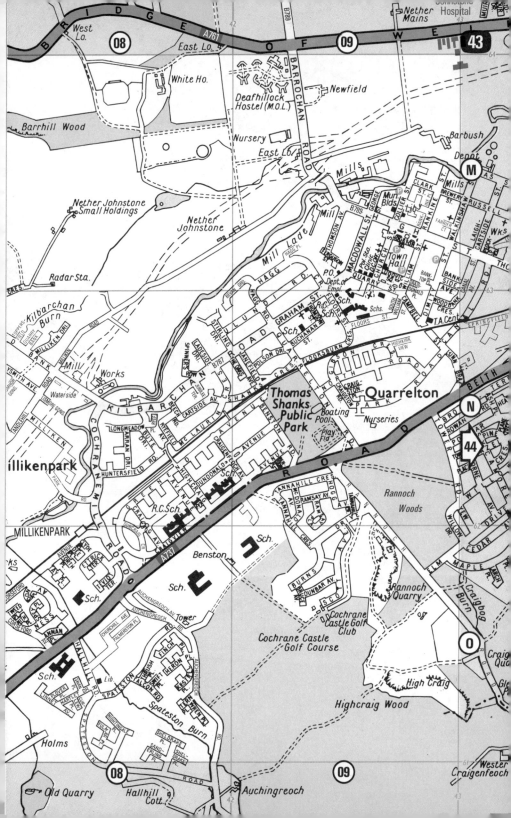

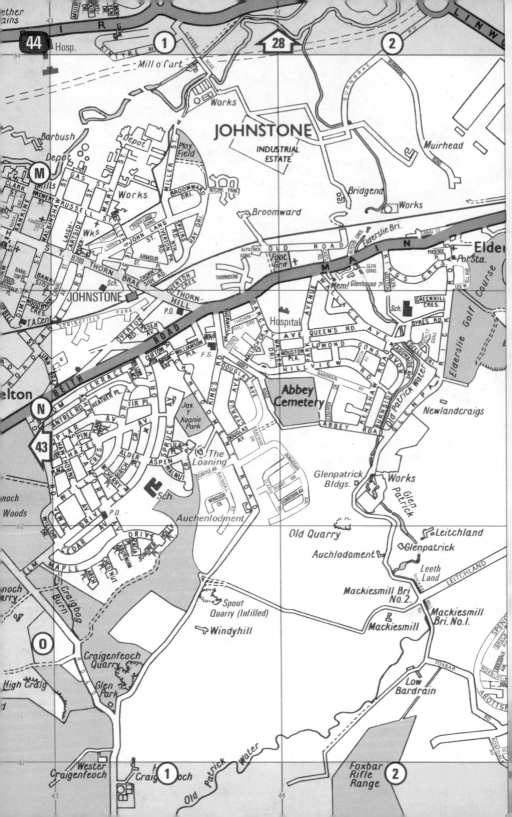

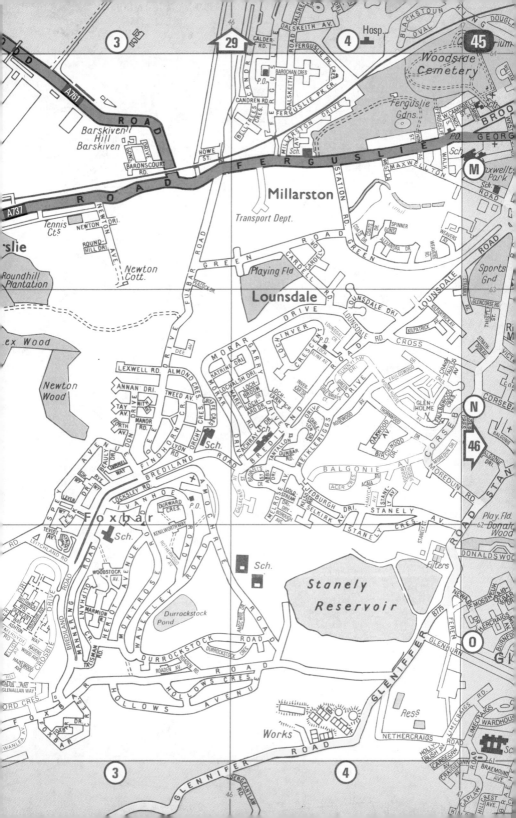

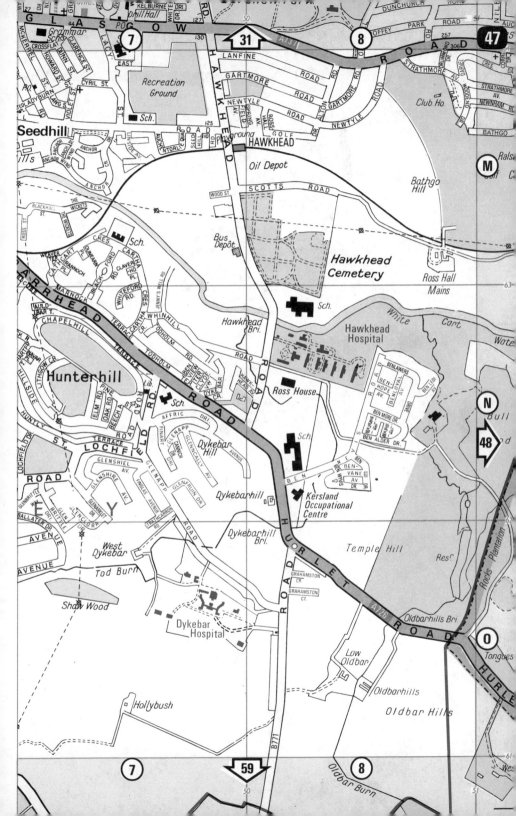

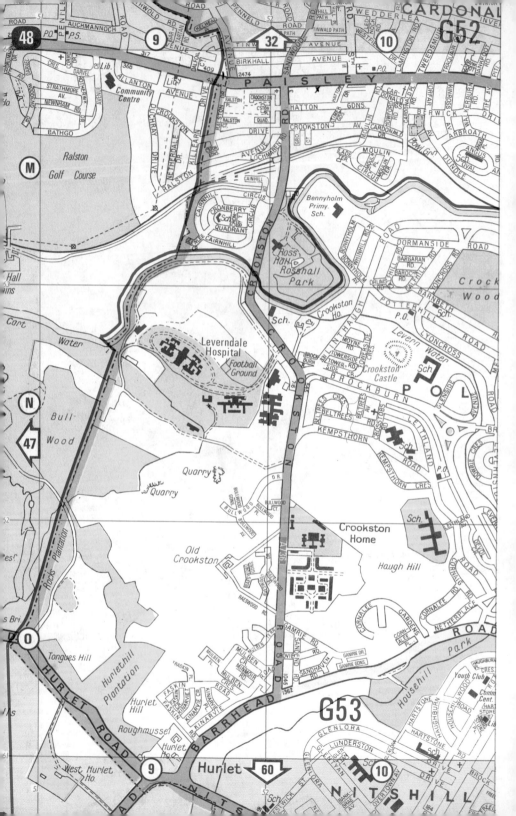

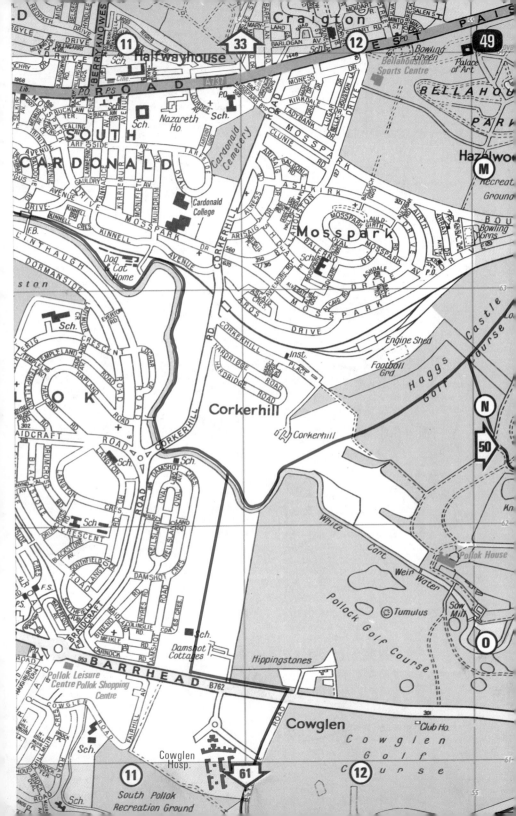

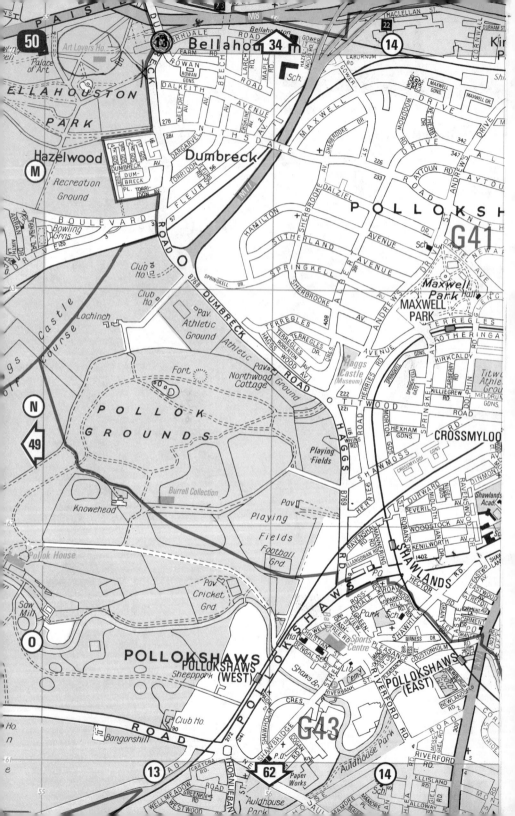

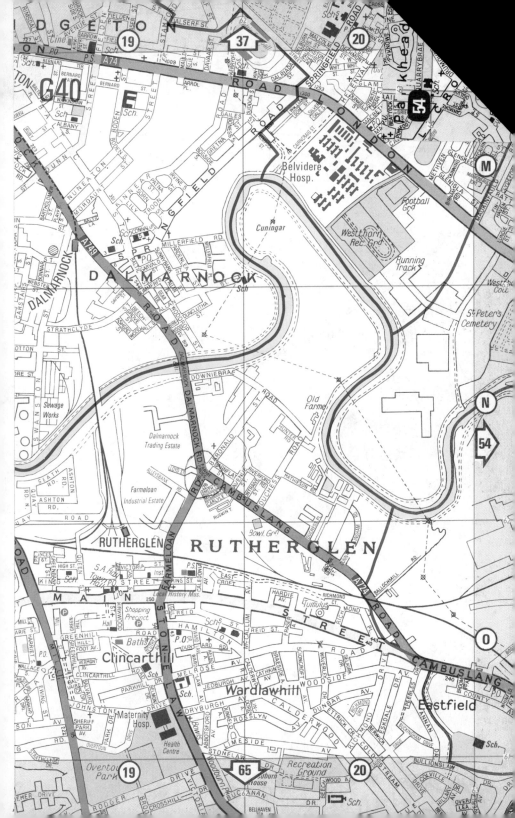

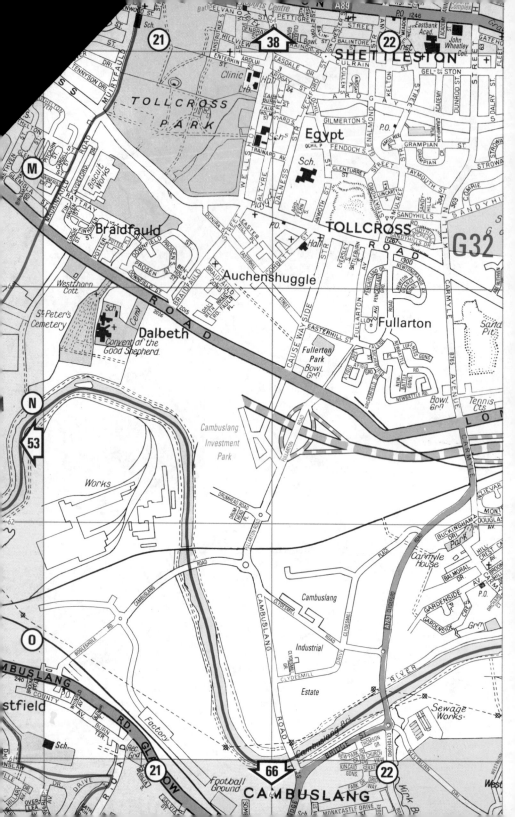

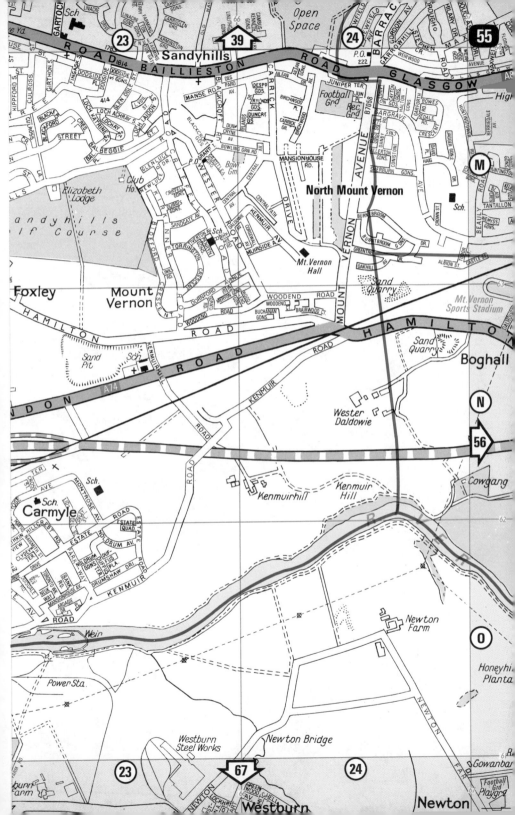

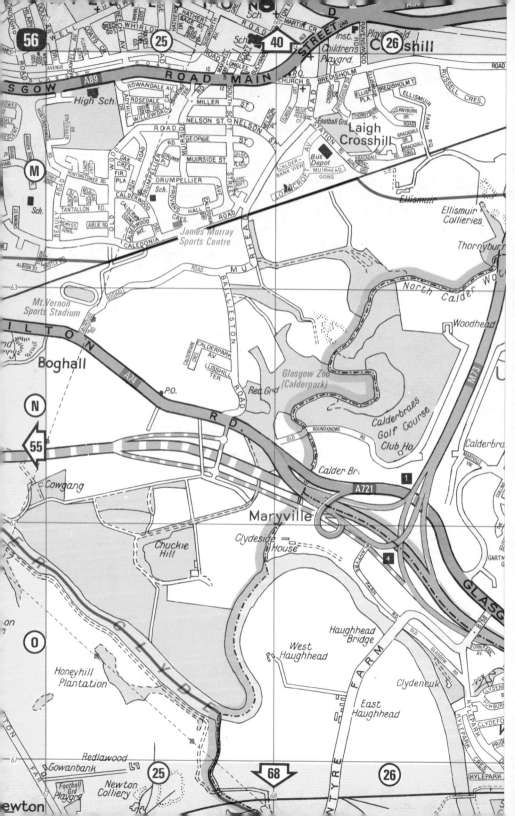

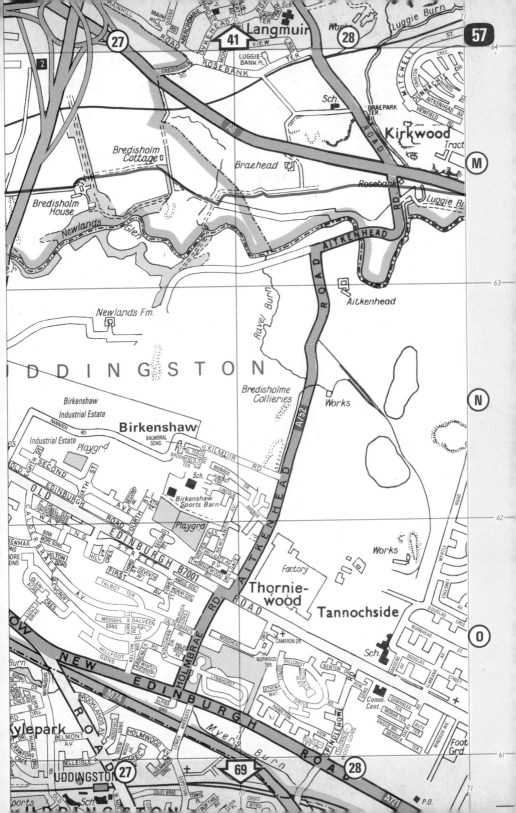

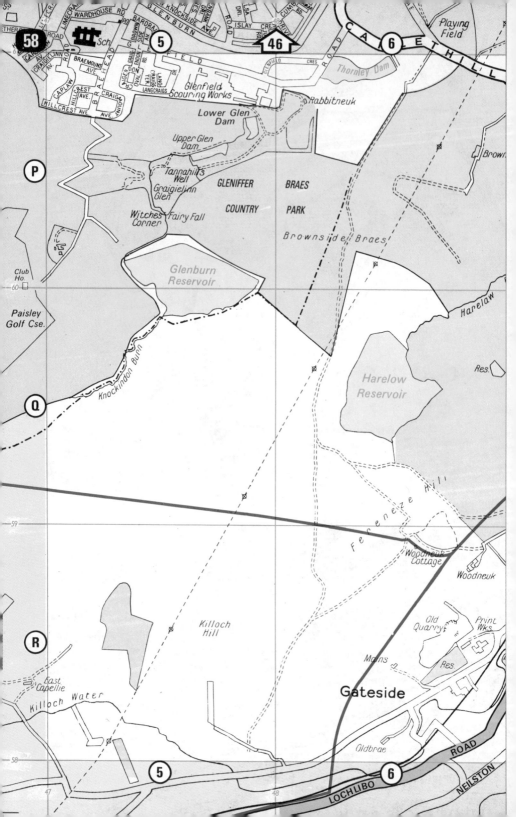

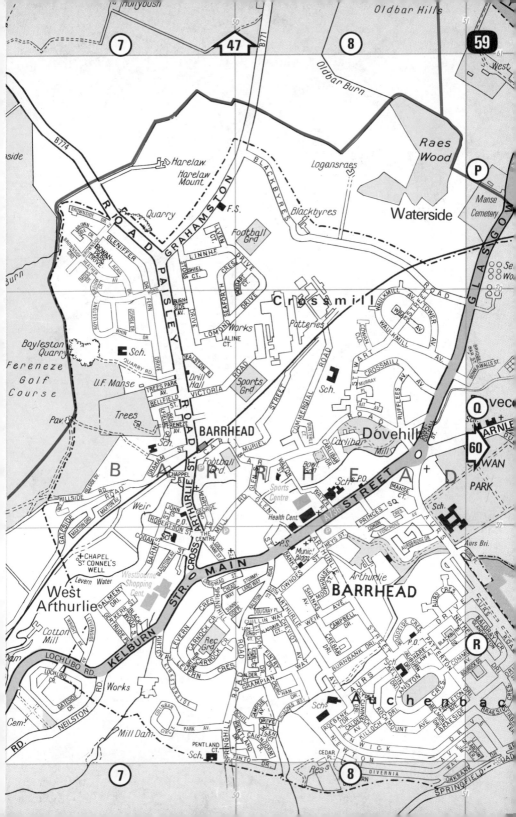

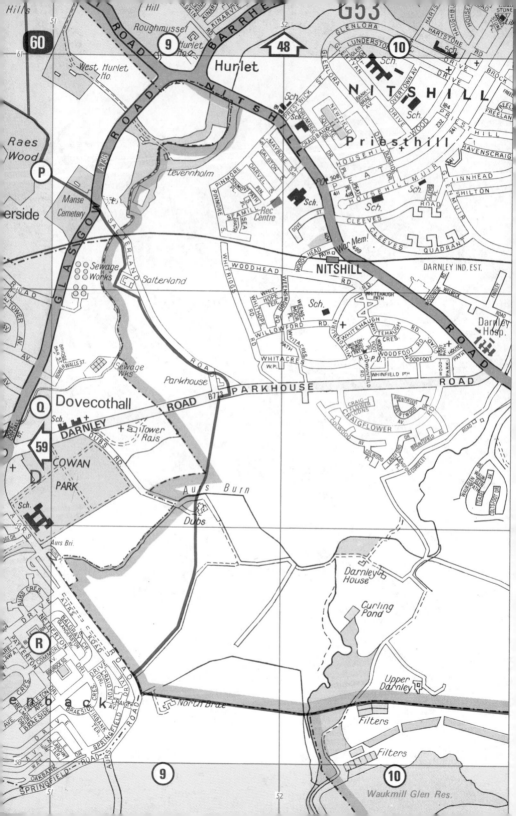

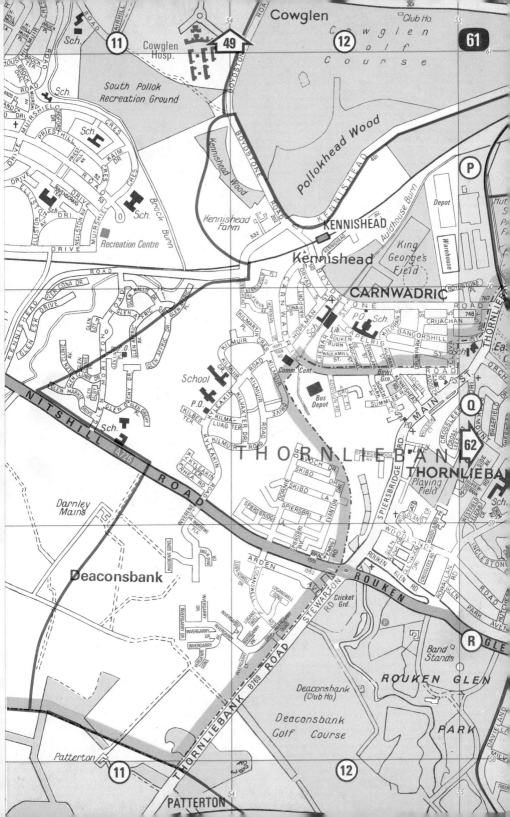

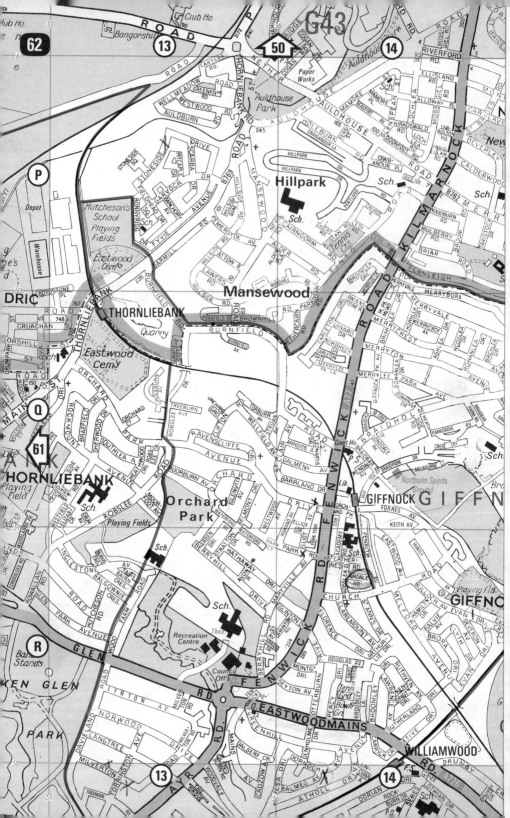

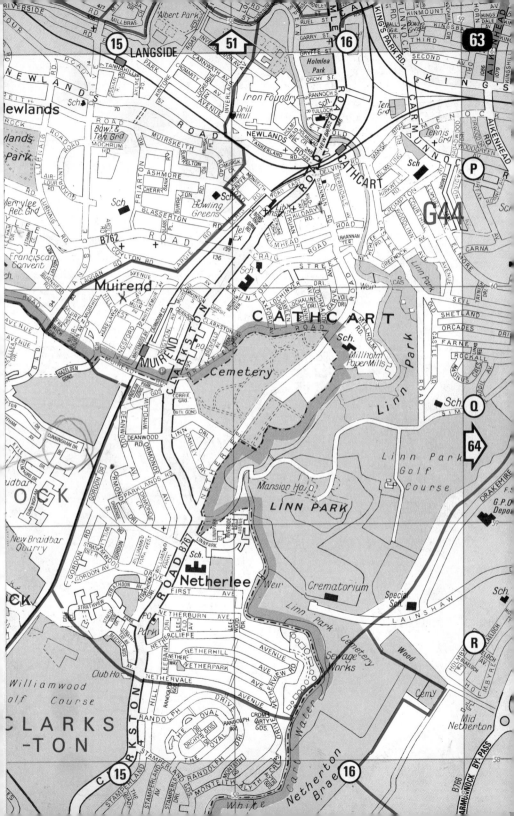

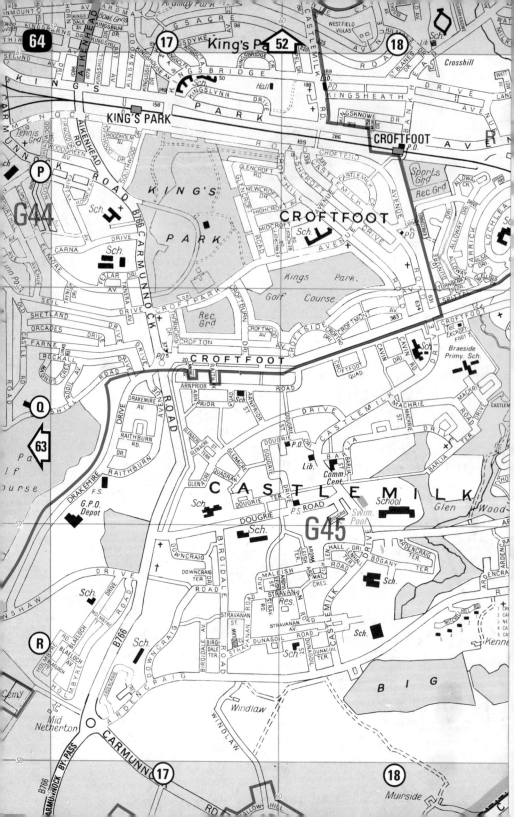

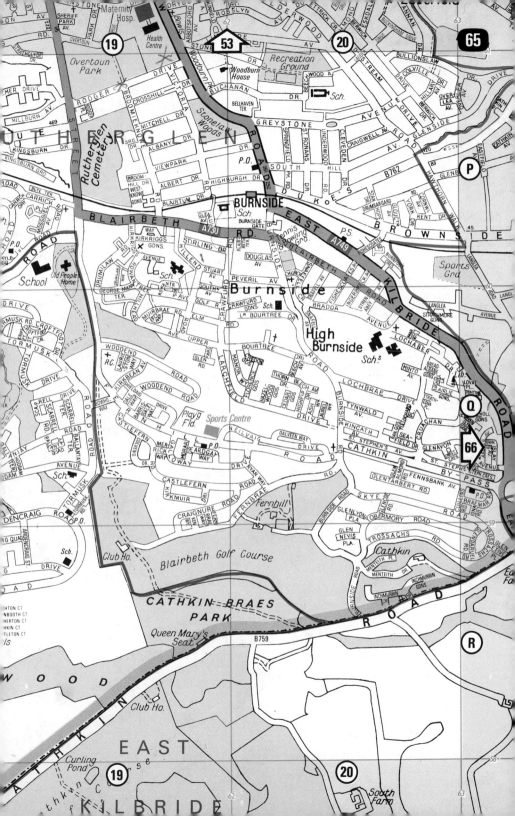

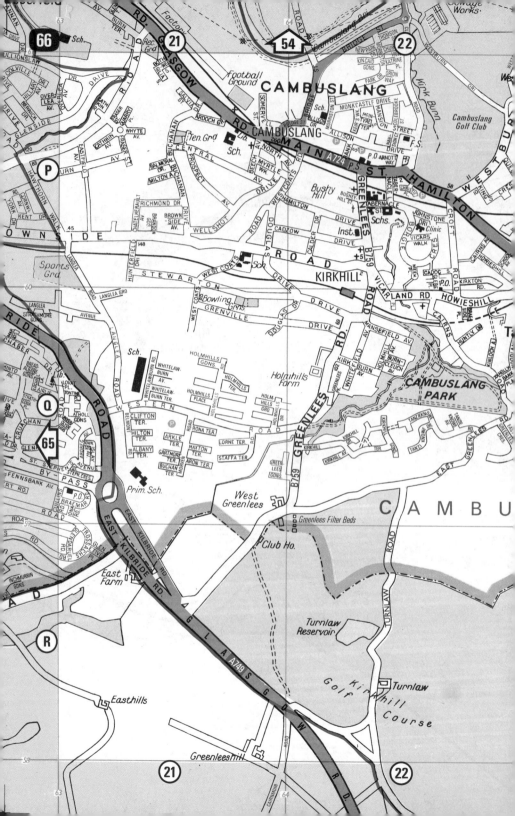

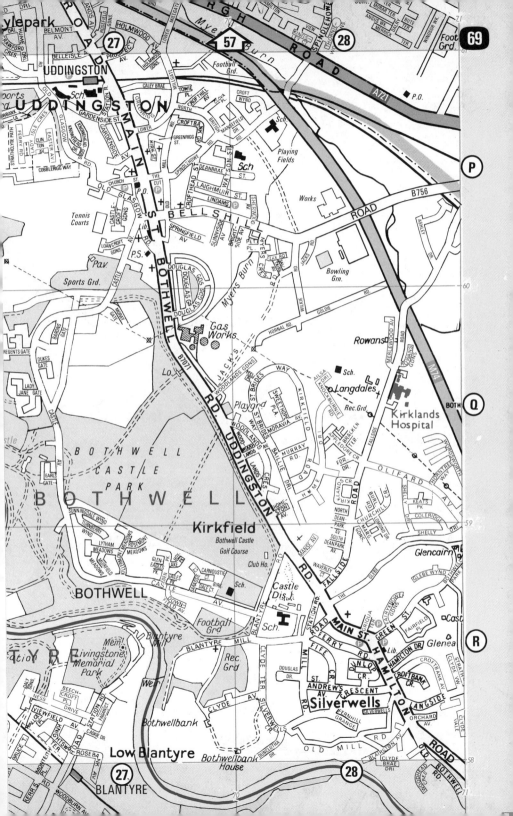

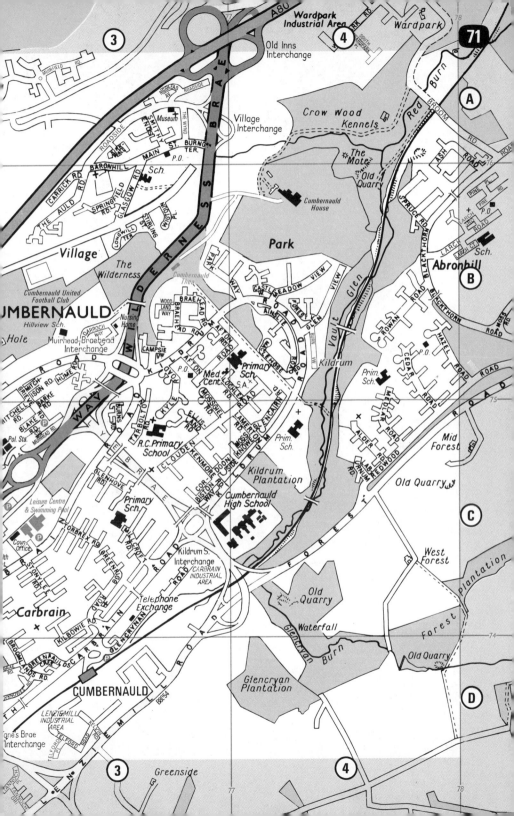

Glasgow

Local Information Guide

Contents

City of Glasgow
Local Information Guide

Useful information
Area of City 79 sq. miles (approx)

Population (Glasgow City)
(1989 estimate) 696,577

Early Closing Days
Tuesday with alternative of Saturday.
Most of the shops in the central area
operate six-day trading.

Electricity 240 volts A.C.

Emergency Services
Police, Fire and Ambulance. Dial 999
on any telephone.

Licensing Hours
Public Houses
Daily (except Sundays) 11 a.m. to
2.30 p.m. and 5 to 11 p.m. (many
open continuously 11 a.m. to
11 p.m.)
Sundays, 12.30 to 2.30 p.m. and 6.30
to 10.30 p.m.
Restaurants, Hotels and Public
Houses with catering facilities, same
as above but can be extended for
drinks with meals.

Information Bureau
Tourist Information Centres:
35–39 St. Vincent Place
Glasgow. 041-227 4880

Town Hall, Abbey Close
Paisley. 041-889 0711

Glasgow Airport 041-848 4440

Strathclyde Transport Travel Centre
St. Enoch Square
Open Monday–Saturday 9.30 a.m.
to 5.30 p.m. 041-226 4826 (Monday
to Saturday 7 a.m. to 9 p.m.,
Sunday 9 a.m.to 7-30 p.m.) for City
services, ferry services, local airlines,
train and express services. Free
timetables are available.

Help & Advice
British Broadcasting Corporation
Queen Margaret Drive, G12.
041-339 8844

British Council
6 Belmont Crescent, G12 8ES
041-339 8651

British Telecom Scotland

Glasgow Area
Westergate Chambers, 11 Hope Street,
Glasgow G2 6AB
All Enquires 041-220 1234 or dial
100 and ask for FREEFONE BT
GLASGOW

Chamber of Commerce
30 George Square, G2.
041-204 2121

Citizens Advice Bureau
212 Bath Street, Glasgow G2 4HW.
041-331 2345/6/7/8
119 Main Street, Glasgow G40 1HA.
041-554 0336

27 Dougrie Drive, Castlemilk,
Glasgow G45 9AD 041-634 0338
139 Main Street (Town Hall)
Rutherglen G73 4HG 041-647 5100
216 Main Streeet, Barrhead
041-881 2032
Civic Centre, East Kilbride
East Kilbride 21295
1143 Maryhill Road, Glasgow G20
041-946 6373/4
46 Township Centre, Easterhouse,
Glasgow G34 9DS 041-771 2328

Consumer Advice Centre
St. Enoch House, 1 St. Enoch Square
Glasgow G1 4BH. 041-204 0262

Customs and Excise
21 India Street, G2 4PZ
041-221 3828

H.M. Immigration Office
Admin Block D, Argyll Avenue
Glasgow Airport
Tel. 041-887 4115

Housing Aid and Advice
Shelter, 53 St. Vincent Crescent
Glasgow G3 8NQ. 041-221 8995/6

Legal Aid and Advice
Castlemilk Advice & Law Centre
27 Dougrie Drive, Glasgow G45.
041-634 0338

Law Centre
30 Dougrie Drive
041-634 0313

Lost Property
Strathclyde Passenger Transport
Executive
St. Enoch Underground Station
Tel. 041-248 6950 (City Buses)
12 West George Street G32
041-332 6811. (Underground)
Other Buses–Office of Bus Company.
Trains–Station of arrival.
Elsewhere in City–Strathclyde Police
Lost Property Department,
173 Pitt Street, G2
041-204 2626

Passport Office
Northgate 96 Milton Street
Glasgow G4. Tel. 041-332 0271

**Registrar of Births, Deaths and
Marriages**
1 Martha Street, G1. 041-227 6343
Hours – Monday to Friday 9.15 a.m.
to 4.00 p.m.

Births must be registered within
twenty-one days, deaths within eight
days, and marriages within three
days. The Registrar should be
consulted at least one month before
intended date of marriage.

**Royal Scottish Society for the
Prevention of Cruelty to Children**
15 Annfield Place, G31.
041-556 1156

**RNID–
Royal National Institute for the
Deaf**
9   Clairmont Gardens, Glasgow
G3 7LW. 041-332 0343

Samaritans
218 West Regent Street, Glasgow
G2 4DQ. 041-248 4488

**Scottish Society for the Mentally
Handicapped**
13 Elmbank Street, Glasgow G2.
041-226 4541

Scottish Television
Cowcaddens. G2. 041-332 9999

**Society for the Prevention of
Cruelty to Animals**
15 Royal Terrace, G3.
(Business Hours)   041-332 0716

Newspapers

Morning Daily
Daily Record
Anderston Quay, G3.   041-248 7000

Glasgow Herald
195 Albion Street, G1.   041-552 6255

Scottish Daily Express
Park Circus Place, G3. 041-332 9600

The Scotsman
181-195 West George St., G2 2LB
                         041-221 6485
Evening Daily
Evening Times
195 Albion Street, G1.   041-552 6255

Weekly
Scottish Sunday Express
Park Circus Place, G3. 041-552 3550

Sunday Mail
Anderston Quay, G3.   041-248 7000

Sunday Post
144 Port Dundas Road, G4.
041-332 9933

Parking

Car parking in the central area of Glasgow is controlled. Parking meters are used extensively and signs indicating restrictions are displayed at kerbsides and on entry to the central area. Traffic Wardens are on duty.

British Rail Car Parks
(Open 24 hours)
Central Station
Queen Street Station

Multi-Storey Car Parks
(Open 24 hours)
Anderston Cross: Cambridge Street: George Street: Mitchell Street: Port Dundas Road: Waterloo Street.

(Limited Opening)
Charing Cross
Sauchiehall Street Centre

Surface Car Parks
Carrick Street: Holland Street: Ingram Street: McAlpine Street: North Frederick Street: Albion Street: Oswald Street: Shuttle Street.

Post Offices
Head Post Office
George Square, G2   041-248 2882
Open Monday to Thursday 9 a.m. to 5.30 p.m. Fridays 9.30 a.m. to 5.30 p.m. Saturdays 9.a.m. to 12.30 p.m. Closed Sunday.
Branch Offices
85–91 Bothwell Street, G2.
4 Dixon Street, G1.

216 Hope Street, G2.
533 Sauchiehall Street, G3.

Taxis

Glasgow has over 1400 traditional London type taxis, all licensed by the Glasgow District Council and all fitted with meters sealed and approved by the Council. A fare card stating the current tariff is displayed in a prominent position within each taxi. At the time of publishing a three mile journey costs £2.40 and waiting time is charged at 10p per minute the total price of each journey is shown on the meter. Fares are normally revued annually by the council. Each taxi can carry a maximum of five passengers.

The major taxi companies in the city offer City tours at fixed prices, listing the places of interest to be visited, leaflets are available at all major hotel reception areas. Tours vary from 2 to 3 hours and in price between £17 and £24.

Any passenger wishing to travel to a destination outside the Glasgow District Boundary should ascertain from the driver the fare to be charged or the method of calculating the fare PRIOR to making the journey.

Complaints

Any complaints regarding the conduct of a taxi driver should be addressed to the Senior Enforcement Officer, Town Clerk's Office, City Chambers, Glasgow. Tel: 041-227-4535.

Local Government

Strathclyde Regional Council
Strathclyde House, 20 India Street
Glasgow G2 4PF
041-204 2900

District Councils:

Argyll & Bute
District Council Headquarters
Kilmory, Lochgilphead PA31 8RT
0546 2127

Bearsden & Milngavie
Municipal Building, Boclair
Bearsden G61 2TQ
041-942 2262

Clydebank
Council Offices, Rosebery Place
Clydebank G81 1TG
041-941 1331

Clydesdale
Clydesdale District Offices
Lanark ML11 7JT
0555 61331

Cumbernauld & Kilsyth
Council Offices, Bron Way
Cumbernauld G67 1DZ
02367 22131

Cummock & Doon Valley
Council Offices, Lugar
Cumnock KA18 3JQ
0290 22111

Cunninghame
Cunninghame House
Irvine KA12 8EE
0294 74166

Dumbarton
Crosslet House
Dumbarton G82 3NS
0389 65100

East Kilbride
Civic Centre
East Kilbride G74 1AB
035-52 28777

Eastwood
Council Offices
Eastwood Park, Rouken Glen Road
Rouken Glen, Giffnock
Glasgow G46 6UG
041-638 6511
041-638 1101

Glasgow City
City Chambers
Glasgow G2 1DU
041-221 9600

Hamilton
Town House
102 Cadzow Street
Hamilton ML3 6HH
0698 282323

Inverclyde
Municipal Buildings
Greenock PA15 1LY
0475 24400

Kilmarnock & Loudoun
Civic Centre
Kilmarnock KA1 1BY
0563 21140

Kyle & Carrick
Burns House
Burns Statue Square
Ayr KA7 1UT
0292 281511

Monklands
Municipal Buildings
Dunbeth Road
Coatbridge ML5 3LF
0236 41200

Motherwell
PO Box 14
Civic Centre
Motherwell ML1 1TW
0698 66166

Renfrew
Municipal Buildings
Cotton Street
Paisley PA1 1BU
041-889 5400

Strathkelvin
Tom Johnston House
Civic Way
Kirkintilloch
Glasgow G66 4TJ
041-776 7171

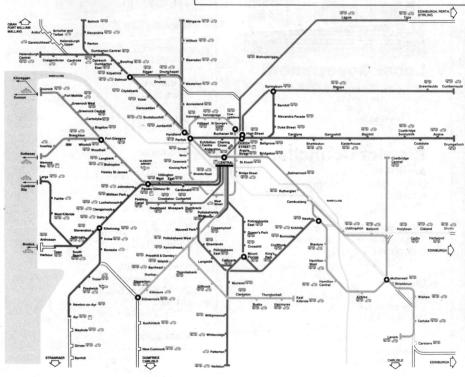

History & Development

The City of Glasgow began life as a makeshift hamlet of huts huddled round a 6thC church, built by St Mungo on the banks of a little salmon river — the Clyde. It was called Gleschow, meaning 'beloved green place' in Celtic. The cathedral was founded in 1136; the university, the second oldest in Scotland, was established in the 15thC; and in 1454 the flourishing mediaeval city wedged between the cathedral and the river was made a Royal burgh. The city's commercial prosperity dates from the 17thC when the lucrative tobacco, sugar and cotton trade with the New World flourished. The River Clyde, Glasgow's gateway to the Americas, was dredged, deepened and widened in the 18thC to make it navigable to the city's heart.

By the 19thC, Glasgow was the greatest shipbuilding centre in the world. From the 1820s onwards, it grew in leaps and bounds westwards along a steep ridge of land running parallel with the river. The hillside became encased in an undulating grid of streets and squares. Gradually the individualism, expressed in one-off set pieces characteristic of the 18thC and early 19thC, gave way to a remarkable coherent series of terraced squares and crescents of epic proportions — making Glasgow one of the finest of Victorian cities. But the price paid for such rapid industrialisation, the tremendous social problems manifest in the squalor of some of the worst of 19thC slums, was high. Today the city is still the commercial and industrial capital of the West of Scotland. The most notorious of the slums have been cleared but the new buildings lack that sparkling clench-fisted Glaswegian character of the 19thC. Ironically, this character was partially destroyed when the slums were cleared for it wasn't the architecture that had failed, only the bureaucrats, who designated such areas as working class ghettos.

Districts
Little remains of mediaeval Glasgow, which stood on the wedge of land squeezed between the cathedral and the River Clyde. Its business centre was The Cross, a space formed by the junction of several streets — the tall, square Tolbooth Steeple, 1626, in the middle. Opposite is Trongate, an arch astride a footpath, complete with tower and steeple salvaged from 17thC St Mary's Church — destroyed by fire in 1793. The centre of 20thC Glasgow is George Square, a tree-lined piazza planned in 1781 and pinned down by more than a dozen statues including an 80-foot-high Doric column built in 1837 to carry a statue of Sir Walter Scott. Buildings of interest: the monumental neo-Baroque City Chambers 1883-88 which take up the east side and the Merchants' House 1874, on the west. To the south of the square, in a huddle of narrow streets, is the old Merchant City. Of interest here is the elegant Trades House, 85 Glassford Street, built by Robert Adam in 1794. An elegant Ionic portico stands on a rusticated ground storey flanked by domed towers. Hutcheson's Hospital, 158 Ingram Street, is a handsome Italianate building designed by David Hamilton in 1805. Nearby is Stirling's Library, originally an 18thC private residence, it became the Royal Exchange in 1827 when the Corinthian portico was added. To the north west is Kelvingrove, Victorian Glasgow at its best. Built around a steep saddle of land, landscaped by Paxton in 1850 and lined along its edge with handsome terraces. Last but not least are the banks of the River Clyde. From Clyde Walkway on the north bank you can see: the Suspension Bridge of 1871 with its pylons in the form of triumphal arches; the old clipper ship, C. V. Carrick, a contemporary of the Cutty Sark, moored by Victoria bridge; 17thC Merchants' Steeple; the Gothic Revival St Andrew's R.C. Cathedral of 1816; the church, built 1739, in nearby St Andrew's Square is a typical copy of London's St Martin-in-the-Fields.

Buildings & Shops

Interesting buildings

Victorian Glasgow was extremely eclectic architecturally. Good examples of the Greek Revival style are Royal College of Physicians 1845, by W. H. Playfair and the Custom House 1840, by G. L. Taylor. The Queen's Room 1857, by Charles Wilson, is a handsome temple used now as a Christian Science church. The Gothic style is seen at its most exotic in the Stock Exchange 1877, by J. Burnet. The new Victorian materials and techniques with glass, wrought and cast iron were also ably demonstrated in the buildings of the time. Typical are: Gardener's Stores 1856, by J. Baird; the Buck's Head, Argyle Street, an amalgam of glass and cast iron; and the Egyptian Halls of 1873, in Union Street, which has a masonry framework. Both are by Alexander Thomson. The Templeton Carpet Factory 1889, Glasgow Green, by William Leiper, is a Venetian Gothic building complete with battlemented parapet.

Glasgow University

The great genius of Scottish architecture is Charles Rennie Mackintosh whose major buildings are in Glasgow. In the Scotland Street School 1904-6, he punctuated a 3-storey central block with flanking staircase towers in projecting glazed bays. His most famous building — Glasgow School of Art 1897-9 — is a magnificent Art Nouveau building of taut stone and glass; the handsome library, with its gabled facade, was added later in 1907-9.

Stirling's Library

Galleries & museums

Scotland's largest tourist attraction, The Burrell Collection, is situated in Pollok Country Park, Haggs Road and has more than 8,000 objects, housed in an award-winning gallery. The Museum and Art Gallery, Kelvingrove Park, Argyle Street, a palatial sandstone building with glazed central court, has one of the best municipal collections in Britain; superb Flemish, Dutch and French paintings, drawings, prints, also ceramics, silver, costumes and armour, as well as a natural history section. Provand's Lordship c1471, in Castle Street, is Glasgow's oldest house and now a museum of 17th-18thC furniture and household articles. Pollok House, Pollok Country Park, a handsome house designed by William Adam in 1752, has paintings by William Blake and a notable collection of Spanish paintings, including works by El Greco. The Museum of Transport, housed in Kelvin Hall, Bunhouse Road, has a magnificent collection of trams, cars, ships models, bicycles, horse-drawn carriages and 7 steam locos. The People's Palace, The Green, built 1898 with a huge glazed Winter Garden, has a lively illustrated history of the city. But the oldest museum in Glasgow is the Hunterian Museum, University of Glasgow, University Avenue, opened in 1807, it has a fascinating collection of manuscripts, early printed books, as well as some fine archaeological and geological exhibits. 400-year-old Haggs Castle, St Andrew's Drive, is now a children's museum with practical demonstrations and exhibits showing how everyday life has changed over the centuries.

Streets & shopping

The Oxford Street of Glasgow is Sauchiehall (meaning 'willow meadow') Street. This with Buchanan Street and Argyle Street is the main shopping centre. Here you will find the department stores, boutiques and general shops. All three streets are

Old Sheriff Court

partly pedestrianised, but the most exhilarating is undoubtedly Buchanan Street. Of particular interest is the spatially elegant Argyll Arcade 1828, the Venetian Gothic-style Stock Exchange 1877, the picturesque Dutch gabled Buchanan Street Bank building 1896 and the Glasgow Royal Concert Hall (opened 1990). In Glasgow Green is The Barrows, the city's famous street market, formed by the junction of London Road and Kent Street. The Market is *open weekends*. Some parts of the city have *EC Tue*.

Museum & Art Gallery Kelvingrove

Cathedrals & Churches

Glasgow Cathedral is a perfect example of pre-Reformation Gothic architecture. Begun in 1238, it has a magnificent choir and handsome nave with shallow projecting transepts. On a windy hill to the east is the Necropolis, a cemetery with a spiky skyline of Victoriana consisting of pillars, temples and obelisks, dominated by an 1825 Doric column carrying the statue of John Knox. Other churches of interest: Lansdowne Church built by J. Honeyman in 1863; St George's Tron Church by William Stark 1807; Caledonian Road Church, a temple and tower atop a storey-high base, designed by Alexander Thomson in 1857; a similar design is to be found at the United Presbyterian Church, St Vincent Street, 1858, but on a more highly articulated ground storey; Queen's Cross Church 1897 is an amalgam of Art Nouveau and Gothic Revival by the brilliant Charles Rennie Mackintosh.

Churches within the central area of Glasgow are:

Church of Scotland
Glasgow Cathedral
Castle Street
Renfield St. Stephen's Church
262 Bath Street
St. George's Tron Church
165 Buchanan Street
St. Columba Church (Gaelic)
300 St. Vincent Street

Baptist
Adelaide Place Church
209 Bath Street

Congregational
Hillhead Centre
1 University Avenue

Episcopal Church in Scotland
Cathedral Church of St. Mary
300 Great Western Road, G4.

First Church of Christ Scientist
1 la Bell Place, Clifton Street, G3.
(off Sauchiehall Street)

Free Church of Scotland
265 St. Vincent Street

German Speaking Congregation
Services held at 7 Hughenden Terrace, G12.

Greek Orthodox Cathedral
St. Luke's, 27 Dundonald Road, G12.

Jewish Orthodox Synagogue
Garnethill, 29 Garnet Street

Methodist
Woodlands Church
229 Woodlands Road

Roman Catholic
St. Andrew's Cathedral
190 Clyde Street
St. Aloysius' Church
25 Rose Street

Unitarian Church
72 Berkeley Street

United Free
Wynd Church,
427 Crown Street, G5.

Glasgow Cathedral

Entertainment

As Scotland's commercial and industrial capital, Glasgow offers a good choice of leisure activities. The city now has 6 theatres where productions ranging from serious drama to pantomime, pop and musicals are performed. The Theatre Royal, Hope Street, is Scotland's only opera house and has been completely restored to its full Victorian splendour. The Royal Scottish National Orchestra gives concerts at the Glasgow Royal Concert Hall, every *Sat night in winter* and is the venue for the proms in *Jun*. Cinemas are still thriving in Glasgow, as are the many public houses, some of which provide meals and live entertainment. In the city centre and Byres Road, West End, there is a fair number of restaurants where traditional home cooking, as well as international cuisines, can be sampled. More night life can be found at the city's discos and dance halls – Tiffany's, Sauchiehall Street and the Plaza, Eglinton Toll. Outdoors, apart from the many parks and nature trails, there is Calderpark Zoological Gardens, situated 6 miles from the centre between Mount Vernon and Uddingston. Here you may see white rhinos, black panthers and iguanas among many species. Departing from Stobcross Quay, you can also cruise down the Clyde in 'P.S. Waverley' – the last sea-going paddle-steamer in the world.

Cinemas

Cannon Cinema, 380 Clarkston Rd, G44.
041-637 2641
Cannon Film Centre–
326 Sauchiehall St, G2.   041-332 9513
(Admin Dept), 326 Sauchiehall St, G2
041-332 1592
326 Sauchiehall St, G2.   041-332 1593
Caledonian Associated Cinemas Ltd–
Regent House, 72 Renfield St, G2
041-332 0606
Cannon Grand–
18 Jamaica St, G1.   041-248 4620
Glasgow Film Theatre–
12 Rose St, G3. (Box Off)   041-332 6535

Grosvenor Cinema–
Ashton Lane, G12.   041-339 4298
Kelburne Cinema–
(Manager), Glasgow Rd, Paisley
041-889 3612
Odeon Film Centre, 56 Renfield St, G2.
041-332 8701
Salon Cinema, Vinicombe St, G12.
041-339 4256

Halls

City Halls, Candleriggs, G1.
Couper Institute
86 Clarkston Road, G44.
Dixon Halls, 650 Cathcart Road, G42.
Glasgow Royal Concert Hall
2 Sauchiehall Street , G3
Govan Hall, Summertown Road, G51.
Kelvin Hall, Argyle Street, G3.
Langside Hall, 5 Langside Avenue, G41.
Partick Hall, 9 Burgh Hall Street, G11.
Pollokshaws Hall
2025 Pollokshaws Road, G43.
Woodside Hall, Glenfarg Street, G20.

(More information about the above G.D.C. halls and others from the Director, Halls and Theatres Department, Candleriggs, G1. 041-552 1201).

Theatres

Citizens' Theatre
Gorbals Street.   041-429 0022
King's Theatre, Bath Street.
Mitchell Theatre and Moir Hall
Granville Street.
Pavilion Theatre
Renfield Street.   041-332 1846
Theatre Royal
Hope Street.   041-331 1234
Tron Theatre
38 Parnie Street.   041-552 3748
The Ticket Centre
Glasgow's Central Box Office for King's Theatre, Mitchell Theatre, Kelvin Hall, Citizen's Theatre, Theatre Royal and City Hall at Candleriggs, G1.
Open Monday to Saturday 10.30 a.m. to 6.30 p.m.
041-227 5511

Glasgow (Abbotsinch) Airport

Glasgow Airport is located eight miles West of Glasgow alongside the M8 motorway at Junction 28. It is linked by a bus service to Anderston Cross Bus Station, the journey time is 25 minutes and buses leave at 30 minute intervals. There is a frequent coach service linking the Airport with

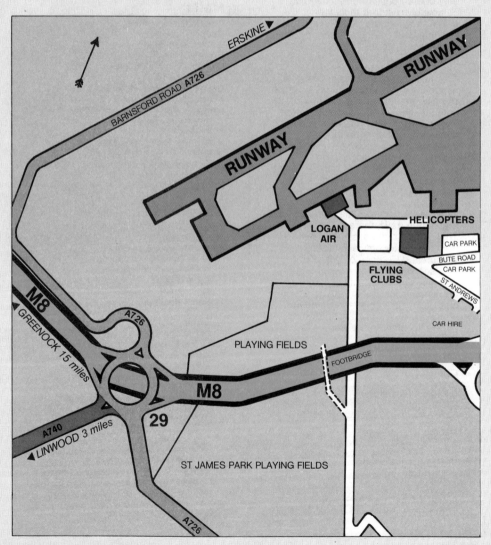

all major bus and rail terminals in the City and a Coach/Air link to and from Prestwick Airport.

The Airport Terminal has a restaurant, grill, buffet, three bars, lounges, shop, post office and banking facilities.

Car parking is available with a graduated scale of charges.

The Airport telephone no is 041-887 1111.

Airlines

(Domestic Routes)
British Airways
66 Gordon Street
Glasgow G1
Reservations Tel: 041-332 9666
British Caledonian Airways
(contact British Airways)
British Midland
Merlin House, Mossland Road,
Hillington, Glasgow
Reservations Tel: 041-204 2436
Loganair Ltd.
Glasgow Airport (administration)
Tel: 041-889 3181.
Trident House, Renfrew Road, Paisley

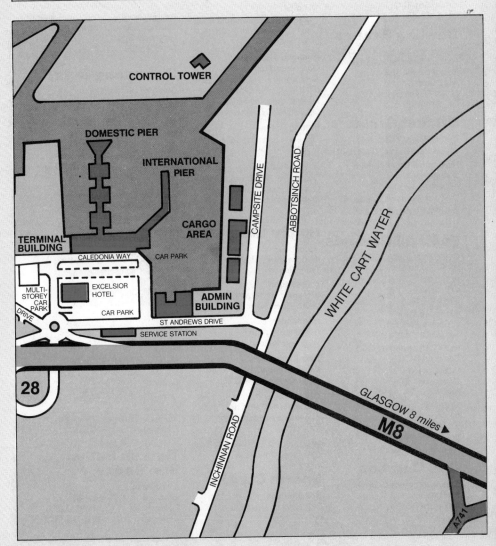

Sport & Recreation

For both spectator and participant, football is Glasgow's favourite sport. Both Celtic and Rangers, Scotland's most famous rival teams, have their grounds within the City. Glasgow houses Scotland's national football stadium at Hampden Park.

Badminton
Scottish Badminton Union's
Cockburn Centre, Bogmoor
Place, G51 4TQ.
041-445 1218

Bowling Greens
There are greens in all the main Parks. Information about clubs from the Scottish Bowling Association:
50 Wellington Street, G2.
041-221 8999.

Cricket Grounds
Cartha Haggs Road, G41.
Clydesdale Beaton Road, G41.
Huntershill Crowhill Road, Bishopbriggs.
Poloc 'Shawholm'
2060 Pollokshaws Road, G43.
West of Scotland Peel Street, G11.

Football Grounds
Celtic Park (Celtic F.C.)
95 Kerrydale St. G40
Firhill Park (Partick Thistle F.C. & Clyde F.C.)
Firhill Rd. G20
Hampden Park (Queen's Park F.C.)
Somerville Dr., G42
Ibrox Park (Rangers F.C.)
Edmiston Dr., G51
Kilbowie Park (Clydebank F.C.)
Argyll Rd., Clydebank
Mertland
Kirkintilloch
St. Mirren Park (St. Mirren F.C.)
Love St., Paisley

Golf Courses
Glasgow District Council
9 holes
Alexandra Park
King's Park.

Knightswood, Lincoln Avenue, G13.
Ruchill, Brassey Street, G20.

18 holes
Lethamhill, Cumbernauld Road,
Littlehill, Auchinairn Road, G64.
Linn Park.

(Charges displayed)
Dougalston Golf Course
Strathblane Road, Milngavie.
(Five miles from Glasgow).
Open to the public daily.
041-956 5750 for charges.

Putting Greens
There are putting greens in some of the main Parks.

Pitch & Putt
Courses at Bellahouston Park, Queen's Park, Rouken Glen and several others.

Rugby Grounds
Auldhouse
(Hutchesons'/Aloysians)
Thornliebank
Garscadden
(Glasgow University)
Garscadden Road South, G15.
Hughenden
(Hillhead High School)
Hughenden Road, G12.
New Anniesland
(Glasgow Acad.)
Helensburgh Drive, G13.
Old Anniesland
(Glasgow High School F.P. & Kelvinside Academicals)
Crow Road, G11
Westerlands
(Glasgow University)
Ascot Avenue, G12

Sports Centres
Bellahouston
Bellahouston Drive, G52.
041-427 5454.

Burnhill
Toryglen Road, Rutherglen.
041-643 0327.

James Murray
Caledonia Road, Baillieston.
041-773 0881

Springburn
Springburn Way, Springburn.
041-558 7358.

Helenvale Park
Outdoor Sports Complex
Helenvale Street, G31.
041-554 4109.

Swimming Baths
Glasgow District Council
Castlemilk, 137 Castlemilk Drive, G45.
Drumchapel, 199 Drumry Road East.
Easterhouse, Bogbain Road, G34.
Govan, Harhill Street, G51.
Govanhill, 99 Calder Street, G42.
North Woodside, Braid Square.
Pollokshaws (Dry-Land/Water Sports Complex) Ashtree Road, G43.
Rutherglen, 44 Greenhill Road, G73.
Shettleston, Elvan Street, G32.
Temple, Knightscliffe Avenue, G13.
Whitehill, Onslow Drive, G31.
Whiteinch, Medwyn Street, G14.

Hours
Monday to Friday 9 a.m. to 9 p.m.
Saturday 9 a.m. to 1 p.m.
*Sunday 9 a.m. to 1 p.m.

Charges
Admission charges are minimal.
OAPs free at certain times.

Turkish Baths/ Sun Beds
available at:
Govanhill   041-423 0233
Pollokshaws   041-632 2200
Shettleston   041-778 1346

and Whiteinch, 041-959 2465
Men and women on separate days. Telephone direct to baths for more information.

Hours
(All the year round).
Monday to Friday 9 a.m. to 9 p.m.
Saturday 9 a.m. to 1 p.m.

SAUNA at:
Castlemilk,   041-634 8254
Drumchapel,   041-944 5812
Rutherglen,   041-647 4530
and Whitehill,   041-551 9969

Tennis
There are courts in some of the main parks. Information about clubs from the Secretary of the West of Scotland Lawn Tennis Association:
Mr. N. Floyd, 1 Boclair Road
Bearsden   041-942 0162

Weather

The City of Glasgow is on the same latitude as the City of Moscow, but because of its close proximity to the warm Atlantic Shores, and the prevailing westerly winds, it enjoys a more moderate climate. Summers are generally cool and winters mostly mild, this gives Glasgow fairly consistent summer and winter temperatures. Despite considerable cloud the City is sheltered by hills to the south-west and north and the average rainfall for Glasgow is usually less than 40 inches per year.

The following table shows the approximate average figures for sunshine, rainfall and temperatures to be expected in Glasgow throughout the year:

Weather Forecasts
For the Glasgow Area including Loch Lomond and the Clyde Coast:
Weatherline
0898 500421 (Recording)
The Glasgow Weather Centre
(Meteorological Office)
33 Bothwell Street, G2
041-248 3451

Month	Hours of Sunshine	Inches of Rainfall	Temperature °C		
			Ave. Max.	Ave. Min.	High/Low
Jan	36	3.8	5.5	0.8	−18
Feb	62	2.8	6.3	0.8	−15
Mar	94	2.4	8.8	2.2	21
Apr	147	2.4	11.9	3.9	22
May	185	2.7	15.1	6.2	26
June	181	2.4	17.9	9.3	30
July	159	2.9	18.6	10.8	29
Aug	143	3.5	18.5	10.6	31
Sept	106	4.1	16.3	9.1	−4
Oct	76	4.1	13.0	6.8	−8
Nov	47	3.7	8.7	3.3	−11
Dec	30	4.2	6.5	1.9	−12

Renfrew District

A selection of leisure, recreational and cultural attractions in Renfrew District:

Barrhead Sports' Centre

The Centre contains swimming-pools, sports halls, activity rooms and sauna suite. Bar and restaurant facilities add to the wide range of sporting and leisure activities available.

Barshaw Park, Glasgow Road, Paisley

The park is extensive with formal and informal areas. It adjoins the public golf course and incorporates a boating-pond, playgrounds, model "ride-on" railway and a nature corner.

Castle Semple Country Park, Lochwinnoch

Castle Semple Loch is a popular feature for sailing and fishing. Canoes, rowing boats and sailing boards for hire. Fishing permits available. Tel: Lochwinnoch 842882.

Coats Observatory

The Observatory has traditionally recorded astronomical and meteorological information since 1882. Now installed with a satellite picture receiver, it is one of the best equipped Observatories in the country. Monday, Tuesday, Thursday 2 p.m.-8 p.m., Wednesday, Friday, Saturday 10 a.m.-5 p.m, October to end March 7-15 p.m.-9.45 p.m. Tel: 041 889 3151

Erskine Bridge

The bridge is an impressive high level structure opened by HRH Princess Anne in 1971 and provides a direct link from Renfrew District to Loch Lomond and the Trossachs. The bridge replaced the Erskine Ferry and affords extensive views up and down river to pedestrian users.

Finlayston Estate

Off the A8 at Langbank. The Estate is now a garden centre with woodland walks. The house has connections with John Knox and Robert Burns and is open April to August on Sundays from 2.30—4.30pm. At other times groups by appointment. Tel: Langbank 285.

Formakin Estate, By Bishopton

A group of buildings and landscaped grounds designed in the Arts and Crafts style at the turn of the century. Currently being restored, the estate has a visitor centre, tea room and guided tours. Open Saturday and Sunday 11 a.m.-6 p.m. Tel: 0505 863400

Gleniffer Braes Country Park, Glenfield Road, Paisley

1,000 breathtaking acres including Glen Park nature trail, picnic and children's play areas. Open dawn till dusk, the park affords extensive walks and spectacular views from this elevated moorland area, and contains an area reserved for model aero flying. Tel: 041-884 3794

Houston Village

Houston was developed in the 18th century as an estate village. The traditional smiddy building, village pubs and terraced houses combine to create a quiet, sleepy atmosphere which has successfully survived the development of extensive modern housing on its periphery.

Inchinnan Bridges

Early 19th century stone bridges over the White Cart and Black Cart rivers close to St Conval's stone, and the site of the Inchinnan Church which houses the graves of the Knights Templar, whose order was introduced to Scotland in 1153 by King David I.

Johnstone Castle

The remnants of a 1700 building formerly a much larger structure but largely demolished in the 1950's. The castle has significant historical links with the Cochrane and Houston families, major landowners who were instrumental in the development of the Burgh of Johnstone.

Kilbarchan Village

A good example of an 18 Century weaving village with many original buildings still fronting the narrow streets. A focal point is the steeple building in the square, orginally a school and meal market and now used as public meeting rooms. A cycle route/footpath system links it to Glasgow and the Clyde Coast.

Laigh Kirk, Paisley

Originally built in 1738, the Laigh Kirk has been converted to an Arts Centre, with a theatre, workshop, bistro and bar open daily 10 a.m.-11 p.m. For further information telephone 041-887 1010

Linwood Sports Centre

A wide range of indoor and outdoor sporting activities include football and Rugby pitches, games hall, squash courts, BMX track, fitness trail, tennis courts and conditioning suite.

Lochwinnoch Village

An attractive rural village close to the Castle Semple Water Park, Muirshiel Country Park and the R.S.P.B. nature reserve, Lochwinnoch contains a small local museum with displays reflecting agricultural, social and industrial aspects of village life. Museum open Monday, Wednesday and Friday 10am–1pm, 2–5pm and 6–8pm. Tuesday and Saturday 10am–1pm and 2–5pm. Open most days throughout the year, visitors should telephone Lochwinnoch 842615.

Muirshiel Country Park

Four miles north of Lochwinnoch, the park features trails of varying length radiating from the Information Centre. open daily 9 a.m.-4-30 p.m. (Winter), 9 a m.-7-30 p.m. (Summer). Tel: Lochwinnoch 842803

Paisley Town Trail

An easy-to-follow route taking in the town's historic and architecturally significant buildings. Visitors can spend an hour or two walking round the trail and referring to a printed guide and wall plaques on the main buildings.

Paisley, Lagoon Leisure Centre

Ultra-modern complex with extensive "fun" pool featuring artificial wave machine and water slides. Also has cafe/bar facilities. Unique within the area, the complex is easily reached by public trasport and has ample parking. Monday-Friday 10 a.m.-10 p.m., Saturday and Sunday 10 a.m.-5.00 p.m. Tel: 041-889 4000.

Paisley Abbey

Birthplace of the Stewart Dynasty, the Abbey dates, in part, to the 12th century and features regimental flags, relics, the Barochan Cross and beautiful stained glass windows. Monday-Saturday 10.00 a.m.-12.00 p.m., 1.00-3.00p.m. Tel: 041-889 3630.

Paisley Town Hall

A Renaissance style building by the River Cart in the heart of Paisley, it features a slim clock tower and houses a Tourist Information Centre. It accommodates many exhibitions during the year and is also available for conferences and functions. Monday–Saturday 9am–5pm. Tel: 041-887 1007.

Paisley Museum and Art Gallery, High Street, Paisley

In addition to the world famous collection of Paisley shawls, the Museum traces the history of the Paisley pattern, the development of weaving techniques and houses collections of local and natural history, ceramics and paintings. Monday-Saturday 10 a.m.-5 p.m. Tel: 041-889 3151.

Renfrew Town Hall

The Town Hall has a "fairy-tale" style to its 105 feet high spire and was the administrative centre of the Royal Burgh of Renfrew. Originally the principal town in the area, Renfrew was strategically placed on the River Clyde, and a passenger ferry continues to operate daily.

Robert Tannahill, Weaver Poet

The works of Tannahill ranks with those of Burns. Born 1774 he took his own life in 1810 and is buried in a nearby graveyard. Visitors can visit his early home, site of his death, and his grave, and read his works in Paisley Library.

Royal Society for Protection of Birds, Lochwinnoch

An interesting visitor centre with observation tower, hides, displays and gift shop. Thursday, Friday, Saturday and Sunday 10 a.m.-5.15 p.m. Shop open 7 days. Tel: Lochwinnoch 842663

Sma' Shot Cottages, Paisley

Fully restored and furnished artisan's house of the Victorian era; exhibition room displaying photographs plus artefacts of local interest. 18th century weaver's loomshop with combined living quarters. Open May-September 1-5 p.m. Group visits arranged by appointment. Tel: 041-812 2513 or 041-889 0530.

The Clyde Estuary

Visitors travelling along the rural route of the Old Greenock Road above Langbank village at the western end of the District are able to take advantage of extensive views of the upper and lower Clyde Estuary, the Gareloch and the mountains beyond.

Thomas Coats Memorial Church

Open Monday-Friday 9 a.m.-12 noon. Visitors should check in advance. Another gift from the Coats family to Paisley, the church was built in 1894 and constructed of red sandstone, is one of the finest Bapist Churches in the country. Tel: 041 889 9980.

Wallace Monument, Elderslie

The monument was erected in 1912 and marks the birthplace of the Scottish Patriot, Sir William Wallace. It stands adjacent to the reconstructed foundation plan of the adjacent Wallace Buildings which dated from the 17th century.

Weaver's Cottage, Kilbarchan

This cottage, built in 1723, houses the last of the village's 800 looms and demonstrations are still given. It contains displays of weaving and domestic utensils, with Cottage garden and refreshments. Open April 1–May 31 and September 1–October 31 on Tuesdays, Thursdays, Saturdays and Sundays 2–5pm, June 1–August 31 from 2–5pm daily.

Public Transport

The City of Glasgow has one of the most advanced, fully integrated public transport systems in the whole of Europe. The Strathclyde Transport network consists of; the local British Rail network, the local bus services and the fully modernised Glasgow Underground, with links to Glasgow Airport and the Steamer and Car Ferry Services.
Note: Although the information in this section is correct at the time of printing it should be checked before use.

Bus Services and Tours

Long Distance Coach Service
Scottish Citylink Coaches Ltd
041-332 9191

Shorter Journeys
Tel: 041-226 4826(0630-2300 Daily)
for City Services and buses to Airdrie, Clydebank, Cumbernauld, Dumbarton, East Kilbride, Erskine, Hamilton, Johnstone, Kirkintilloch, Paisley, Wishaw
Buses leave from Anderston Cross Bus Station 041-248 7432.
for Ayr, Bearsden, Bellshill, Blantyre, Cumbernauld, Edinburgh, Glasgow Airport, Gourock, Hamilton, Kilmarnock, Lanark, Motherwell, Prestwick, Renfrew, Newmains, Wishaw etc.

Buses leave from Buchanan Bus Station 041-332 7133.
for Aberfoyle, Airdrie, Bishopbriggs Callander, Coatbridge, Cumbernauld, Dundee, Dunfermline, Edinburgh, Glasgow Airport, Glencoe, Kirkintilloch,

Kilsyth, Leven, Milngavie, Perth, St.Andrews, Stirling etc.

Day and Half Day Tours
Scottish City Link
Buchanan Bus Station.
041-332 8055

Haldane's of Cathcart, Delvin Road, G44. 041-637 2234.

Strathclyde Buses Ltd.
197 Victoria Road, G42 7AD
041-636 3190
(Glasgow City Bus Tour and Glimpses of Charles R. Mackintosh Architecture with C.R.M. Society) 041-636 3195

British Rail
Passenger enquiries: 041-204 2844.
Sleeper reservations: 041-221 2305.

Central Station
Inter-City electric services for English destinations, including Carlisle, Preston, Liverpool, Manchester (3 hours 35 minutes), Leeds, Nottingham, Crewe, Birmingham (4 hours 20 minutes), London (Euston) (5 hours). Also connections for Wales and West of England.
Scottish destinations in South and West include Ayr (for Burns country), Kilmarnock, Dumfries, Stranraer (for Ireland via Larne), Ardrossan and Largs. Electric trains include Gourock and Wemyss Bay (for Clyde steamers).

Queen Street Station
Trains for scenic West Highland Line to Oban, Fort William and Mallaig. Steamer connections to the Islands. Inter-City expresses for Edinburgh, connecting with trains to England including Newcastle, York, London (King's Cross). Services for North and East Scotland, including Fife, Stirling, Perth, Dundee, Aberdeen, Inverness, Wick, Thurso, Kyle of Lochalsh.
Electric trains: Dumbarton, Balloch (for Loch Lomond), Helensburgh. City Rail Link Service bus connects Queen Street Station and Central Station.

Parks & Gardens

There are over 70 public parks within the city. The most famous is Glasgow Green. Abutting the north bank of the River Clyde, it was acquired in 1662. Of interest are the Winter Gardens attached to the People's Palace. Kelvingrove Park is an 85-acre park laid out by Sir Joseph Paxton in 1852. On the south side of the city is the 148-acre Queen's Park, Victoria Road, established 1857-94. Also of interest: Rouken Glen, Thornliebank, with a spectacular waterfall, walled garden, nature trail and boating facilities; Victoria Park, Victoria Park Drive, with its famous Fossil Grove flower gardens and yachting pond. In Great Western Road are the Botanic Gardens. Founded in 1817, the gardens' 42 acres are crammed with natural attractions, including the celebrated Kibble Palace glasshouse with its fabulous tree ferns, exotic plants and white marble Victorian statues.

The main public parks in Glasgow are:

Alexandra
671 Alexandra Parade, G31.
Bellahouston
Paisley Road West, G52.
Botanic Gardens
730 Gt. Western Road, G12.
Hogganfield Loch
Cumbernauld Road, G33.
Kelvingrove
Sauchiehall Street, G3.
King's
325 Carmunnock Road, G44.
Linn
Clarkston Road at Netherlee Road, G44.
Queen's
Victoria Road, G42.
Rouken Glen
Rouken Glen Road, G46.
Springburn
Broomfield Road, G21.
Tollcross
461 Tollcross Road, G32.
Victoria
Victoria Park Drive North, G14.

Kibble Palace

Strathclyde Further Education

Anniesland College
Hatfield Drive, Glasgow, G12 0YE.
041-357 3969

Ayr College
Dam Park, Ayr, KA8 0EU.
Ayr (0292) 265184

Barmulloch College
186 Rye Road, Glasgow, G21 3JY.
041-558 9071

Bell College of Technology
Almada Street, Hamilton,
Lanarkshire, ML3 0JB.
Hamilton (0698) 283100

Cambuslang College
Hamilton Road,
Cambuslang, Glasgow, G72 7BS.
041-641 6197

Cardonald College of Further Education
690 Mosspark Drive, Glasgow,
G52 3AY.
041-883 6151

Central College of Commerce
300 Cathedral Street, G1 2TA.
041-552 3941

Clydebank College
Kilbowie Road, Clydebank,
Dunbartonshire, G81 2AA.
041-952 7771

Coatbridge College
Kildonan Street, Coatbridge,
Lanarkshire, ML5 3LS.
Coatbridge (0236) 22316

Cumbernauld College
Town Centre, Cumbernauld,
Glasgow, G67 1HU.
Cumbernauld (0236) 731811

Glasgow College of Building and Printing
60 North Hanover Street, Glasgow,
G1 2BP.
041-332 9969

Glasgow College of Food Technology
230 Cathedral Street, Glasgow,
G1 2TG.
041-552 3751

Glasgow College of Nautical Studies
21 Thistle Street, Glasgow, G5 9XB.
041-429 3201

Glasgow College of Technology
Cowcaddens Road, Glasgow,
G4 0BA.
041-332 7090

James Watt College
Finnart Street, Greenock,
Renfrewshire, PA16 8HF.
Greenock (0475) 24433

John Wheatley College
1346-1364 Shettleston Road,
Glasgow G32 9AT
041-778 2426

Kilmarnock College
Holehouse Road, Kilmarnock,
Ayrshire, KA3 7AT.
Kilmarnock (0563) 23501

Langside College
50 Prospecthill Road, Glasgow,
G42 9LB.
041-649 4991

Motherwell College
Dalzell Drive, Motherwell,
Lanarkshire, ML4 2DD.
Motherwell (0698) 59641

Reid Kerr College, The
Renfrew Road, Paisley, Renfrewshire,
PA13 4DR
041-889 4225

Springburn College
110 Flemington Street, Glasgow,
G21 4BX.
041-558 9001

Stow College
43 Shamrock Street, Glasgow,
G4 9LD.
041-332 1786

University of Glasgow
University Avenue, Glasgow
041-339 8855

University of Strathclyde,
George Street, Glasgow
G11XQ
041 552 4400

Hospitals

**Greater Glasgow Health Board
(Adminstration)
112 Ingram St., Glasgow G1 1ET
041-552-6222**

Acorn Street Psychiatric Day Hospital
23 Acorn Street, Bridgeton,
Glasgow G40 4AA
041-556 4789

Baillieston Health Centre
20 Muirside Road,
Glasgow G69 7AD
041-771 0871

Belvidere Hospital
London Road, Glasgow G31 4PG
041-554 1855

Birdston Hospital, Milton of Campsie
Glasgow G65 8BY
041-776 6114

Blawarthill Hospital,
129 Holehouse Drive,
Knightswood.Glasgow G13 3TG
041-954 9547

Bridgeton Health Centre
201 Abercromby Street
Glasgow G40 2EA
041-554 1866

Broomhill & Lanfine Hospitals
Kirkintilloch, Glasgow G66 1RR
041-776 5141

Carsewell House (Psychiatric
Outpatient)
5 Oakley Terrace, Glasgow G31 2HX
041-554 6267

Castlemilk Health Centre
Dougrie Drive, Castlemilk,
Glasgow G45
041-634 3434

Canniesburn Hospital
Switchback Road, Bearsden,
Glasgow G61 1QL
041-942 2255

Charing Cross (Alcohol and Drug)
Day Centre, 8 Woodside Crescent,
Glasgow G3 7UL
041-332 5463

Children's Home Hospital
Strathblane, Glasgow G63 9EP
0360 70203

Clydebank Health Centre
Kilbowie Road, Clydebank G81 2TQ
041-952 2080

Cowglen Hospital
Boydstone Road, Glasgow G53 6XJ
041-632 9106

Darnley Hospital
755 Nitshill Road, Glasgow G53 7RR
041-881 1005

David Elder Infirmary
503 Langlands Road, Glasgow G51 4DY
041-445 2466

Douglas Inch Centre
2 Woodside Terrace,
Glasgow G3 7UY
041-332 3844

Drumchapel Hospital
129 Drumchapel Road,
Glasgow G15 6PX
041-944 2344

Duke Street Hospital
253 Duke Street, Glasgow G31 1HY
041-556 5222

Duntocher Hospital
Duntocher, Clydebank G81 5QU
Duntocher 74294

Easterhouse Health Centre
9 Auchinlea Road, Glasgow G34 9QU
041-771 0781

Gartloch Hospital, Gartloch Road,
Gartcosh, Glasgow G69 8EJ
041-771 0771

Gartnavel General Hospital
1053 Great Western Road,
Glasgow G12 0YN
041-334 8122

Gartnavel Royal Hospital
1055 Great Western Road,
Glasgow G12 0XH
041-334 6241

Glasgow Dental Hospital and School
378 Sauchiehall Street
Glasgow G2 3JZ
041-332 7020

Glasgow Eye Infirmary
3 Sandyford Place, Glasgow G3 7NB
041-204 0721

Glasgow Homeopathic Hospital
1000 Great Western Road,
Glasgow G12 0AA
041-339 0382

Glasgow Royal Infirmary
84 Castle Street, Glasgow G4 0SF
041-552 3535

Glasgow Royal Maternity Hospital
Rottenrow, Glasgow G4 0NA
041-552 3400

Glasgow School of Chiropody
757 Crookston Road,
Glasgow G53 7UA
041-883 0418

Glasgow School of Occupational
Therapy, 29 Sherbrooke Avenue,
Glasgow G41 4ER
041-427 3032

Gorbals Health Centre
45 Pine Place, Glasgow G5 0BQ
041-429 6291

Govan Health Centre
5 Drumoyne Road,
Glasgow G51 4BJ
041-440 1212

Govanhill Health Centre
233 Calder Street
Glasgow G42 7DR
041-424 3003

Knightswood Hospital
125 Knightswood Road,
Glasgow G12 2XG
041-954 9641

Lennox Castle Hospital
Lennoxtown, Glasgow G65 7LB
Lennoxtown 313000

Lenzie Hospital
Auchinloch Road, Kirkintilloch,
Glasgow G66 5DF
041-776 1208

Leverndale Hospital
510 Crookston Road
Glasgow G53 7TU
041-882 6255

Lightburn Hospital
Carntyne Road, Glasgow G32 6ND
041-774 5102

Maryhill Health Centre
41 Shawpark Street,
Glasgow G20 9DR
041-946 7151

Mearnskirk Hospital
Newton Mearns, Glasgow G77 5RZ
041-639 2251

Parkhead Health Centre
101 Salamanca Street,
Glasgow G31 5BA
041-556 5232

Parkhead Hospital
81 Salamanca Street,
Glasgow
041-554 7951

Philipshill Hospital
East Kilbride Road, Busby,
Glasgow G76 9HW
041-644 1144

Pollock Health Centre
21 Cowglen Road
Glasgow G53 6EQ
041-880 8899

Possilpark Health Centre
85 Denmark Street,
Glasgow G22 5EG
041-336 5311

Queen Mother's Hospital
Yorkhill, Glasgow G3 8SH
041-339 8888

Royal Hospital for Sick Children
129 Drumchapel Road
Glasgow G15 6PX
041-944 2344

Royal Hospital for Sick Children
Yorkhill, Glasgow G3 8SJ
041-339 8888

Royal Samaritan Hospital for Women
69 Coplaw Street, Glasgow G42 7JF
041-423 3033

Ruchill Hospital
Bilsland Drive, Glasgow G20 9NB
041-946 7120

Rutherglen Health Centre
130 Stonelaw Road, Rutherglen,
Glasgow G73 2PQ
041-647 7171

Rutherglen Maternity Hospital
120 Stonelaw Road, Rutherglen,
Glasgow G73 2PG
041-647 0011

Shettleston Health Centre
420 Old Shettleston Road,
Glasgow G32 7JZ
041-778 9191

Southern General Hospital
1345 Govan Road, Glasgow G51 4TF
041-445 2466

Springburn Health Centre
200 Springburn Way,
Glasgow G21 1TR
041-558 0101

Stobhill General Hospital
133 Balornock Road,
Glasgow G21 3UW
041-558 0111

Stoneyetts Hospital
Chryston, Glasgow G69 0JG
041-776 1026

Thornliebank Health Centre
20 Kennishead Road
Glasgow G46 8NY
041-620 2222

Townhead Health Centre
16 Alexandra Parade
Glasgow G31 2ES
041-552 3477

Victoria Geriatric Unit
Mansionhouse Road,
Glasgow G41 3DX
041-649 4511

Victoria Infirmary
Langside Road, Glasgow G42 9TY
041-649 4545

Waverley Park Hospital
Kirkintilloch, Glasgow G66 2HE
041-776 2461

Western Infirmary
Dumbarton Road, Glasgow G11 6NT
041-339 8822

Woodilee Hospital
Kirkintilloch, Glasgow G66 3UG
041-776 2451

Woodside Health Centre
Barr Street, Glasgow G20 7LR
041-332 9977

INDEX TO STREETS

General Abbreviations

All.	Alley	Ct.	Court	Mans.	Mansions
App.	Approach	Dr.	Drive	Mkt.	Market
Arc.	Arcade	E.	East	Ms.	Mews
Av.	Avenue	Est.	Estate	Mt.	Mount
Bldgs.	Buildings	Esp.	Esplanade	N.	North
Boul.	Boulevard	Gdns.	Gardens	Par.	Parade
Bri.	Bridge	Gra.	Grange	Pass.	Passage
Circ.	Circus	Grn.	Green	Pk.	Park
Cft.	Croft	Gro.	Grove	Pl.	Place
Clo.	Close	Ho.	House	Prom.	Promenade
Cor.	Corner	Ind.	Industrial	Quad.	Quadrant
Cotts.	Cottages	La.	Lane	Ri.	Rise
Cres.	Crescent	Lo.	Lodge	Rd.	Road

S.	South
Sq.	Square
Sta.	Station
St.	Street
Ter.	Terrace
Trd.	Trading
Vills.	Villas
Vw.	View
W.	West
Wf.	Wharf
Wk.	Walk
Yd.	Yard

District Abbreviations

Bail.	Baillieston	Clark.	Clarkston	Giff.	Giffnock	Old K.	Old Kilpatrick
Barr.	Barrhead	Clyde.	Clydebank	John.	Johnstone	Pais.	Paisley
Bear.	Bearsden	Coat.	Coatbridge	Kilb.	Kilbarchan	Renf.	Renfrew
Bish.	Bishopbriggs	Cumb.	Cumbernauld	Kirk.	Kirkintilloch	Step.	Stepps
Blan.	Blantyre	Dalm.	Dalmuir	Lenz.	Lenzie	Thorn.	Thornliebank
Both.	Bothwell	E.K.	East Kilbride	Linw.	Linwood	Udd.	Uddingston
Chr.	Chryston	Gart.	Gartcosh	Neil.	Neilston		

NOTES

The figures and letters following a street name indicate the postal district for that street with the square and page number where it will be found in the atlas. Thus the postal district for Abbey Drive is G14, and it will be found in square H12 on page 19.

A street name followed by the name of another street in italics does not appear on the map, but will be found adjoining or near the latter.

Abbey Clo., Pais.	M	6	46	Abington St. G20	H16	21	Aikenhead Rd. G42	M16	51
Abbey Dr. G14	H12	19	Aboukir St. G51	K12	33	Ailean Dr. G32	M24	55
Abbey Rd., John.	N	2	44	Aboyne Dr., Pais.	N	6	46	Ailean Gdns. G32	M24	55
Abbeycraig Rd. G34	J26	40	Aboyne St. G51	L12	33	Ailort Av. G44	P16	63
Abbeydale Way G73	Q20	65	Acacia Av. G78	P	7	59	*Lochinver Dr.*		
Neilvaig Dr.			Acacia Dr., Pais.	N	4	45	Ailsa Dr. G42	O15	51
Abbeyhill St. G32	K21	38	Acacia Pl., John.	O	1	44	Ailsa Dr. G73	P18	64
Abbeylands Rd., Clyde.	B	8	5	Academy Rd., Giff.	R14	62	Ailsa Dr., Clyde.	C	8	5
Abbot St. G41	N15	51	Academy St. G32	M22	54	Ailsa Dr., Pais.	O	5	46
Frankfort St.			Acer Cres. G78	N	4	45	Ailsa Dr., Udd.	Q28	69
Abbot St., Pais.	L	6	30	Achamore Pl. G15	D	9	6	Ailsa Rd., Bish.	E19	11
Abbotsburn Way, Pais.	K	5	30	*Achamore Rd.*			Ailsa Rd., Renf.	J	8	31
Abbotsford Av. G73	O19	53	Achamore Rd. G15	D	9	6	Ainslie Rd. G52	K10	32
Abbotsford Cres., Pais.	O	2	44	Achray Dr., Pais.	N	4	45	Ainslie Rd., Cumb.	B	4	71
Abbotsford Ct., Cumb.	D	2	70	Acorn Ct. G4	M18	52	Airdale Rd., Giff.	R14	62
Abbotsford La. G5	M16	51	*Acorn St.*			Airgold Dr. G15	D	9	6
Cumberland St.			Acorn St. G40	M18	52	Airgold Pl. G15	D	9	6
Abbotsford Pl. G5	M16	51	Acre Dr. G20	E14	8	Airlie Av., Bear.	C12	7
Abbotsford Pl., Cumb.	D	2	70	Acre Rd. G20	E13	8	*Tweedsmuir Dr.*		
Abbotsford Rd., Bear.	C11	7	Acredyke Cres. G21	F20	23	Airlie Gdns. G73	Q20	65
Abbotsford Rd., Clyde.	E	7	5	Acredyke Pl. G21	G20	23	Airlie Rd., Bail.	M25	56
Abbotsford Rd., Cumb.	D	2	70	Acredyke Rd. G21	F19	23	Airlie St. G12	H13	20
Abbotsford, Bish.	E20	11	Acredyke Rd. G73	O18	52	Airlour Rd. G43	P15	63
Abbotshall Av. G15	D	9	6	Acrehill St. G33	J20	37	Airth Dr. G52	M12	49
Abbotsinch Rd.,	J	6	30	Adams Court La. G2	K16	35	Airth La. G51	M12	49
Pais. & Renf.			*Howard St.*			Airth Pl. G51	M12	49
Abbott Cres., Clyde.	F	8	17	Adamswell St. G21	H18	22	Airthrey Av. G14	H12	19
Aberconway St., Clyde.	F	8	17	Adamswell Ter., Chr.	E28	15	Aitken St. G31	K20	37
Abercorn Av. G52	K	9	32	Addiewell St. G32	K22	38	Aitkenhead Av., Coat.	M28	57
Abercorn Pl. G23	E15	9	Addison Gro., Thorn.	Q12	61	Aitkenhead Rd., Udd.	O28	57
Abercorn St., Pais.	L	6	30	Addison Pl., Thorn.	Q12	61	Alasdair Ct., Barr.	R	8	59
Abercrombie Cres., Bail.	L27	41	Addison Rd. G12	H14	20	Albany Av. G32	L23	39
Abercromby Dr. G40	L18	36	Addison Rd., Thorn.	Q12	61	Albany Cotts. G13	G12	19
Abercromby Sq. G40	L18	36	Adelphi St. G5	L17	36	*Crow Rd.*		
Abercromby St. G40	L18	36	Admiral St. G41	L15	35	Albany Dr. G73	P19	65
Aberdalgie Path G34	K25	40	Advie Pl. G42	O16	51	Albany Pl., Both.	R28	69
Aberdalgie Rd. G34	K25	40	*Prospecthill Rd.*			*Marguerite Gdns.*		
Aberdour St. G31	K20	37	Affric Dr., Pais.	N	7	47	Albany Quad. G32	L23	39
Aberfeldy St. G31	K20	37	Afton Cres., Bear.	D13	8	*Mansionhouse Dr.*		
Aberfoyle St. G31	K20	37	Afton Dr., Renf.	H	9	18	Albany St. G40	M19	53
Aberlady Rd. G51	K12	33	Afton Rd., Cumb.	B	3	71	Albany Ter. G72	Q21	66
Abernethy Dr., Linw.	L	1	28	Afton St. G41	O15	51	Albany Way, Pais.	K	6	30
Abernethy St. G31	K20	37	Agamemnon St., Dalm.	E	6	4	*Abbotsburn Way*		
Aberuthven Dr. G32	M22	54	Aigas Cotts. G13	G12	19	Albert Av. G42	N15	51
Abiegail Pl., Blan.	R26	68	*Crow Rd.*			Albert Cross G41	M15	51

95

Albert Ct. G41	M15	51
Albert Dr.		
Albert Dr. G41	N14	50
Albert Dr. G73	P19	65
Albert Dr., Bear.	E13	8
Albert Rd. G42	N16	51
Albert Rd., Clyde.	D 7	5
Albert Rd., Lenz.	D23	13
Albert Rd., Renf.	H 8	17
Alberta Pl. G12	H14	20
Saltoun St.		
Albion St. G1	K17	36
Albion St., Bail.	M24	55
Albion St., Pais.	L 6	30
Alcaig Rd. G52	N12	49
Alder Av., Lenz.	C22	12
Alder Ct., Barr.	R 8	59
Alder Pl. G43	P14	62
Alder Pl., John.	N 1	44
Alder Rd. G43	P14	62
Alder Rd., Cumb.	C 4	71
Alder Rd., Dalm.	C 6	4
Alderman Pl. G13	G11	19
Alderman Rd. G13	F 9	18
Aldersdyke Pl., Blan.	R26	68
Alderside Dr., Udd.	O27	57
Alexander St., Clyde.	E 7	5
Alexandra Av. G33	G23	25
Alexandra Av., Lenz.	D23	13
Alexandra Cross G31	K19	37
Duke St.		
Alexandra Ct. G31	K19	37
Roebank St.		
Alexandra Dr., Pais.	M 4	45
Alexandra Dr., Renf.	H 8	17
Alexandra Gdns., Lenz.	D23	13
Alexandra Par. G31	K19	37
Alexandra Park St. G31	K19	37
Alexandra Rd., Lenz.	D23	13
Alford St. G21	H17	22
Alfred Ter. G52	H14	20
Great Western Rd.		
Algie St. G41	O15	51
Alice St. G5	M17	52
Alice St., Pais.	N 6	46
Aline Ct., Barr.	Q 7	59
Allan Av., Renf.	J 9	32
Allan Pl. G40	M19	53
Allan St. G40	N19	53
Allander Gdns., Bish.	D18	10
Allander Rd., Bear.	D11	7
Allander St. G22	H17	22
Allands Av., Renf.	G 5	16
Allanfauld Rd., Cumb.	B 2	70
Allanton Av., Pais.	M 9	48
Allanton Dr. G52	L10	32
Allerton Gdns., Bail.	M24	55
Alleysbank G73	N19	53
Allison Dr. G72	P22	66
Allison Pl. G42	N16	51
Prince Edward St.		
Allison Pl. Gart.	H27	27
Allison St. G42	N16	51
Allnach Pl. G34	K27	41
Alloway Cres. G73	P18	64
Alloway Dr. G73	P18	64
Alloway Dr., Clyde.	D 8	5
Alloway Rd. G43	P14	62
Alma St. G40	L19	37
Almond Av., Renf.	J 9	32
Almond Cres., Pais.	N 3	45
Almond Dr., Lenz.	C22	12
Almond Rd. G33	G23	25
Almond Rd., Bear.	E11	7
Almond St. G33	J20	37
Almond Vale, Udd.	O28	57
Hamilton Vw.		
Alness Cres. G52	M12	49
Alpatrick Gdns., John.	M 1	44
Alpine Gro., Udd.	O27	57
Alsatian Av., Clyde	E 8	5
Alston La. G40	L18	36
Claythorn St.		
Altnacreag Gdns., Chr.	D28	15
Alton Gdns. G12	H14	20
Great George St.		
Alton Rd., Pais.	M 8	47
Altyre St. G32	M21	54
Alva Gate. G52	N12	49
Alva Gdns. G52	N12	49
Alva Pl., Lenz.	D24	13
Alyth Cres., Clark.	S16	63
Alyth Gdns. G52	M12	49
Alyth Gdns., Clark.	S16	63
Ambassador Way, Renf.	J 8	31
Cockels Loan		
Amisfield St. G20	G15	21
Amochrie Dr., Pais.	O 4	45
Amochrie Rd., Pais.	N 3	45
Amulree Pl. G32	M22	54
Amulree St. G32	L22	38
Ancaster Dr. G13	G12	19
Ancaster La. G13	F11	19
Great Western Rd.		
Anchor Av., Pais.	M 7	47
Anchor Cres., Pais.	M 7	47
Anchor Dr., Pais.	M 7	47
Anchor Wynd, Pais.	M 7	47
Ancroft St. G20	H16	21
Anderson Dr., Renf.	H 8	17
Anderson Gdns., Blan.	R27	69
Station Rd.		
Anderson Quay G3	L15	35
Anderson St. G11	J13	34
Andrew Av., Lenz.	D23	13
Andrew Av., Renf.	H 9	18
Andrew Dr., Clyde.	F 8	17
Andrew Sillars Av. G72	P23	67
Andrews St., Pais.	L 6	30
Anglegate G14	H11	19
Angus Av. G52	M11	49
Angus Av., Bish.	F20	23
Angus Gdns., Udd.	O27	57
Angus La. G64	E20	11
Angus Oval G52	M10	48
Angus Pl. G52	M10	48
Angus St. G21	H18	22
Angus St., Clyde.	F 9	18
Angus Wk., Udd.	O28	57
Annan Dr. G73	O20	53
Annan Dr., Bear.	D11	7
Annan Dr., Pais.	N 3	45
Annan Pl., John.	O08	43
Annan St. G42	O16	51
Annandale St. G42	M16	51
Annbank St. G31	L18	36
Anne Av., Renf.	H 8	17
Anne Cres., Lenz.	D23	13
Annette St. G42	N16	51
Annfield Gdns., Blan.	R26	68
Annfield Pl. G31	K18	36
Annick Dr., Bear.	E11	7
Annick St. G32	L22	38
Annick St. G72	P23	67
Anniesdale Av. G33	G23	25
Anniesland Cres. G14	G10	18
Anniesland Mansions G13	G12	19
Ancaster Dr.		
Anniesland Rd. G13	G11	19
Anniesland Rd. G14	G10	18
Anson St. G40	M18	52
Anson Way, Renf.	J 8	31
Britannia Way		
Anstruther St. G32	L21	38
Antonine Gdns., Clyde.	C 7	5
Antonine Rd., Bear.	C10	6
Anworth St. G32	M22	54
Appin Rd. G31	K19	37
Appin Ter. G73	Q20	65
Lochaber Dr.		
Appin Way, Udd.	Q28	69
Bracken Ter.		
Appleby St. G22	H16	21
Applecross Gdns., Chr.	D27	15
Applecross St. G22	H16	21
Appledore Cres., Udd.	Q28	69
Apsley La. G11	J13	34
Apsley St. G11	J13	34
Aray St. G20	G14	20
Arbroath Av. G52	M10	48
Arcadia St. G40	L18	36
Arcadia St. G40	L18	36
Drake St.		
Arcan Cres. G15	E10	6
Archerfield Av. G32	N22	54
Archerfield Cres. G32	N22	54
Archerfield Dr. G32	N22	54
Archerfield Gro. G32	N22	54
Archerhill Av. G13	F 9	18
Archerhill Cotts. G13	F10	18
Archerhill Rd.		
Archerhill Cres. G13	F10	18
Archerhill Gdns. G13	F10	18
Archerhill Rd.		
Archerhill Rd. G13	F10	18
Archerhill Sq. G13	F10	18
Kelso St.		
Archerhill St. G13	F10	18
Archerhill Rd.		
Archerhill Ter. G13	F10	18
Archerhill Rd.		
Ard Pl. G42	O18	52
Ard Rd., Renf.	H 7	17
Ard St. G32	M22	54
Ardagie Dr. G32	O23	55
Ardagie Pl. G32	O23	55
Ardbeg Av. G73	Q21	66
Ardbeg Av., Bish.	E20	11
Ardbeg St. G42	N16	51
Ardconnel St. G46	Q12	61
Arden Av. G46	R12	61
Arden Dr., Giff.	R13	62
Arden Pl. G46	R12	61
Stewarton Rd.		
Ardencraig Cres. G44	R17	64
Ardencraig Dr. G45	R18	64
Ardencraig La. G45	R17	64
Ardencraig Rd.		
Ardencraig Quad. G45	R18	64
Ardencraig Rd. G45	R17	64
Ardencraig St. G45	R19	65
Ardencraig Ter. G45	R18	64
Ardenlea Rd., Udd.	O27	57
Ardenlea St. G40	M19	53
Ardery St. G11	J13	34
Apsley St.		
Ardessie Pl. G20	G14	20
Ardessie St. G23	E14	8
Torrin Rd.		
Ardfern St. G32	M22	54
Ardgay Pl. G32	M22	54
Ardgay St. G32	M22	54
Ardgay Way G73	Q19	65
Ardgour Dr., Linw.	L 1	28
Ardgowan Av., Pais.	M 6	46
Ardgowan Dr., Udd.	O27	57
Ardgowan St., Pais.	N 6	46
Ardholm St. G32	L22	38
Ardhu Pl. G15	D 9	6
Ardlamont Sq., Linw.	L 2	28
Ardlaw St. G51	L12	33
Ardle Rd. G43	P15	63
Ardlui St. G32	M21	54
Ardmaleish Cres. G45	R18	64
Ardmaleish Rd. G45	R17	64
Ardmaleish St. G45	R18	64
Ardmaleish Ter. G45	R18	64
Ardmay Cres. G44	O17	52
Ardmillan St. G33	K21	38
Ardmore Oval, Pais.	L 4	29
Ardmore St. G31	K19	37
Ardmory Av. G42	O17	52
Ardmory La. G42	O18	52
Ardnacross Dr. G33	J23	39
Ardnahoe Av. G42	O17	52
Ardnahoe Pl. G42	O17	52
Ardneil Rd. G51	L12	33
Ardnish St. G51	K12	33
Ardo Gdns. G51	L13	34
Ardoch Gro. G72	P21	66
Ardoch Rd., Bear.	C13	8
Ardoch St. G22	H17	22
Ardoch Way, Chr.	E27	15
Braeside Av.		
Ardshiel Rd. G51	K12	33
Ardsloy La. G14	H10	18
Ardsloy Pl.		
Ardsloy Pl. G14	H10	18
Ardtoe Cres. G33	G24	25
Ardtoe Pl. G33	G24	25
Arduthie Rd. G51	K12	33
Ardwell Rd. G52	M12	49
Argosy Way, Renf.	J 8	31
Britannia Way		
Argyle St. G3	J14	34
Argyle St., Pais.	M 5	46
Argyll Arc. G2	K16	35
Argyll Av., Renf.	H 7	17
Argyll Rd., Bear.	B12	7

Street	Grid	Page
Argyll Rd., Clyde.	E 8	5
Arisaig Dr. G52	M12	49
Arisaig Dr., Bear.	D13	8
Arisaig Pl. G52	M12	49
Ark La. G31	K18	36
Arkle Ter. G72	Q21	66
Arkleston Cres., Pais.	K 7	31
Arkleston Rd., Pais.	K 7	31
Arklet Rd. G51	L12	33
Arklie Av., Bear.	B12	7
Tweedsmuir Cres.		
Arlington St. G3	J15	35
Armadale Ct. G31	K19	37
Armadale Path G31	K19	37
Armadale Pl. G31	K19	37
Armadale St. G31	K19	37
Armour Pl., John.	M 1	44
Armour St. G31	L18	36
Armour St., John.	M 1	44
Arngask Rd. G51	K12	33
Arnhall Pl. G52	M12	49
Arnholm Pl. G52	M12	49
Arnisdale Pl. G34	K25	40
Arnisdale Rd. G34	K25	40
Arnisdale Way G73	Q19	65
Shieldaig Dr.		
Arniston St. G32	K21	38
Arnol Pl. G33	K24	39
Arnold Av., Bish.	E19	11
Arnold St. G20	G16	21
Arnott Way G72	P22	66
Arnprior Gdns., Chr.	E27	15
Braeside Av.		
Arnprior Quad. G45	Q17	64
Arnprior Rd. G45	Q17	64
Arnprior St. G45	Q17	64
Arnside Av., Giff.	Q14	62
Arnthern St. G72	P23	67
Arnwood Dr. G12	G13	20
Aron Ter. G72	Q21	66
Aros Dr. G52	N12	49
Arran Dr. G52	M12	49
Arran Dr., Cumb.	D 1	70
Arran Dr., Giff.	R13	62
Arran Dr., John.	N08	43
Arran Dr., Pais.	O 6	46
Arran La., Chr.	E28	15
Burnbrae Av.		
Arran Pl., Clyde.	E 8	5
Arran Pl., Linw.	L 1	28
Arran Rd., Renf.	J 8	31
Arran Ter. G73	P18	64
Arranthrue Cres., Renf.	H 8	17
Arranthrue Dr., Renf.	H 8	17
Arriochmill Rd. G20	H14	20
Kelvin Dr.		
Arrochar Ct. G23	F15	21
Sunningdale Rd.		
Arrochar Dr. G23	E14	8
Arrochar St. G23	F14	20
Arrol Pl. G40	M19	53
Arrol St. G52	K 9	32
Arrowchar Ct. G23	F15	21
Arrowchar St.		
Arrowchar St. G23	F14	20
Arrowsmith Av. G13	F11	19
Arthur Av., Barr.	R 7	59
Arthur Rd., Pais.	O 6	46
Arthur St. G3	J14	34
Arthur St., Pais.	L 5	30
Arthurlie Av., Barr.	R 8	59
Arthurlie Dr., Giff.	R14	62
Arthurlie St. G51	K12	33
Arthurlie St., Barr.	R 8	59
Arundel Dr. G42	O16	51
Arundel Dr., Bish.	D19	11
Asbury Ct., Linw.	L 2	28
Ascaig Cres. G52	N12	49
Ascog Rd., Bear.	E12	7
Ascog St. G42	N16	51
Ascot Av. G12	G12	19
Ascot Ct. G12	G13	20
Ash Gro., Bish.	E19	11
Ash Gro., Lenz.	C22	12
Ash Gro., Udd.	O28	57
Douglas Cres.		
Ash Pl., John.	N 1	44
Ash Rd., Bail.	M25	56
Ash Rd., Cumb.	A 4	71
Ash Rd., Dalm.	C 6	4
Ash Wk. G73	Q20	65
Ashburton Rd. G12	G13	20
Ashby Cres. G13	E12	7
Ashcroft Dr. G44	P18	64
Ashdale Dr. G52	M12	49
Ashdene Rd. G22	F16	21
Ashfield St. G22	H17	22
Ashfield, Bish.	D19	11
Ashgill Pl. G22	G17	22
Ashgill Rd. G22	G16	21
Ashgrove St. G40	N19	53
Ashgrove, Bail.	L27	41
Ashkirk Dr. G52	M12	49
Ashlea Dr., Giff.	Q14	62
Ashley La. G3	J15	35
Woodlands Rd.		
Ashley St. G3	J15	35
Ashmore Rd. G43	P15	63
Ashton Gdns. G12	J14	34
Ashton Rd.		
Ashton La. G12	J14	34
University Av.		
Ashton Pl. G12	H14	20
Byres Rd.		
Ashton Rd. G12	J14	34
University Av.		
Ashton Rd. G73	N19	53
Ashton Ter. G12	J14	34
Ashton Rd.		
Ashton Way G78	O 3	45
Ashtree Rd. G43	O14	50
Ashvale Cres. G21	H18	22
Ashvale Row E. G21	H18	22
Ashvale Row		
Ashvale Row W. G21	H18	22
Ashvale Row		
Aspen Pl., John.	N 1	44
Athelstane Dr., Cumb.	D 1	70
Athelstane Rd. G13	F11	19
Athena Way, Udd.	O28	57
Athol Av. G52	K 9	32
Athol Gdns., Bear.	B12	7
Athol Ter., Udd.	N27	57
Lomond Rd.		
Athole Gdns. G12	H14	20
Athole La. G12	H14	20
Saltoun St.		
Atholl Cres., Pais.	L 9	32
Atholl Dr., Giff.	S14	62
Atholl Gdns. G73	Q21	66
Atholl Gdns., Bish.	D19	11
Atholl La., Chr.	E28	15
Atholl Pl., Linw.	L 1	28
Atlas Pl. G21	H18	22
Atlas Rd. G21	H18	22
Atlas St., Clyde.	F 7	17
Attlee Av., Clyde.	E 8	5
Attlee Pl., Clyde.	E 8	5
Attlee Av.		
Attow Rd. G43	P13	62
Auburn Dr., Barr.	R 8	59
Auburn Pl. G78	L20	37
Auchans Rd., Linw.	J 1	28
Auchencrow St. G34	K26	40
Auchendale, Lenz.	C24	13
Auchengeich Rd., Chr.	D26	14
Auchengill Path G34	J26	40
Auchengill Rd.		
Auchengill Pl. G34	J26	40
Auchengill Rd. G34	J26	40
Auchenglen Dr., Chr.	E27	15
Auchenlodment Rd., John.	N 1	44
Auchentorlie Quad. Pais.	M 7	47
Auchentorlie St. G11	J12	33
Auchentoshan Av., Clyde.	C 6	4
Auchentoshan Ter. G21	J18	36
Auchentoshen Cotts., Old K.	C 5	4
Auchinairn Rd., Bish.	F18	22
Auchinbee Loop Rd., Cumb.	B 1	70
Auchinlea Rd. G34	J24	39
Auchinleck Av. G33	G21	24
Auchinleck Cres. G33	G21	24
Auchinleck Dr. G33	G21	24
Auchinleck Gdns. G33	G21	24
Auchinleck Rd. G33	F21	24
Auchinleck Rd., Clyde,	B 7	5
Auchinleck Ter., Clyde.	B 7	5
Auchinleck Rd.		
Auchinloch Rd., Lenz.	D23	13
Auchinloch St. G21	H18	22
Auchmannoch Av., Pais.	L 9	32
Auckengreoch Av., John.	O08	43
Auckengreoch Rd., John.	O08	43
Auckland Pl., Dalm.	D 5	4
Auckland St. G22	H16	21
Auld Kirk Rd. G72	Q23	67
Auld Rd., The, Cumb.	B 3	71
Auld St., Dalm.	D 6	4
Auldbar Rd. G52	M12	49
Auldbar Ter., Pais.	N 7	47
Auldburn Rd. G43	P13	62
Auldearn Rd. G21	F20	23
Auldgirth Rd. G52	M12	49
Auldhouse Av. G42	P13	62
Harriet St.		
Auldhouse Rd. G43	P13	62
Auldhouse Ter. G43	P14	62
Auldhouse Rd.		
Aultbea St. G22	F16	21
Aultmore Rd. G33	K24	39
Aurs Cres., Barr.	R 8	59
Aurs Dr., Barr.	R 8	59
Aurs Pl., Barr.	R 8	59
Aurs Rd., Barr.	Q 8	59
Aursbridge Dr., Barr.	R 8	59
Austen La. G13	G12	19
Skaterig La.		
Austen La. G13	G12	19
Woodend Dr.		
Austen Rd. G13	G12	19
Avenel Rd. G13	E12	7
Avenue End Rd. G33	H22	24
Avenue St. G40	L19	37
Avenue St. G73	N19	53
Avenue, The, Kilb.	N07	42
Low Barholm		
Avenuehead Rd., Chr.	D27	15
Avenuehead Rd., Gart.	F28	27
Avenuepark St. G20	H15	21
Aviemore Gdns., Bear.	C13	8
Aviemore Rd. G52	N12	49
Avoch Dr. G46	Q12	61
Avoch St. G34	J25	40
Avon Av., Bear.	D13	8
Avon Dr. G64	F19	23
Avon Dr., Linw.	L 1	28
Avon Rd., Bish.	F19	23
Avon Rd., Giff.	R13	62
Avon St. G5	L15	35
Avonbank Rd. G73	O18	52
Avondale Dr., Pais.	L 7	31
Avondale St. G33	J22	38
Avonhead Av. G67	D 1	70
Avonhead Gdns. G67	D 1	70
Avonhead Pl. G67	D 1	70
Avonhead Rd. G67	D 1	70
Avonspark St. G21	H19	23
Aylmer Rd. G43	P15	63
Ayr Rd., Giff.	R13	62
Ayr St. G21	H18	22
Aytoun Rd. G41	M14	50
Back Causeway G31	L20	37
Back Sneddon St., Pais.	L 6	30
Backmuir Rd. G15	D10	6
Bagnell St. G21	G18	22
Bailie Dr., Bear.	B11	7
Baillie Dr., Both.	Q28	69
Baillieston Rd. G32	M23	55
Baillieston Rd., Udd.	N25	56
Bain Sq. G40	L18	36
Bain St.		
Bain St. G40	L18	36
Bainsford St. G32	L21	38
Baird Av. G52	K 9	32
Baird Dr., Bear.	C11	7
Baird St. G4	J17	36
Bairdsbrae G4	H16	21
Possil Rd.		
Baker Pl. G41	N15	51
Baker St.		
Baker St. G41	N15	51
Bakewell Rd., Bail.	L25	40

Name	Ref		Name	Ref		Name	Ref	
Balaclava St. G2	L16	35	Balvicar Dr. G42	N15	51	Barnkirk Av. G15	D10	6
McAlpine St.			Balvicar St. G42	N15	51	Barns St., Clyde.	E 8	5
Balado Rd. G33	K24	39	Balvie Av. G15	E10	6	Barnsford Av., Renf.	H 4	16
Balbeg St. G51	L12	33	Balvie Av., Giff.	R14	62	Barnsford Rd., Pais.	J 4	29
Balbeggie Pl. G32	M23	55	Banavie Rd. G11	H13	20	Barnton St. G32	K21	38
Balbeggie St. G32	M23	55	Banchory Av. G43	P13	62	Barnwell Ter. G51	K12	33
Balblair Rd. G52	N12	49	Banchory Av., Renf.	F 5	16	Barochan Cres., Pais.	M 4	45
Balcarres Av. G12	G14	20	Banchory Cres., Bear.	E13	8	Barochan Rd. G53	M10	48
Balcomie St. G33	J22	38	Banff St. G33	J22	38	Baron Rd., Pais.	L 7	31
Balcurvie Rd. G34	J25	40	Bangorshill St. G46	Q12	61	Baron St., Renf.	J 8	31
Baldinnie Rd. G34	K25	40	Bank Rd. G32	O23	55	Baronald Dr. G12	G13	20
Baldorran Cres., Cumb.	B 1	70	Bank St. G12	J15	35	Baronald Gate G12	G13	20
Baldoven Cres. G33	K24	39	Bank St. G72	P22	66	Baronald St. G73	N19	53
Baldovie Rd. G52	M11	49	Bank St., Barr.	R 8	59	Baronhill, Cumb.	A 3	71
Baldragon Rd. G34	J25	40	Bank St., Pais.	M 6	30	Barons Court Dr., John.	M 3	45
Baldric Rd. G13	G11	19	Bankbrae Av. G53	P10	60	Barons Court Gdns.,	M 3	45
Baldwin Av. G13	E11	7	Bankend St. G33	J22	38	John.		
Balerno Dr. G52	M12	49	Bankfoot Dr. G52	M10	48	Barons Court Rd., John.	M 3	45
Balfluig St. G34	J24	39	Bankfoot Rd. G52	M10	48	Barons Gate, Both.	Q27	69
Balfour St. G20	G14	20	Bankfoot Rd., Pais.	L 4	29	Barr Cres., Clyde.	C 7	5
Balfron Rd. G51	K12	33	Bankglen Rd. G15	D10	6	Barr Pl., Pais.	M 5	46
Balfron Rd., Pais.	L 8	31	Bankhall St. G42	N16	51	Barr St. G20	H16	21
Balgair Dr., Pais.	L 7	31	Bankhead Av. G13	G10	18	Barra Av., Renf.	J 8	31
Balgair St. G22	G16	21	Bankhead Dr. G73	O19	53	Barra St. G20	F14	20
Balgair Ter. G32	L22	38	Bankhead Rd. G73	P18	64	Barrachnie Cres., Bail.	L24	39
Balglass St. G22	H16	21	Bankhead Rd., Waterside	B25	14	Barrachnie Rd., Bail.	L24	39
Balgonie Av. G78	N 4	45	Bankier St. G40	L18	36	Barrack St. G4	L18	36
Balgonie Av., Pais.	N 4	46	Banknock St. G32	L21	38	Barrhead Rd. G43	O 9	48
Balgonie Dr., Pais.	N 5	46	Bankside Av., John.	M09	43	Barrhead Rd., Pais.	M 7	47
Balgonie Rd. G52	M12	49	Banktop Pl., John.	M09	43	Barrie Quad., Clyde.	D 7	5
Balgonie Woods, Pais.	N 5	46	Banling Green Rd. G44	P16	63	Barrie Rd. G52	K10	32
Balgownie Cres., Thorn.	R13	62	*Clarkston Rd.*			Barrington Dr. G4	J15	35
Balgray Cres., Barr.	R 9	60	Bannatyne Av. G31	K19	37	Barrisdale Rd. G20	F14	20
Balgraybank St. G21	H19	23	Banner Dr. G13	E11	7	Barrisdale Way G73	Q19	65
Balgrayhill Rd. G21	G18	22	Banner Rd. G13	E11	7	Barrland Dr., Giff.	Q14	62
Balintore St. G32	L22	38	Bannercross Av., Bail.	L25	40	Barrland St. G41	M16	51
Baliol La. G3	J15	35	Bannercross Dr., Bail.	L23	40	Barrochan Rd., John.	M09	43
Woodlands Rd.			Bannercross Gdns., Bail.	L25	40	Barrowfield St. G40	L19	37
Baliol St. G3	J15	35	*Bannercross Dr.*			Barrwood St. G33	J21	38
Ballaig Av., Bear.	C11	7	Bannerman Pl., Clyde.	E 8	5	Barscube Ter., Pais.	M 7	47
Ballaig Cres. G33	G23	25	Bannerman St., Clyde.	E 7	5	Barshaw Dr., Pais.	L 7	31
Ballantay Quad. G45	Q19	65	Bantaskin St. G20	F14	20	Barshaw Pl., Pais.	L 8	31
Ballantay Rd. G45	Q19	65	Banton Pl. G33	K25	40	Barshaw Rd. G52	L 9	32
Ballantay Ter. G45	Q19	65	Barassie Cres., Cumb.	A 2	70	Barterholm Rd., Pais.	N 6	46
Ballantyne Rd. G52	K10	32	Barassie Ct., Both.	R27	69	Bartholomew St. G40	M19	53
Ballater Dr., Bear.	E12	7	Barbae Pl., Udd.	Q28	69	Bartiebeith Rd. G33	K24	39
Ballater Dr., Pais.	N 7	47	*Hume Dr.*			Basset Av. G13	F10	18
Ballater Dr., Renf.	F 5	16	Barbreck Rd. G42	N15	51	Basset Cres. G13	F10	18
Ballater St. G5	L17	36	*Pollokshaws Rd.*			Bath La. G2	K16	35
Ballayne Dr., Chr.	E28	15	Barcaldine Av., Chr.	E25	14	*Blythswood St.*		
Ballindalloch Dr. G31	K19	37	Barcaple St. G21	H18	22	Bath La. W. G3	K15	35
Balloch Gdns. G52	M12	49	Barclay Av., John.	N 1	44	*North St.*		
Balloch Vw., Cumb.	C 2	70	Barclay Sq., Renf.	J 7	31	Bath St. G2	K16	35
Ballochmill Rd. G73	O20	53	Barclay St. G21	G18	22	Bathgate St. G31	L19	37
Ballogie Rd. G44	O16	51	*Balgrayhill Rd.*			Bathgo Av., Pais.	M 9	48
Balmarino Pl. G64	E20	11	Barcraigs Dr., Pais.	O 6	46	Batson St. G42	N16	51
Balmartin Rd. G23	E14	8	Bard Av. G13	F10	18	Battle Pl. G41	O15	51
Balmeg Av., Giff.	S14	62	Bardowie St. G22	H16	21	Battleburn St. G32	M22	54
Balmerino Pl., Bish.	F20	23	Bardrain Av., John.	N 2	44	Battlefield Av. G42	O16	51
Angus Av.			Bardrain Rd., Pais.	O 5	46	Battlefield Cres. G42	O16	51
Balmoral Cres. G42	N16	51	Bardrill Dr., Bish.	E18	10	*Battlefield Gdns.*		
Queens Dr.			Bardykes Rd., Blan.	R26	68	Battlefield Gdns. G42	O16	51
Balmoral Cres., Renf.	G 6	16	Barfillan Dr. G52	L12	33	Battlefield Rd. G42	O16	51
Balmoral Dr. G32	O22	54	Barfillan Rd. G52	L12	33	Bavelaw St. G33	J23	39
Balmoral Dr., Bear.	E13	8	Bargaran Rd. G53	M10	48	Bayfield Av. G15	D10	6
Balmoral Dr., G72	P21	66	Bargarron Dr., Pais.	K 7	31	Bayfield Ter. G15	D10	6
Balmoral Gdns., Blan.	R26	68	Bargeddie St. G33	J20	37	Beaconsfield Rd. G12	G13	20
Balmoral Gdns., Udd.	N27	57	Barhill Cres., Kilb.	NO7	42	Beard Cres., Gart.	G 6	16
Balmoral Rd., John.	N 1	44	Barholm Sq. G33	J23	39	Beardmore Cotts., Renf.	G 6	16
Balmoral St. G14	H10	18	Barke Rd., Cumb.	B 3	71	Beardmore St., Dalm.	D 5	4
Balmore Pl. G22	G16	21	Barlanark Av. G32	K23	39	Beardmore Way, Dalm.	D 5	4
Balmore Rd. G23	C15	9	Barlanark Pl. G32	L23	39	Bearford Dr. G52	L10	32
Balmore Sq. G22	G16	21	*Hallhill Rd.*			Bearsden Rd. G13	F12	19
Balmuildy Rd., Bish. G23	D16	9	Barlanark Pl. G33	K24	39	Beaton Rd. G41	N15	51
Balornock Rd. G21	G19	23	Barlanark Rd. G33	K23	39	Beattock St. G31	L20	37
Balruddery Pl. G64	F20	23	Barlia Dr. G45	Q18	64	Beatty St., Dalm.	D 4	4
Balshagray Av. G11	H12	19	Barlia St. G45	Q18	64	Beaufort Av. G43	P14	62
Balshagray Cres. G11	J12	19	Barlia Ter. G45	Q18	64	Beaufort Gdns., Bish.	E18	10
Balshagray La. G11	H12	19	Barloch St. G22	H17	22	Beauly Dr., Pais.	N 3	45
Balshagray Pl. G11	H12	19	Barlogan Av. G52	L12	33	Beauly Pl. G20	G14	20
Balshagray Dr.			Barlogan Quad. G52	L12	33	Beauly Pl., Bish.	E20	11
Baltic Ct. G40	M19	53	Barmill Rd. G43	P13	62	Beauly Pl., Chr.	E26	14
Baltic St.			Barmulloch Rd. G21	H19	23	Beauly Rd., Bail.	M25	56
Baltic La. G40	M19	53	Barn Grn. G78	M07	42	Beaumont Gate G12	J14	34
Baltic Pl. G40	M18	52	Barnard Gdns., Bish.	D19	11	Bedale Rd., Bail.	M24	55
Baltic St. G40	M19	53	Barnard Ter. G40	M19	53	Bedford Av., Clyde.	E 8	5
Balure St. G31	K20	37	Barnbeth Rd. G53	N10	48	*Onslow Rd.*		
Balvaird Cres. G73	O19	53	Barnes Rd. G20	G16	21	Bedford La. G5	L16	35
Balvaird Dr. G73	O19	53	Barnes St., Barr.	R 7	59	Bedford Row G5	L16	35
Balveny St. G33	J23	39	Barnflat St. G73	N19	53	*Dunmore St.*		

Name	Grid	Page
Bedford St. G5	L16	35
Bedlay Ct., Chr.	D28	15
Bedlay St. G21	H18	22
Linsburn St.		
Bedlay St. G21	H18	22
Petershill Rd.		
Bedlay Wk., Chr.	D28	15
Beech Av. G41	M13	50
Beech Av. G72	P21	66
Beech Av. G73	Q20	65
Beech Av., Bail.	L25	40
Beech Av., Bear.	C13	8
Beech Av., John.	N 2	44
Beech Av., Pais.	N 7	47
Beech Av. North Av. G72	P21	66
Beech Dr., Dalm.	C 7	5
Beech Gdns., Bail.	L25	40
Beech Gro., Barr.	R 8	59
Arthurlie Av.		
Beech Pl., Bish.	F19	23
Beech Rd., Bish.	F19	23
Beech Rd., John.	N08	43
Beech Rd., Lenz.	C23	13
Beechcroft Pl., Blan.	R27	69
Beeches Av., Clyde.	C 6	4
Beeches Rd., Clyde.	C 6	4
Beeches Ter., Clyde.	C 7	4
Beechgrove St. G40	N19	53
Beechlands Av., Giff.	R15	63
Beechmount Cotts. G14	G 9	18
Dumbarton Rd,		
Beechmount Rd., Lenz.	D23	13
Beechwood Av. G11	H12	19
Beechwood Dr.		
Beechwood Av. G73	P20	65
Beechwood Ct., Bear.	D12	7
Beechwood Dr. G11	H12	19
Beechwood Dr., Renf.	J 7	31
Beechwood La., Bear.	D12	7
Beechwood Ct.		
Beechwood Pl. G11	H12	19
Beechwood Dr.		
Beechwood Rd., Cumb.	C 2	70
Beil Dr. G13	F 9	18
Beith Rd., John.	O07	42
Beith St. G11	J13	34
Belgrave La. G12	H15	21
Belgrave La.		
Belgrave Ter. G12	H15	21
Lorraine Rd.		
Belhaven Cres. La. G12	H14	20
Belhaven Ter. G12	H14	20
Belhaven Ter. W. G12	H14	20
Bell St. G1	L17	36
Bell St., Clyde.	F 8	17
Bell St., Renf.	H 8	17
Bellahouston Dr. G52	M12	49
Bellahouston La. G52	M12	49
Bellairs Pl., Blan.	R26	68
Belleisle Av., Udd.	O27	57
Belleisle St. G42	N16	51
Bellevue Pl. G21	J18	36
Bellfield Cres., Barr.	Q 7	59
Bellfield St. G31	L19	37
Bellfield St., Barr.	Q 7	59
Bellgrove St. G31	L18	36
Bellrock Cres. G33	K22	38
Bellrock St. G33	K22	38
Bellscroft Av. G73	O18	52
Bellshaugh La. G12	G14	20
Bellshaugh Pl. G12	G14	20
Bellshaugh Rd. G12	G14	20
Bellshill Rd., Both.	R28	69
Bellshill Rd., Udd.	P27	69
Belltrees Cres., Pais.	M 4	45
Bellwood St. G41	O15	51
Belmar Ct., Linw.	L 2	28
Belmont Av., Udd.	O27	57
Belmont Cres. G12	H15	21
Belmont Dr. G73	O19	53
Belmont Dr., Barr.	R 8	59
Belmont Dr., Giff.	Q13	62
Belmont La. G12	H14	20
Great Western Rd.		
Belmont Rd. G21	G18	22
Belmont Rd. G72	Q21	66
Belmont Rd., Pais.	L 7	31
Belmont St. G12	H15	21
Belmont St., Clyde.	F 7	17
Belses Dr. G52	L11	33
Belstane Pl., Udd.	Q28	69
Appledore Cres.		
Belsyde Av. G15	E10	6
Beltane St. G3	K15	35
Beltrees Av. G53	N10	48
Beltrees Cres. G53	N10	48
Beltrees Rd. G53	N10	48
Belvidere Cres., Bish.	D19	11
Belvoir Pl., Bish.	S26	68
Bemersyde Av. G43	P13	62
Bemersyde Rd. G78	O 3	45
Bemersyde, Bish.	E20	11
Ben Alder Dr., Pais.	N 8	47
Ben Buie Way, Pais.	N 8	47
Ben Ledi Av., Pais.	N 8	47
Ben Lui Dr., Pais.	N 8	47
Ben More Dr., Pais.	N 8	47
Ben Nevis Rd., Pais.	N 8	47
Ben Venue Way, Pais.	N 8	47
Ben Wyvis Dr., Pais.	N 8	47
Benalder St. G11	J14	34
Benarty Gdns., Bish.	E19	11
Bencroft Dr. G44	P18	64
Bengairn St. G31	K20	37
Bengal Pl. G43	O14	50
Christian St.		
Bengal St. G43	O14	50
Benhar Pl. G33	K21	38
Benholme St. G32	M21	54
Benhope Av., Pais.	N 8	47
Benlawers Dr., Pais.	N 8	47
Benloyal Av., Pais.	N 8	47
Benmore St. G21	G18	22
Bennan Sq. G42	N17	52
Benston Pl., John.	N09	43
Benston Rd., John.	N09	43
Bentall St. G5	M17	52
Bentinck St. G3	J15	35
Bents Rd., Bail.	L25	40
Benvane Av., Pais.	N 8	47
Benvie Gdns., Bish.	E19	11
Benview St. G20	H15	21
Benview Ter., Pais.	N 7	47
Berelands Cres. G73	O18	52
Berelands Pl. G73	O18	52
Beresford Av. G14	H12	19
Berkeley St. G3	K15	35
Berkeley Terrace La. G3	J15	35
Elderslie St.		
Berkley Dr., Blan.	R26	68
Bernard Path G40	M19	53
Bernard St. G40	M19	53
Bernard Ter. G40	M19	53
Berneray St. G22	F17	22
Berridale Av. G44	P16	63
Berriedale Av., Bail.	M25	56
Berryburn Rd. G21	H20	23
Berryhill Dr., Giff.	R13	62
Berryhill Rd., Cumb.	C 2	70
Berryhill Rd., Pais.	R13	62
Berryknowes Av. G52	L11	33
Berryknowes La. G52	L11	33
Berryknowes Rd. G52	M11	49
Berryknowes Rd., Chr.	F26	26
Bertram St. G41	N15	51
Bertrohill Ter. G33	K23	39
Stepps Rd.		
Bervie St. G51	L12	33
Berwick Cres., Linw.	K 1	28
Berwick Dr. G52	M10	48
Berwick Dr. G73	O20	53
Betula Dr., Dalm.	C 7	5
Bevan Gro., John.	O08	43
Beverley Rd. G43	P14	62
Bevin Av., Clyde.	E 8	5
Bideford Cres. G32	M23	55
Biggar Pl. G31	L19	37
Biggar St. G31	L19	37
Bigton St. G33	J22	38
Bilbao St. G45	M17	52
Bilsland Dr. G20	G15	21
Binend Rd. G53	O11	49
Binnie Pl. G40	L18	36
Binniehill Rd., Cumb.	B 1	70
Binns Rd. G33	J23	39
Birch Cres., John.	N 1	44
Birch Dr., Lenz.	C23	13
Birch Gro., Udd.	O28	57
Burnhead St.		
Birch Knowle, Bish.	F19	23
Birch Rd., Dalm.	C 7	5
Birch Vw., Bear.	C13	8
Birchfield Dr. G14	H10	18
Birchlea Dr., Giff.	Q14	62
Birchwood Av. G32	M24	55
Birchwood Dr., Pais.	N 4	45
Birchwood Pl. G32	M24	55
Birdston Rd. G21	G20	23
Birgidale Av. G45	R17	64
Birgidale Rd. G45	R17	64
Birgidale Ter. G45	R17	64
Birkdale Ct., Both.	R27	69
Birken Rd., Lenz.	D24	13
Birkenshaw St. G31	K19	37
Birkenshaw Way, Pais.	K 6	30
Abbotsburn Way		
Birkhall Av. G52	M 9	48
Birkhall Av., Renf.	F 5	16
Birkhall Dr., Bear.	E12	7
Birkhill Av., Bish.	D19	11
Birkhill Gdns., Bish.	D20	11
Birkmyre Rd. G51	L12	33
Birks Rd., Renf.	J 7	31
Tower Dr.		
Birkwood St. G40	N19	53
Birmingham Rd., Renf.	J 7	31
Birnam Av., Bish.	D19	11
Birnam Cres., Bear.	C13	8
Birnam Gdns., Bish.	E19	11
Birnam Rd. G31	M20	53
Birness Dr. G43	O14	50
Birness St. G43	O14	50
Birnie Ct. G21	H20	23
Birnie Rd. G21	H20	23
Birnock Av., Renf.	J 9	32
Birsay Rd. G22	F16	21
Bishop Gdns., Bish.	E18	10
Bishop St. G2	K16	35
Bishopmill Pl. G21	H20	23
Bishopmill Rd. G21	H20	23
Bisset Cres., Clyde.	C 6	4
Black St. G4	J17	36
Blackburn Sq., Barr.	R 8	59
Blackburn St. G51	L14	34
Blackburn St. G51	L15	35
Blackbyres Rd., Barr.	P 8	59
Blackcraig Av. G15	D10	6
Blackcroft Gdns. G32	M23	55
Blackcroft Rd. G32	M23	55
Blackfaulds Rd. G73	O18	52
Blackford Cres. G32	M23	55
Blackford Pl. G32	M23	55
Blackford Rd., Pais.	M 7	47
Blackfriars St. G1	K17	36
Blackhall La., Pais.	M 6	46
Blackhall St., Pais.	M 6	46
Blackhill Cotts. G23	E16	9
Blackhill Pl. G33	J20	37
Blackhill Rd. G23	E14	8
Blackie St. G3	J14	34
Blacklands Pl., Lenz.	D24	13
Blacklaw La., Pais.	L 6	30
Blackstone Av. G53	O11	49
Blackstone Cres. G53	N11	49
Blackstone Rd., Candren	K 3	29
Blackstoun Av., Linw.	L 1	28
Blackstoun Oval, Pais.	L 4	29
Blackstoun Rd., Pais.	L 4	29
Blackthorn Av., Lenz.	C22	12
Blackthorn Gro., Lenz.	C22	12
Blackthorn Rd., Cumb.	B 4	71
Blackthorn St. G22	G18	22
Blackwood Av., Linw.	L 1	28
Blackwood St. G13	F12	19
Blackwood St., Barr.	R 7	59
Blackwoods Cres., Chr.	E27	15
Blacurvie Rd. G34	J25	40
Bladda La., Pais.	M 6	46
Blades Ct., Gart.	G28	27
Bladnoch Dr. G15	E11	7
Moraine Av.		
Blaeloch Av. G45	R17	64
Blaeloch Dr. G45	R17	64
Blaeloch Ter. G45	R17	64
Blair Cres., Bail.	M25	56
Blair Rd., Pais.	L 9	32
Blair St. G32	L21	38
Blairatholl Av. G11	H13	20
Blairatholl Gdns. G11	H13	20

Street	Ref		Street	Ref		Street	Ref
Blairbeth Dr. G44	O16 51		Botanic Cres. G20	H14 20		Braeside Dr., Barr.	R 8 59
Blairbeth Rd. G73	P19 65		Bothlyn Cres., Gart.	F27 27		Braeside Pl. G72	Q22 66
Blairbeth Ter. G73	Q19 65		Bothlynn Dr. G33	G23 25		Braeside St. G20	H15 21
Blairdardie Rd. G15	E10 6		Bothlynn Rd., Chr.	F26 26		Braid Sq. G4	J16 35
Blairdenan Av., Chr.	D28 15		Bothwell La. G2	K16 35		Braid St. G4	J16 35
Blairgowrie Rd. G52	M11 49		*West Campbell St.*			Braidbar Farm Rd., Giff.	Q14 62
Blairhall Av. G41	O15 51		Bothwell Park Rd. G71	R28 69		Braidbar Rd., Giff.	Q14 62
Blairhill Av., Chr. &	C25 14		Bothwell Rd., Udd. &	P27 69		Braidcraft Rd. G53	N11 49
Waterside			Both.			Braidfauld Gdns. G32	M21 54
Blairlogie St. G33	J22 38		Bothwell St. G72	P21 66		Braidfauld Pl. G32	N21 54
Blairston Av., Both.	R28 69		Bothwell Ter. G12	J15 35		Braidfauld St. G32	N21 54
Blairston Gdns., Both.	R28 69		*Bank St.*			Braidfield Rd., Clyde.	C 7 5
Blairston Av.			Bothwick Way, Pais.	O 3 45		Braidholm Cres., Giff.	Q14 62
Blairtum Dr. G73	P19 65		*Crosbie Dr.*			Braidholm Rd., Giff.	Q14 62
Blairtummock Rd. G32	K23 39		Boundary Rd. G73	N18 52		Braidpark Cres., Giff.	Q14 62
Blake Rd., Cumb.	C 3 71		Bourne Cres., Renf.	F 5 16		Braidpark Dr., Giff.	Q14 62
Blane St. G4	J17 36		Bourne Ct., Renf.	F 5 16		Braids Rd., Pais.	N 6 46
Blantyre Cres., Clyde.	B 6 4		Bourock Sq., Barr.	R 9 60		Bramley Pl., Lenz.	D24 13
Blantyre Farm Rd.,	R26 68		Bourtree Dr. G73	Q20 65		Branchock Av. G72	Q23 67
Blan. & Udd.			Bouverie St. G14	G 9 18		Brand St. G51	L14 34
Blantyre Mill Rd., Both.	R27 69		Bouverie St. G73	O18 52		Brandon Gdns. G72	P21 66
Blantyre Rd., Both.	R28 69		Bowden Dr. G52	L10 32		Brandon St. G31	L18 36
Blantyre St. G3	J14 34		Bower St. G12	H15 21		Branscroft G78	M07 42
Blaven Ct., Bail.	M26 56		Bowerwalls St., Barr.	Q 9 60		Brassey St. G20	G15 21
Bracadale Rd.			Bowes Cres., Bail.	M24 55		Breadalbane Gdns. G73	Q20 65
Blawarthill St. G14	G 9 18		Bowfield Av. G52	L 9 32		Breadalbane St. G3	K15 35
Blenheim Av. G33	G23 25		Bowfield Cres. G52	L 9 32		Brech Av., Bail.	L27 41
Blenheim Ct. G33	G24 25		Bowfield Dr. G52	L 9 32		Brechin Rd., Bish.	E20 11
Blenheim Av.			Bowfield Pl. G52	L 9 32		Brechin St. G3	K15 35
Blenheim La. G33	G24 25		Bowfield Ter. G52	L 9 32		Breck Av. G78	O 2 44
Blesdale Ct., Clyde.	E 7 5		*Bowfield Cres.*			Brediland Rd., Linw.	L 1 28
Blochairn Rd. G21	J19 37		Bowhouse Way G73	Q19 65		Brediland Rd., Pais.	N 3 45
Bluevale St. G31	L19 37		Bowling Green La. G14	H11 19		Bredisholm Dr., Bail.	M26 56
Blyth Pl. G32	L23 39		*Westland Dr.*			Bredisholm Rd., Bail.	M27 57
Blyth Rd., G33	L24 39		Bowling Green Rd. G14	H11 19		Bredisholm Ter., Bail.	M26 56
Blythswood Av., Renf.	H 8 17		Bowling Green Rd. G32	M23 55		Brenfield Av. G44	Q15 63
Blythswood Dr., Pais.	L 6 30		Bowling Green Rd. G44	P16 63		Brenfield Dr. G44	Q15 63
Blythswood Rd., Renf.	G 8 17		Bowman St. G42	N16 51		Brentwood Av. G53	Q10 60
Blythswood Sq. G2	K16 35		Bowmont Gdns. G12	H14 20		Brentwood Dr. G53	Q10 60
Blythswood St. G2	K16 35		Bowmont Hill, Bish.	D19 11		Brentwood Sq. G53	Q10 60
Boclair Av., Bear.	D12 7		Bowmont Ter. G12	H14 20		*Brentwood Dr.*	
Boclair Cres., Bear.	D13 8		Bowmore Gdns. G73	Q21 66		Brereton St. G42	N17 52
Boclair Cres., Bish.	E19 11		Bowmore Gdns., Udd.	O27 57		Bressey Rd. G33	L24 39
Boclair Rd., Bear.	D13 8		Bowmore Rd. G52	L12 33		Breval Cres., Clyde.	B 7 5
Boclair Rd., Bish.	E19 11		Boyd St. G42	N16 51		Brewery St., John.	M09 43
Boclair St. G13	F12 19		Boydstone Pl. G46	P12 61		Brewster Av., Pais.	K 7 31
Boden St. G40	M19 53		Boydstone Rd. G43	P12 61		Briar Dr., Clyde.	D 7 5
Bodmin Gdns., Chr.	D27 15		Boyle St., Clyde.	F 8 17		Briar Neuk, Bish.	F19 23
Gartferry Rd.			Boyleston Rd., Barr.	Q 7 59		Briar Rd. G43	P14 62
Bogany Ter. G45	R18 64		Boyndie Path G34	K25 40		Briarlea Dr., Giff.	Q14 62
Bogbain Rd. G34	K25 40		Boyndie St. G34	K25 40		Briarwood Ct. G32	N24 55
Boghall Rd., Udd.	N25 56		Brabloch Cres., Pais.	L 6 30		Brick La., Pais.	L 6 30
Boghall St. G33	J22 38		Bracadale Dr., Bail.	M26 56		Bridge of Weir Rd.	L08 43
Boghead Rd. G21	H19 23		Bracadale Gdns., Bail.	M26 56		Kilb. & Linw.	
Boghead Rd., Lenz.	D22 12		Bracadale Gro., Bail.	M26 56		Bridge St., Dalm.	D 6 4
Bogleshole Rd. G72	O21 54		Bracadale Rd., Bail.	M26 56		Bridge St., G72	P22 66
Bogmoor Rd. G51 \	K11 33 \		Bracken Rd., Barr.	P 7 59		Bridge St., Linw.	L 2 28
Bogside Pl., Bail.	K26 40		Bracken St. G22	G16 21		Bridge St., Pais.	M 6 46
Whamflet Av.			Bracken Ter., Udd.	Q28 69		Bridgebar St., Barr.	Q 9 60
Bogside Rd. G33	G22 24		Brackenbrae Av., Bish.	E18 10		Bridgeburn Dr., Chr.	E27 15
Bogside St. G40	M19 53		Brackenbrae Rd., Bish.	E18 10		Bridgegate G1	L17 36
Bogton Av. G44	Q15 63		Brackenrig Rd. G46	R12 61		Bridgend Rd. G53	O11 49
Bogton Avenue La. G44	Q15 63		Brackla Av. G13	F 9 18		Bridgeton Cross G40	L18 36
Bogton Av.			Bracora Pl. G20	G14 20		Brigham Pl. G23	F15 21
Boleyn Rd. G41	N15 51		*Glenfinnan Dr.*			*Broughton Rd.*	
Bolivar Ter. G42	O17 52		Bradan Av. G13	F 9 18		Brighton Pl. G51	L13 34
Bolton Dr. G42	O16 51		Bradda Av. G73	Q20 65		Brighton St. G51	L13 34
Bon Accord St., Clyde.	F 7 17		Bradfield Av. G12	G14 20		Brightside Av., Udd.	P28 69
Bonawe St. G20	H15 21		Brae Av., Clyde.	B 7 5		Brisbane St. G42	O16 51
Kirkland St.			Brae Cres., Clyde.	B 7 5		Brisbane St., Dalm.	D 5 4
Boness St. G40	M19 53		Braeface Rd., Cumb.	C 2 70		Britannia Way, Clyde.	E 7 5
Bonhill St. G22	H16 21		Braefield Dr., Thorn.	Q13 62		Britannia Way, Renf.	J 8 31
Bonnar St. G40	M19 53		Braefoot Cres., Pais.	O 6 46		Briton St. G51	L13 34
Bonnaughton Rd., Bear.	C10 6		Braehead Rd., Clyde.	B 7 5		Broad Pl. G40	L18 36
Bonnyholm Av. G53	M10 48		Braehead Rd., Cumb.	B 3 71		*Broad St.*	
Bonnyrigg Dr. G43	P13 62		Braehead Rd., Pais.	P 5 58		Broad St. G40	L18 36
Bonyton Av. G13	G 9 18		Braehead St. G5	M17 52		Broadford St. G4	J17 36
Boon Dr. G15	E10 6		Braemar Av., Dalm.	D 6 4		*Harvey St.*	
Boquhanran Pl., Clyde.	D 7 5		Braemar Cres., Bear.	E12 7		Broadholm St. G22	G16 21
Albert Rd.			Braemar Dr., John.	N 1 44		Broadleys Av., Bish.	D18 10
Boquhanran Rd., Clyde	E 6 4		Braemar Rd. G73	Q21 66		Broadlie Dr. G13	G10 18
Borden La. G13	G12 19		Braemar Rd., Renf.	G 5 16		Broadloan, Renf.	J 8 31
Borden Rd. G13	G12 19		Braemar St., G42	O15 51		Broadwood Dr. G44	P16 63
Boreland Dr. G13	F10 18		Braemar Vw., Dalm.	C 6 4		Brock Oval G53	P11 61
Boreland Pl. G13	G10 18		Braemount Av., Pais.	P 5 58		Brock Pl. G53	O11 49
Borgie Cres. G72	P22 66		Braes Av., Clyde.	F 8 17		Brock Rd. G53	O11 49
Borland Rd., Bear.	D13 8		Braeside Av. G73	O20 53		Brock Ter. G53	P11 61
Borron St. G4	H17 22		Braeside Av., Chr.	E27 15		Brock Way G67	C 3 71
Borthwick St. G33	J22 38		Braeside Cres., Bail.	L27 41		*North Carbrain Rd.*	
Boswell Sq. G52	K 9 32		Braeside Cres., Barr.	R 9 60			

Street	Ref	Pg
Brockburn Rd. G53	N10	48
Brockburn Ter. G53	O11	49
Brockville St. G32	L21	38
Brodick Sq. G64	F19	23
Brodick St. G21	J19	37
Brodie Park Av., Pais.	N 6	46
Brodie Pl., Renf.	J 7	31
Brodie Rd. G21	F20	23
Brogknowe, Udd.	O26	56
Glasgow Rd.		
Brook St. G40	L18	36
Brooklands Av., Udd.	O27	57
Brooklea Dr., Giff.	P14	62
Brookside St. G40	L19	37
Broom Cres., Barr.	P 7	59
Broom Dr., Clyde.	D 7	5
Broom Gdns., Lenz.	C22	12
Broom Rd. G43	P14	62
Broom Rd. G67	A 4	71
Broom Ter., John.	N 1	44
Broomdyke Way, Pais.	K 5	30
Broomfield Av. G21	H19	23
Broomfield Rd.		
Broomfield Av. G72	O20	53
Broomfield Pl. G21	G18	22
Broomfield Rd.		
Broomfield Rd. G21	G18	22
Broomfield Ter., Udd.	N27	57
Broomhill Av. G11	J12	33
Broomhill Av. G32	O22	54
Broomhill Cres. G11	H12	19
Broomhill Dr. G11	H12	19
Broomhill Dr. G73	P19	65
Broomhill Gdns. G11	H12	19
Broomhill La. G11	H12	19
Broomhill Path G11	J12	33
Broomhill Pl. G11	H12	19
Broomhill Rd. G11	J12	33
Broomhill Ter. G11	J12	33
Broomieknowe Dr. G73	P19	65
Broomieknowe Rd. G73	P19	65
Broomielaw G1	L16	35
Broomknowe Pl. G66	D24	13
Broomknowe, Cumb.	B 1	70
Broomknowes Rd. G21	H19	23
Broomlands Av., Renf.	F 5	16
Broomlands Cres., Renf.	F 5	16
Broomlands Gdns., Renf.	F 5	16
Broomlands Rd., Cumb.	D 3	71
Broomlands St., Pais.	M 5	46
Broomlands Way, Renf.	F 6	16
Broomlea Cres., Renf.	F 5	16
Broomley Dr. G46	R14	62
Broomley La., Giff.	R14	62
Broomloan Ct. G51	L13	34
Broomloan Pl. G51	L13	34
Broomloan Rd. G51	L13	34
Broompark Circus G31	K18	36
Broompark Dr. G31	K18	36
Broompark Dr., Renf.	F 5	16
Broompark St. G31	K18	36
Broomton Rd. G21	F20	23
Broomward Dr., John.	M 1	44
Brora Dr., Bear.	D13	8
Brora Dr., Giff.	R14	62
Brora Dr., Renf.	H 9	18
Brora Gdns., Bish.	E19	11
Brora La. G31	J20	37
Brora St.		
Brora Rd., Bish.	E19	11
Brora St. G33	J20	37
Broughton Dr. G23	F15	21
Broughton Gdns. G23	E15	9
Broughton Rd. G23	F15	21
Brown Av., Clyde.	F 8	17
Brown Rd., Cumb.	C 2	70
Brown St. G2	K16	35
Brown St., Pais.	L 5	30
Brown St., Renf.	J 7	31
Brownhill Rd. G43	Q13	62
Brownlie St. G42	O16	51
Browns La., Pais.	M 6	46
Brownsdale Rd. G73	O18	52
Brownside Av. G72	P21	66
Brownside Av., Barr.	P 7	59
Brownside Av., Pais.	O 5	46
Brownside Cres., Barr.	P 7	59
Brownside Dr. G13	G 9	18
Brownside Dr., Barr.	P 7	59
Brownside Gro., Barr.	P 7	59
Brownside Rd.	P20	65
G72 & G73		
Bruce Av., John.	O09	43
Bruce Av., Pais.	K 7	31
Bruce Rd. G41	M15	51
Bruce Rd., Pais.	L 7	31
Bruce Rd., Renf.	J 7	31
Bruce St., Clyde.	E 7	5
Bruce Ter., Blan.	R27	69
Brucefield Pl. G34	K26	40
Brunstane Rd. G34	J25	40
Brunswick Ho., Dalm.	C 5	4
Perth Cres.		
Brunswick St. G1	K17	36
Brunton St. G44	P16	63
Brunton Ter. G44	Q15	63
Bruntsfield Av. G53	Q10	48
Bruntsfield Gdns. G53	Q10	60
Brydson Pl., Linw.	L 1	28
Fulwood Av.		
Buccleuch Av. G52	K 9	32
Buccleuch La. G3	J16	35
Scott St.		
Buccleuch St. G3	J16	35
Norfolk St.		
Buchan St. G5	L16	35
Buchan Ter., G72	Q21	66
Buchanan Cres. G64	F20	23
Buchanan Dr. G64	F20	23
Buchanan Dr. G72	P21	66
Buchanan Dr. G73	P19	65
Buchanan Dr., Bear.	D13	8
Buchanan Dr., Bish.	F20	23
Buchanan Dr., Lenz.	D23	13
Buchanan Gdns. G32	N24	55
Buchanan St. G1	K16	35
Buchanan St., Bail.	M25	56
Buchanan St., John.	N09	43
Buchlyvie Path G34	K25	40
Buchlyvie Rd., Pais.	L 9	32
Buchlyvie St. G34	K25	40
Buckingham Bldgs.	H14	20
G12		
Great Western Rd.		
Buckingham Dr. G32	O22	54
Buckingham Dr. G73	O20	53
Buckingham St. G12	H14	20
Buckingham Ter. G12	H14	20
Great Western Rd.		
Bucklaw Gdns. G52	M11	49
Bucklaw Pl. G52	M11	49
Bucklaw Ter. G52	M11	49
Buckley St. G22	G17	22
Bucksburn Rd. G21	H20	23
Buddon St. G40	M20	53
Budhill Av. G32	L22	38
Bulldale St. G14	G 9	18
Bullionslaw Dr. G73	P20	65
Bulloch Av., Giff.	R14	62
Bullwood Av. G53	N 9	48
Bullwood Ct. G53	N 9	48
Bullwood Dr. G53	N 9	48
Bullwood Gdns. G53	N 9	48
Bullwood Pl. G53	N 9	48
Bunessan St. G52	L12	33
Bunhouse Rd. G3	J14	34
Burgh Hall La. G11	J13	34
Fortrose St.		
Burgh Hall St. G11	J13	34
Burgh La. G12	H14	20
Vinicombe St.		
Burghead Dr. G51	K12	33
Burghead Pl. G51	K12	33
Burgher St. G31	L20	37
Burleigh Rd., Udd.	Q28	69
Burleigh St. G51	K13	34
Burlington Av. G12	G13	20
Burmola St. G22	H16	21
Burmouth Rd. G33	L24	39
Burn Gdns., Blan.	R26	68
Burn Ter. G72	O21	54
Burn Vw., Cumb.	B 4	71
Burnacre Gdns., Udd.	O27	57
Burnbank Dr., Barr.	R 8	59
Burnbank Gdns. G20	J15	35
Burnbank Pl. G4	K18	36
Drygate		
Burnbank Ter. G20	J15	35
Burnbrae Av., Bear.	B13	8
Burnbrae Av., Chr.	E28	15
Burnbrae Av., Linw.	L 2	28
Bridge St.		
Burnbrae Ct., Lenz.	D23	13
Auchinloch Rd.		
Burnbrae Dr. G73	P20	65
East Kilbride Rd.		
Burnbrae Rd., John.	M 2	44
Burnbrae Rd., Lenz.	E24	13
Burnbrae St. G21	H19	23
Burnbrae, Clyde.	C 7	5
Burncleuch Av., G72	Q22	66
Burncrooks Ct., Clyde.	C 6	4
Burndyke Ct. G51	K14	34
Burndyke Sq. G51	K14	34
Burndyke St. G51	K13	34
Burnett Rd. G33	K24	39
Burnfield Av., Giff.	Q13	62
Burnfield Cotts., Giff.	Q13	62
Burnfield Dr. G43	Q13	62
Burnfield Gdns., Giff.	Q14	62
Burnfield Rd.		
Burnfield Rd., Giff.	P13	62
Burnfoot Cres. G73	P20	65
Burnfoot Cres., Pais.	O 5	46
Burnfoot Dr. G52	L10	32
Burngreen Ter., Cumb.	A 3	71
Burnham Rd. G14	H10	18
Burnham Ter. G14	H10	18
Burnham Rd.		
Burnhead Rd. G43	P15	63
Burnhead Rd., Cumb.	C 1	70
Burnhead St., Udd.	O28	57
Burnhill Quadrant G73	O18	52
Burnhill St. G73	O18	52
Burnhouse St. G20	G14	20
Burnmouth Ct. G33	L24	39
Pendeen Rd.		
Burnpark Av., Udd.	O26	56
Burns Dr., John.	O09	43
Burns Gro., Thorn.	R13	62
Burns Rd., Cumb.	C 3	71
Burns St. G4	J16	35
Burns St., Dalm.	D 6	4
Burnside Av., Barr.	Q 7	59
Burnside Cres., Clyde.	B 7	5
Burnside Ct., Dalm.	D 6	4
Scott St.		
Burnside Gate G73	P20	65
Burnside Gdns., Kilb.	N 7	42
Burnside Rd. G73	P20	65
Burnside Rd., John.	N 2	44
Burnside Ter. G72	Q24	67
Burntbroom Dr., Bail.	M24	55
Burntbroom Gdns.,	M24	55
Bail.		
Burntbroom Rd.,	M24	55
Udd. & Bail.		
Burntbroom St. G33	K23	39
Burntshields Rd.,	N06	42
Kilb.		
Burr Gdns., Bish.	E20	11
Solway Rd.		
Burrells La. G4	K18	36
High St.		
Burrelton Rd. G43	P15	63
Burton La. G43	N16	51
Langside Rd.		
Bushes Av., Pais.	N 5	46
Busheyhill St. G72	P22	66
Bute Av., Renf.	J 8	31
Bute Cres., Bear.	E12	7
Bute Cres., Pais.	O 5	46
Bute Dr., John.	N08	43
Bute Gdns. G12	J14	34
Bute Gdns. G44	Q16	53
Bute Ter. G73	P19	65
Bute Ter., Udd.	O28	57
Butterbiggins Rd. G42	M16	51
Butterfield Pl. G41	N15	51
Pollokshaws Rd.		
Byrebush Rd. G53	N11	49
Byres Av., Pais.	L 7	31
Byres Cres.		
Byres Cres., Pais.	L 7	31
Byres Rd. G11	J14	34
Byres Rd., John.	N 2	44
Byron Ct., Udd.	R28	69
Shelly Dr.		
Byron La. G11	J12	33
Sandeman St.		

Name	Ref	Pg
Byron St. G11	J12	33
Byron St., Clyde.	D 6	4
Byshot St. G22	H17	22
Cable Depot Rd., Dalm.	E 6	4
Cadder Ct., Bish.	C19	11
Cadder Gro. G20	F15	21
Cadder Rd.		
Cadder Pl. G20	F15	21
Cadder Rd. G20	F15	21
Cadder Rd., Bish.	C19	11
Cadder Way, Bish.	C19	11
Cadoc St., G72	P22	66
Cadogan St. G2	K16	35
Cadzow Av., Giff.	S13	62
Cadzow Dr., G72	P21	66
Caird Dr. G11	J13	34
Cairn Av., Renf.	J 9	32
Cairn Dr., Linw.	L 1	28
Cairn La., Pais.	K 5	30
Mosslands Rd.		
Cairn St. G21	G18	22
Cairnban St. G51	L11	33
Cairnbrook Rd. G34	K26	40
Cairncraig St. G31	M20	53
Cairndow Av. G44	Q15	63
Cairndow Ct. G44	Q15	63
Cairngorm Cres., Barr.	R 8	59
Cairngorm Cres., Bear.	C10	6
Cairngorm Cres., Pais.	N 6	46
Cairngorm Rd. G43	P14	62
Cairnhill Circus G52	M 9	48
Cairnhill Dr. G52	M 9	48
Cairnhill Pl. G52	M 9	48
Cairnhill Circus		
Cairnhill Rd. G61	E12	7
Cairnlea Dr. G51	L13	34
Cairnmuir Rd. G72	R21	66
Cairns Av. G72	P22	66
Cairns Rd. G72	Q22	66
Cairnsmore Pl. G15	E 9	6
Cairnsmore Rd. G15	E 9	6
Cairnswell Av. G72	Q23	67
Cairnswell Pl. G72	Q23	67
Cairntoul Dr. G14	G10	18
Cairntoul Pl. G14	G10	18
Calcots Path G34	J26	40
Auchengill Rd.		
Calcots Pl. G34	J26	40
Caldarvan St. G22	H16	21
Calder Av., Barr.	R 8	59
Calder Dr. G72	P22	66
Calder Gate, Bish.	D18	10
Calder Pl., Bail.	M25	56
Calder Rd., Pais.	L 4	29
Calder Rd., Udd.	P26	68
Calder St. G42	N16	51
Calderbank Vw., Bail.	M26	56
Calderbraes Av., Udd.	O27	57
Caldercuilt Rd. G20	F14	20
Caldercuilt St. G20	F14	20
Calderpark Av., Udd.	N25	56
Calderpark Cres., Udd.	N25	56
Caldervale, Udd.	P26	68
Calderwood Av., Bail.	M25	56
Calderwood Dr., Bail.	M25	56
Calderwood Gdns., Bail.	M25	56
Calderwood Rd. G73	O20	53
Calderwood Rd., G43	P14	62
Caldwell Av. G13	G10	18
Caldwell Av., Linw.	L 1	28
Caledon La. G12	J14	34
Highburgh Rd.		
Caledon St. G12	J14	34
Caledonia Av. G5	M17	52
Caledonia Av. G73	O19	53
Caledonia Dr., Bail.	M25	56
Caledonia Rd. G5	M17	52
Caledonia Rd., Bail.	M25	56
Caledonia St. G5	M17	52
Caledonia St., Dalm.	E 6	4
Caledonia St., Pais.	L 5	30
Caledonian Circuit G72	P23	67
Caledonian Cotts., Both.	R28	69
Caledonian Cres. G12	H14	20
Great Western Rd.		
Caledonian Cres. G12	J15	35
Caledonian Mans. G12	H14	20
Great Western Rd.		
Caledonian Pl. G72	P24	67
Caley Brae, Udd.	P27	69
Calfhill Rd. G53	M10	48
Calfmuir Rd.,	C25	14
Chr. & Waterside		
Calgary St. G4	J17	36
Callander St. G20	H16	21
Callieburn Rd., Bish.	F19	23
Cally Av. G15	D10	6
Calside Av., Pais.	M 5	46
Calside, Pais.	N 6	46
Calton Entry G40	L18	36
Gallowgate		
Calvay Cres. G33	K23	39
Calvay Pl. G33	L24	39
Calvay Rd. G33	K23	39
Cambourne Rd., Chr.	D27	15
Cambridge Av., Clyde.	D 7	5
Cambridge Dr. G20	G14	20
Glenfinnan Dr.		
Cambridge La. G3	J16	35
Cambridge St.		
Cambridge Rd., Renf.	J 8	31
Cambridge St.	K16	35
Camburn St. G32	L21	38
Cambus Pl. G32	J23	39
Cambusdoon Rd. G32	J23	39
Cambuskenneth Gdns.	L24	39
Cambuskenneth Pl. G32	J23	39
Cambuslang Rd. G32	O21	54
Cambuslang Rd.	N19	53
G72 & G73		
Cambusmore Pl. G32	J23	39
Camden St. G5	M17	52
Camelon St. G32	L21	38
Cameron Dr., Bear.	D13	8
Cameron Dr., Udd.	O28	57
Cameron Sq., Clyde.	C 8	5
Glasgow Rd.		
Cameron St. G20	H16	21
Cameron St. G52	K 9	32
Cameron St., Clyde	F 8	17
Camlachie St. G31	L19	37
Camp Rd. G73	N18	52
Camp Rd., Bail.	L25	40
Campbell Dr., Barr.	R 8	59
Campbell Dr., Bear.	C11	7
Campbell St. G20	F14	21
Campbell St., John.	N09	43
Campbell St., Renf.	H 8	17
Camperdown St. G20	H16	21
Garscube Rd.		
Camphill Av. G41	O15	51
Camphill, Pais.	M 5	46
Camps Cres., Renf.	J 9	32
Campsie Av., Barr.	R 8	59
Campsie Dr., Bear.	B12	7
Campsie Dr., Pais.	K 7	31
Campsie Dr., Pais.	O 5	46
Campsie Pl., Chr.	F26	26
Campsie St. G21	G18	22
Campsie Vw., Bail.	L27	41
Campsie Vw., Chr.	F26	26
Campsie Vw., Cumb.	B 3	71
Campsie Vw.G33	H23	25
Campston Pl. G33	J22	38
Camstradden Dr. E.,	D11	7
Bear.		
Camstradden Dr. W.,	D11	7
Bear.		
Camus Pl. G15	D 9	6
Canal Av., John.	M 1	44
Canal Rd., John.	N09	43
Canal St. G4	J17	36
Canal St., Clyde.	F 7	17
Canal St., John.	M 2	44
Canal St., Pais.	M 5	46
Canal St., Renf.	H 8	17
Canal Ter., Pais.	M 6	46
Canberra Av., Dalm.	D 5	4
Cander Rigg, Bish.	D19	11
Candleriggs G1	L17	36
Candren Rd., Linw.	L 2	28
Candren Rd., Pais.	M 4	45
Canmore Pl. G31	M20	53
Canmore St. G31	M20	53
Cannich Dr., Pais.	N 7	47
Canniesburn Rd., Bear.	D11	7
Canniesburn Sq., Bear.	E12	7
Macfarlane Rd.		
Canniesburn Toll, Bear.	D12	7
Canonbie St. G34	J26	40
Canting Way G51	K14	34
Capelrig St. G46	Q12	61
Caplaw Rd., Pais.	P 5	58
Caplethill Rd.,	O 6	46
Pais. & Barr.		
Caprington St. G33	J22	38
Cara Dr. G51	K12	33
Caravelle Way, Renf.	J 8	31
Friendship Way		
Carberry Rd. G41	N14	50
Carbeth St. G22	H16	21
Carbisdale St. G22	G18	22
Carbost St. G23	E14	8
Torgyle St.		
Carbrook St. G21	J19	37
Carbrook St., Pais.	M 5	46
Cardarrach St. G21	H19	23
Cardell Dr., Pais.	M 4	45
Cardell Rd., Pais.	M 4	45
Carding La. G3	K15	35
Argyle St.		
Cardonald Dr. G52	M10	48
Cardonald Gdns. G52	M10	48
Cardonald Place Rd.	M10	48
G52		
Cardow Rd. G21	H20	23
Cardowan Dr. G33	G23	25
Cardowan Rd. G33	G24	25
Cardowan Rd. G33	L21	38
Cardrona St. G33	H22	24
Cardross Ct. G31	K18	36
Cardross St. G31	K18	36
Cardwell St. G41	M16	51
Cardyke St. G21	H19	23
Careston Pl., Bish.	E20	11
Carfin St. G42	N16	51
Carfrae St. G3	K14	34
Cargill St. G31	M21	54
Cargill St. G64	F19	23
Carham Cres. G52	L11	33
Carham Dr. G52	L11	33
Carillon Rd. G51	L14	34
Carisbrooke Cres., Bish.	D19	11
Carlaverock Rd. G43	P14	62
Carleith Av., Clyde.	C 6	4
Carleith Quad. G51	K11	33
Carleith Ter., Clyde.	C 6	4
Carleith Av.		
Carleston St. G21	H18	22
Carleton Dr., Giff.	Q14	62
Carleton Gate, Giff.	Q14	62
Carlibar Av. G13	G 9	18
Carlibar Dr., Barr.	Q 8	59
Carlibar Gdns., Barr.	Q 8	59
Commercial Rd.		
Carlibar Rd., Barr.	Q 7	59
Carlile La., Pais.	L 6	30
New Sneddon St.		
Carlile Pl., Pais.	L 6	30
Carlisle St. G21	H17	22
Carlowrie Av., Blan.	R26	68
Carlton Ct. G5	L16	35
Carlton Pl. G5	L16	35
Carlton Ter. G20	H15	21
Wilton St.		
Carlyle Av. G52	K 9	32
Carlyle Rd., Pais.	L 6	30
Carlyle Ter. G73	N19	53
Carmaben Rd. G33	K24	39
Carment Dr. G41	O14	50
Carment La. G41	O14	50
Carmichael Pl. G42	O15	51
Carmichael St. G51	L13	34
Carmunnock By-pass	R17	64
G44		
Carmunnock La. G44	P16	63
Madison Av.		
Carmunnock Rd. G44	O16	51
Carmyle Av. G32	N22	54
Carna Dr. G44	P17	64
Carnarvon St. G3	J15	35
Carnbooth Ct. G42	R18	64
Carnbroe St. G20	J16	35
Carnegie Rd. G52	L10	32
Carnock Cres., Barr.	R 7	59
Carnock Rd. G53	O11	49
Carnoustie Cres., Bish.	E20	11
Carnoustie Ct., Both.	R27	69
Carnoustie St. G5	L15	35

Name	Map	Pg
Carntyne Pl. G32	K20	37
Carntyne Rd. G31	L20	37
Carntynehall Rd. G32	K21	38
Carnwadric Rd. G46	Q12	61
Carnwath Av. G43	P15	63
Caroline St. G31	L21	38
Carolside Dr. G15	D10	6
Carradale Gdns., Bish.	E20	11
Thrums Av.		
Carradale Pl., Linw.	L 1	28
Carrbridge Dr. G20	G14	20
Glenfinnan Dr.		
Carriagehill Dr., Pais.	N 6	46
Carrick Cres., Giff.	R14	62
Carrick Dr. G32	M24	55
Carrick Dr. G73	P19	65
Carrick Gro. G32	M24	55
Carrick Rd. G73	P18	64
Carrick Rd., Bish.	E20	11
Carrick Rd., Cumb.	B 3	71
Carrick St. G2	K16	35
Carrickarden Rd., Bear.	D12	7
Carrickstone Vw., Cumb.	A 2	70
Carriden Pl. G33	K24	39
Carrington St. G4	J15	35
Carroglen Gdns. G32	L23	39
Carroglen Gro. G32	L23	39
Carron Cres. G22	G17	22
Carron Cres. G66	D24	13
Carron Cres., Bear.	D11	7
Carron Cres., Bish.	E19	11
Carron Ct. G72	P23	67
Carron,La., Pais.	K 7	31
Kilearn Rd.		
Carron Pl. G22	G18	22
Carron St., G22	G18	22
Carrour Gdns., Bish.	E18	10
Carsaig Dr. G52	L12	33
Carse View Dr., Bear.	C13	8
Carsebrook Av., Chr. & Waterside	C25	14
Chryston Rd.		
Carsegreen Av., Pais.	O 4	45
Carstairs St. G40	N19	53
Carswell Gdns. G41	N15	51
Cart St., Clyde.	F 7	17
Cartartan Rd., Pais.	L 9	32
Cartcraigs Rd. G43	P13	62
Cartha Cres., Pais.	M 7	47
Cartha St. G41	O15	51
Cartside Av., John.	N08	43
Cartside Quad. G42	O16	51
Cartside St. G42	O15	51
Cartside Ter., Kilb.	N08	43
Kilbarchan Rd.		
Cartvale La., Pais.	L 6	30
Cartvale Rd. G42	O15	51
Caskie Dr., Blan.	R27	69
Cassley Av., Renf.	J 9	32
Castle Av., Both.	R27	69
Castle Av., John.	N 1	44
Castle Av., Udd.	P27	69
Castle Chimmins Av. G72	Q23	67
Castle Chimmins Rd. G72	Q23	67
Castle Crescent North Ct. G1	K17	36
Royal Exchange Sq.		
Castle Gait, Pais.	M 6	46
Castle Gdns., Chr.	E27	15
Castle Pl., Udd.	P27	69
Ferry Rd.		
Castle Rd. G78	M 2	44
Main Rd.		
Castle Rd., John.	M 2	44
Castle Sq., Dalm.	D 6	4
Castle St. G4	K18	36
Castle St. G73	O19	53
Castle St., Bail.	M25	56
Castle St., Dalm.	D 6	4
Castle St., Pais.	M 5	46
Castle Vw., Clyde.	D 7	5
Granville St.		
Castle Way, Cumb.	B 4	71
Castlebank Cres., G11	J13	34
Meadowside St.		
Castlebank Ct. G13	G12	19
Castlebank Gdns. G13	G12	19
Castlebank St. G11	J12	33
Castlebank Vill. G13	G12	19
Castlebay Dr. G22	E17	10
Castlebay Pl. G22	F17	22
Castlebay St. G22	F17	22
Castlecroft Gdns., Udd.	P27	69
Castlefern Rd. G73	Q19	65
Castlehill Cres., Renf.	H 8	17
Ferry Rd.		
Castlehill Rd., Bear.	C10	6
Castlelaw Gdns. G32	L22	38
Castlelaw Pl. G32	L22	38
Castlelaw St. G32	L22	38
Castlemilk Cres. G44	P18	64
Castlemilk Dr. G45	Q18	64
Castlemilk Mews G44	P18	64
Castlemilk Rd.		
Castlemilk Rd. G44	O18	52
Castleton Av. G21	F18	22
Colston Rd.		
Castleton Ct. G42	R18	64
Cathay St. G22	F17	22
Cathcart Cres., Pais.	M 7	47
Cathcart Pl.	O18	52
Cathcart Rd. G42	O16	51
Cathcart Rd. G73	O18	52
Cathedral Ct. G4	K17	36
Rottenrow East		
Cathedral La. G4	K17	36
Cathedral St.		
Cathedral Sq. G4	K18	36
Cathedral St. G1	K17	36
Cathedral St. G4	K18	36
Catherine Pl. G3	K15	35
Hydepark St.		
Cathkin Av. G72	P21	66
Cathkin Av. G73	O20	53
Cathkin By-pass G73	Q20	65
Cathkin Ct. G42	R18	64
Cathkin Gdns., Udd.	N27	57
Cathkin Pl., G72	P21	66
Cathkin Rd. G42	O15	51
Cathkin Rd., E.K.	R19	65
Cathkin Rd., Udd.	N27	57
Cathkin Vw. G32	O22	54
Cathkinview Rd. G42	O16	51
Catrine Av., Clyde.	D 8	5
Causewayside St. G32	N22	54
Causeyside St., Pais.	M 6	46
Cavendish Pl. G5	M16	51
Cavendish St. G5	M16	51
Cavin Dr. G45	Q18	64
Cavin Rd. G45	Q18	64
Caxton St. G13	G12	19
Cayton Gdns., Bail.	M24	55
Cecil Pl. G11	L15	35
Paisley Rd. W.		
Cecil St. G12	H14	20
Cedar Av. G78	O 1	44
Cedar Av., Dalm.	D 5	4
Cedar Ct. G20	J16	35
Cedar Ct. G78	M07	42
Cedar Dr., Lenz.	C23	13
Cedar Gdns. G73	Q20	65
Cedar Pl., Barr.	R 8	59
Cedar Pl., Blan.	R26	68
Cedar Rd., Bish.	F19	23
Cedar Rd., Cumb.	B 4	71
Cedar St. G20	J16	35
Cedar Wk., Bish.	F19	23
Cedric Pl. G13	F11	19
Cedric Rd. G13	F11	19
Celtic Pl. G20	F14	20
Maryhill Rd.		
Cemetery Rd. G32	L23	39
Cemetery Rd. G52	M11	49
Paisley Rd. W.		
Central Av. G11	J12	33
Broomhill Ter.		
Central Av. G32	M23	55
Central Av. G72	P21	66
Central Av., Udd.	P29	69
Central Chambers G2	K16	35
Hope St.		
Central Path G32	M24	55
Central Way, Cumb.	D 2	70
Central Way, Pais.	L 6	30
Centre St. G5	L16	35
Centre, The, Barr.	R 7	59
Ceres Gdns. G64	E20	11
Cessnock Rd. G33	G22	24
Cessnock St. G51	L14	34
Cessnock St., Clyde.	D 8	5
Chachan Dr. G51	K12	33
Skipness Dr.		
Chalmers Ct. G40	L18	36
Chalmers Gate G40	L18	36
Chalmers Pl. G40	L18	36
Claythorn St.		
Chalmers St. G40	L18	36
Chalmers St., Clyde.	E 7	5
Chamberlain La. G13	G12	19
Chamberlain Rd. G13	G12	19
Chancellor St. G11	J13	34
Chapel Rd., Clyde.	C 7	5
Chapel St. G20	G15	21
Chapel St. G73	O18	52
Chapelhill Rd., Pais.	N 7	47
Chapelton Av., Bear.	D12	7
Chapelton Gdns., Bear.	D12	7
Chapelton St., G22	G16	21
Chaplet Av., G13	F11	19
Chapman St. G42	N16	51
Allison St.		
Chappel St., Barr.	Q 7	59
Charing Cross G2	J15	35
Charing Cross La. G3	K15	35
Granville St.		
Charles Av., Renf.	H 8	17
Charles Cres., Lenz.	D23	13
Charles St. G21	J18	36
Charlotte La. G1	L17	36
London Rd.		
Charlotte La. S. G1	L17	36
Charlotte St.		
Charlotte Pl., Pais.	N 6	46
Charlotte St., G1	L17	36
Chatelherault Av. G72	P21	66
Chatton St. G23	E14	8
Cheapside St. G3	K15	35
Chelmsford Dr. G12	G13	20
Cherry Bank, Lenz.	C22	12
Cherry Cres., Clyde.	D 7	5
Cherry Pl., Bish.	F19	23
Cherry Pl., John.	N 1	44
Cherrybank Rd. G43	P15	63
Chester St. G32	L22	38
Chesterfield Av. G12	G13	20
Chesters Pl. G73	O19	53
Chesters Rd., Bear.	D11	7
Chestnut Dr., Dalm.	C 7	5
Chestnut Dr., Lenz.	C22	12
Chestnut Pl., John.	O 1	44
Chestnut St. G22	G17	22
Cheviot Av., Barr.	R 8	59
Cheviot Rd., G43	P14	62
Cheviot Rd., Pais.	O 6	46
Chirnside Pl. G52	L10	32
Chirnside Rd. G52	L10	32
Chisholm St. G1	L17	36
Christian St. G43	O14	50
Christie La., Pais.	L 6	30
New Sneddon St.		
Christie Pl. G72	P22	66
Christie St., Pais.	L 6	30
Christopher St. G21	J19	37
Chryston Rd., Waterside & Chr.	C25	14
Church Av. G33	G23	25
Church Av. G73	P20	65
Church Dr., Lenz.	C23	13
Church Hill, Pais.	L 6	30
Church La. G42	N16	51
Victoria Rd.		
Church Rd., Chr.	F26	26
Church Rd., Giff.	R14	62
Church St. G11	J14	34
Church St., Bail.	M26	56
Church St., Clyde.	D 7	5
Church St., John.	M09	43
Church St., Kilb.	M07	42
Church St., Udd.	P27	69
Churchill Av., John.	O08	43
Churchill Cres., Udd.	Q28	69
Churchill Dr. G11	H12	19
Churchill Pl., Kilb.	M07	42
Churchill Way, Bish.	E18	10
Kirkintilloch Rd.		

Colvend Dr. G73	Q19 65	
Colvend St. G40	M18 52	
Colville Dr. G73	P20 65	
Colwood Av. G53	Q10 60	
Colwood Gdns. G53	Q10 60	
Colwood Av.		
Colwood Path G53	Q10 60	
Parkhouse Rd.		
Colwood Pl. G53	Q10 60	
Colwood Sq. G53	Q10 60	
Colwood Av.		
Comedie Rd. G33	H24 25	
Comely Park St. G31	L19 37	
Comley Pl. G31	L19 37	
Gallowgate		
Commerce St. G5	L16 35	
Commercial Ct. G5	L17 36	
Commercial Rd. G5	M17 52	
Commercial Rd., Barr.	Q 8 59	
Commonhead Rd. G34	K26 40	
Commonhead Rd., Bail.	K27 41	
Commore Av., Barr.	R 8 59	
Commore Dr. G13	F10 18	
Comrie Rd. G33	G23 25	
Comrie St. G32	M22 54	
Cona St. G46	Q12 61	
Conan Ct. G72	P23 67	
Condorrat Ring Rd.,	D 1 70	
Cumb.		
Congleton St. G53	P 9 60	
Nitshill Rd.		
Congress Rd. G3	K15 35	
Conifer Pl., Lenz.	C22 12	
Conisborough Path G34	J24 39	
Balfluig St.		
Conisborough Rd. G34	J24 39	
Connal St. G40	M19 53	
Conniston St. G32	K21 38	
Conon Av., Bear.	D11 7	
Consett La. G33	K23 39	
Consett St. G33	K23 39	
Consett La.		
Contin Pl. G12	G14 20	
Convair Way, Renf.	J 8 31	
Lismore Av.		
Conval Way, Pais.	K 5 30	
Abbotsburn Way		
Cook St. G5	L16 35	
Coopers Well La. G11	J14 34	
Dumbarton Rd.		
Coopers Well St. G11	J14 34	
Dumbarton Rd.		
Copland Pl. G51	L13 34	
Copland Quad. G51	L13 34	
Copland Rd. G51	L13 34	
Coplaw St. G42	M16 51	
Copperfield La., Udd.	O28 57	
Hamilton Vw.		
Corbett St. G32	M22 54	
Corbiston Way, Cumb.	C 3 71	
Cordiner St. G44	O16 51	
Corkerhill Gdns. G52	M12 49	
Corkerhill Pl. G52	N11 49	
Corkerhill Rd. G52	N11 49	
Corlaich Av. G42	O18 52	
Corlaich Dr. G42	O18 52	
Corn St. G4	J16 35	
Cornaig Rd. G53	O10 48	
Cornalee Gdns. G53	O10 48	
Cornalee Pl. G53	O10 48	
Cornalee Rd. G53	O10 48	
Cornhill St. G21	G19 23	
Cornock St. G23	E14 8	
Torrin Rd.		
Cornock Cres., Clyde.	D 7 5	
Cornock St., Clyde.	D 7 5	
Cornwall Av. G73	P20 65	
Cornwall St. G41	L14 34	
Coronation Pl., Gart.	F27 27	
Coronation Way, Bear.	E13 8	
Corpach Pl. G34	J26 40	
Corran St. G33	K21 38	
Corrie Dr., Pais.	M 9 48	
Corrie Gro. G44	Q15 63	
Corrie Pl., Lenz.	D24 13	
Corrour Rd. G43	O14 50	
Corse Rd. G52	L 9 32	
Corsebar Av., Pais.	N 5 46	
Corsebar Cres., Pais.	N 5 46	
Corsebar Dr., Pais.	N 5 46	

Corsebar La. G78	N 4 45	
Balgonie Av.		
Corsebar Rd., Pais.	N 5 46	
Corseford Av., John.	O08 43	
Corsehill Pl. G34	K26 40	
Corsehill St. G34	K26 40	
Corselet Rd. G53	Q10 60	
Corsewall Av. G32	M24 55	
Corsford Dr. G53	P11 61	
Corsock St. G31	K20 37	
Corston St. G33	K20 37	
Cortachy Pl., Bish.	E20 11	
Coruisk Way	O 3 45	
Spencer Dr.		
Coruisk Way, Pais.	O 3 45	
Spencer Dr.		
Corunna St. G3	K15 35	
Coshneuk Rd. G33	G22 24	
Cottar St. G20	F15 21	
Cotton Av., Linw.	L 1 28	
Cotton St. G40	N19 53	
Cotton St., Pais.	M 6 46	
Coulters La. G40	L18 36	
Countess Wk., Bail.	L28 41	
County Av. G72	O20 53	
County Pl., Pais.	L 6 30	
Moss St.		
County Sq., Pais.	L 6 30	
Couper St. G4	J17 36	
Courthill Av. G44	P16 63	
Coustonhill St. G43	O14 50	
Pleasance St.		
Coustonholm Rd. G43	O14 50	
Coventry Dr. G31	K19 37	
Cowal Dr., Linw.	L 1 28	
Cowal Rd. G20	F14 20	
Cowal St. G20	F14 20	
Cowan Clo., Barr.	Q 8 59	
Cowan Cres.	R 8 59	
Cowan La. G12	J15 35	
Cowan St.		
Cowan Rd., Cumb.	A 1 70	
Cowan St. G12	J15 35	
Cowan Wilson Av., Blan.	S26 68	
Cowcaddens Rd. G2	J16 35	
Cowden Dr., Bish.	D19 11	
Cowden St. G51	K11 33	
Cowdenhill Circus G13	F11 19	
Cowdenhill Pl. G13	F11 19	
Cowdenhill Rd. G13	F11 19	
Cowdie St., Pais.	K 5 30	
Cowdray Cres., Renf.	H 8 17	
Cowell Vw., Clyde.	D 7 5	
Granville St.		
Cowglen Pl. G53	O11 49	
Cowglen Rd.		
Cowglen Rd. G53	O11 49	
Cowglen Ter. G53	O11 49	
Cowie St. G41	L15 35	
Cowlairs Rd. G21	H18 22	
Coxhill St. G21	H17 22	
Coxton Pl. G33	J23 39	
Coylton Rd. G43	P15 63	
Craggan Dr. G14	G 9 18	
Cragielea St. G31	K19 37	
Crags Av., Pais.	N 6 46	
Crags Cres., Pais.	N 6 46	
Crags Rd., Pais.	N 6 46	
Craig Rd. G44	P16 63	
Craig Rd., Linw.	K 1 28	
Craigallian Av. G72	Q23 67	
Craiganour La. G43	P14 62	
Craiganour Pl. G43	P14 62	
Craigard Pl. G73	Q21 66	
Inverclyde Gdns.		
Craigbank Dr. G53	P10 60	
Craigbank St. G22	H17 22	
Craigbarnet Cres. G33	H22 24	
Craigbo Av. G23	E14 8	
Craigbo Ct. G23	F14 20	
Craigbo Dr. G23	F14 20	
Craigbo Pl. G23	F14 20	
Craigbo Rd. G23	F14 20	
Craigbo St. G23	E14 8	
Craigbog Av., John.	N08 43	
Craigdonald Pl., John.	M09 43	
Craigellan Rd. G43	P14 62	
Craigenbay Cres., Lenz.	C23 13	
Craigenbay Rd., Lenz.	D23 13	
Craigenbay St. G21	H19 23	

Craigencart Ct., Clyde.	C 6 4	
Gentle Row		
Craigend Dr., Coat.	M29 57	
Craigend Pl. G13	G12 19	
Craigend St. G13	G12 19	
Craigendmuir Rd. G33	H24 25	
Craigendmuir St. G33	J20 37	
Craigendon Oval, Pais.	P 5 58	
Craigendon Rd., Pais.	P 5 58	
Craigends Dr., Kilb.	M07 42	
High Barholm		
Craigenfeoch Av., John.	N08 43	
Craigfaulds Av., Pais.	N04 45	
Craigflower Gdns. G53	Q10 60	
Craigflower Rd. G53	Q10 60	
Craighalbert Rd. G68	B 1 70	
Craighall Rd. G4	J16 35	
Craighead Av. G33	H20 23	
Craighead St., Barr.	R 7 59	
Craighead Way, Barr.	R 7 59	
Craighouse St. G33	J22 38	
Craigie Pk. G66	C24 13	
Craigie St. G42	N16 51	
Craigiebar Dr., Pais.	O 5 46	
Craigieburn Gdns. G20	F13 20	
Craigieburn Rd., Cumb.	C 2 70	
Craigiehall Pl. G51	L14 34	
Craigielea Dr., Pais.	L 5 30	
Craigielea Rd. G81	B 6 4	
Craigielea Rd., Renf.	H 8 17	
Craigielinn Av., Pais.	P 5 58	
Craigievar St. G33	J24 39	
Craigleith St. G32	L21 38	
Craiglockhart St. G33	J23 39	
Craigmaddie Ter. La. G3	K15 35	
Derby St.		
Craigmillar Rd. G42	O16 51	
Craigmont Dr. G20	G15 21	
Craigmont St. G20	G15 21	
Craigmore Rd., Bear.	B10 6	
Craigmore St. G31	L20 37	
Craigmount Av., Pais.	P 5 58	
Craigmuir Cres. G52	L 9 32	
Craigmuir Pl. G52	L 9 32	
Craigmuir Rd.		
Craigmuir Rd. G52	L 9 32	
Craigneil St. G33	J24 39	
Craignestock St. G40	L18 36	
Craignethan Gdns. G11	J13 34	
Lawrie St.		
Craignure Rd. G73	Q19 65	
Craigpark Dr. G31	K19 37	
Craigpark G31	K19 37	
Craigpark Ter. G31	K19 37	
Craigpark		
Craigpark Way, Udd.	O28 57	
Newton Dr.		
Craigs Av., Clyde.	C 8 5	
Craigston Pl., John.	N09 43	
Craigston Rd., John.	N09 43	
Craigton Av., Barr.	R 9 60	
Craigton Dr. G51	L12 33	
Craigton Dr., Barr.	R 9 60	
Craigton Pl. G51	L12 33	
Craigton Dr.		
Craigton Pl., Blan.	R26 68	
Craigton Rd. G51	L12 33	
Craigvicar Gdns. G32	L23 39	
Hailes Av.		
Craigview Av., John.	O08 43	
Craigwell Av. G73	P20 65	
Crail St. G31	L20 37	
Cramond Av., Renf.	J 9 32	
Cramond St. G5	N17 52	
Cramond Ter. G32	L22 38	
Cranborne Rd. G12	G13 20	
Cranbrooke Dr. G20	F14 20	
Cranhill St. G33	J20 37	
Cranston St. G3	K15 35	
Cranworth La. G12	H14 20	
Great George St.		
Cranworth St. G12	H14 20	
Crarae Av., Bear.	E12 7	
Crathie Dr. G11	J13 34	
Crathie La. G11	J13 34	
Exeter Dr.		
Craw Rd., Pais.	M 5 46	
Crawford Av., Lenz.	D23 13	
Crawford Cres., Blan.	R26 68	
Crawford Cres., Udd.	O27 57	

Name	Ref	Pg
Crawford Ct., Giff.	R13	62
Milverton Rd.		
Crawford Dr. G15	E 9	6
Crawford La. G11	J13	34
Crawford Path G11	J13	34
Crawford St.		
Crawford St. G11	J13	34
Crawford Dr., Pais.	L 4	29
Crawfurd Gdns. G73	Q19	65
Crawfurd Rd. G73	Q19	65
Crawriggs Av., Lenz.	C23	13
Crebar Dr., Barr.	R 8	59
Crebar St. G46	Q12	61
Credon Gdns. G73	Q20	65
Cree Av., Bish.	E20	11
Cree Gdns. G32	L21	38
Kilmany Dr.		
Creran St. G40	L18	36
Tobago St.		
Crescent Ct., Dalm.	D 6	4
Swindon St.		
Crescent Rd. G13	G10	18
Great George St.		
Cresswell La. G12	H14	20
Cresswell St. G12	H14	20
Cressy St. G11	K12	33
Crest Av. G13	F10	18
Crestlea Av., Pais.	O 6	46
Creswell Ter., Udd.	O27	57
Kylepark Dr.		
Crichton Ct. G42	R18	64
Crichton St. G21	H18	22
Crieff Ct. G3	K15	35
North St.		
Criffell Gdns. G32	M23	55
Criffell Rd. G32	M23	55
Crimea St. G2	K16	35
Crinan Gdns., Bish.	E19	11
Crinan Rd., Bish.	E19	11
Crinan St. G31	K19	37
Cripps Av., Clyde.	E 8	5
Croft Rd. G73	P22	66
Croft Wynd, Udd.	P28	69
Croftbank Av. G71	R28	69
Croftbank Cres., Both.	R28	69
Croftbank Cres., Udd.	P27	69
Croftbank St. G21	H18	22
Croftbank St., Udd.	P27	69
Croftburn Dr. G44	Q17	64
Croftcroighn Rd. G33	J22	38
Croftend Av. G44	P18	64
Croftfoor Rd. G44	Q17	64
Croftfoot Cotts., Gart.	G28	27
Croftfoot Cres. G45	Q19	65
Croftfoot Dr. G45	Q18	64
Croftfoot Quad. G45	Q18	64
Croftfoot Rd. G45	Q17	64
Croftfoot St. G45	Q19	65
Croftfoot Ter. G45	Q18	64
Crofthead St., Udd.	P27	69
Crofthill Av., Udd.	P27	69
Crofthill Rd. G44	P17	64
Crofthouse Dr. G44	Q18	64
Croftmont Av. G44	Q18	64
Croftmoraig Av., Chr.	D28	15
Crofton Av. G44	Q17	64
Croftpark Av. G44	Q17	64
Croftpark Rd., Clyde.	B 7	5
Croftside Av. G44	Q18	64
Croftspar Av. G32	L23	39
Croftspar Dr. G32	L23	39
Croftspar Pl. G32	L23	39
Croftwood Av. G44	Q17	64
Croftwood, Bish.	D19	11
Cromart Pl., Chr.	E26	14
Cromarty Av. G43	P15	63
Cromarty Av., Bish.	E20	11
Cromarty Gdns., Clark.	R16	63
Crombie Gdns., Bail.	M25	56
Cromdale St. G51	L12	33
Cromer La., Pais.	K 5	30
Abbotsburn Way		
Cromer St. G20	G15	21
Cromer Way, Pais.	K 5	30
Mosslands Rd.		
Crompton Av. G44	P16	63
Cromwell La. G20	J16	35
Cromwell St.		
Cromwell St. G20	J16	35
Cronberry Quad. G52	M 9	48
Cronberry Ter. G52	M 9	48
Crookedshields Rd. G72	R22	66
Crookston Av. G52	M10	48
Crookston Ct. G52	M10	48
Crookston Dr. G52	M 9	48
Crookston Gdns. G52	M 9	48
Crookston Gro. G52	M10	48
Crookston Pl. G52	M 9	48
Crookston Quad. G52	M 9	48
Crookston Rd. G52	N10	48
Crookston Ter. G52	M10	48
Crookston Rd.		
Crosbie Dr. G78	O 3	45
Crosbie St. G20	F14	20
Crosbie Woods, Pais.	N 4	45
Cross Arthurlie St.,	R 7	59
Barr.		
Cross Rd., Pais.	N 4	45
Cross St. G32	N23	55
Cross St., Pais.	M 5	46
Cross, The, G1	L17	36
Cross, The, Pais.	L 6	30
Crossbank Av. G42	N18	52
Crossbank Dr. G42	N18	52
Crossbank Rd. G42	N17	52
Crossbank Ter. G42	N17	52
Crossflat Cres., Pais.	L 7	31
Crossford Dr. G23	E15	9
Crosshill Av. G42	N16	51
Crosshill Av., Lenz.	C23	13
Crosshill Dr. G73	P19	65
Crosshill Rd.,	C20	11
Bish. & Lenz.		
Crosshill Sq., Bail.	M26	56
Crosslee St. G52	L12	33
Crosslees Ct., Thorn.	Q12	61
Main St.		
Crosslees Dr., Thorn.	Q12	61
Crosslees Pk., Thorn.	Q12	61
Crosslees Rd., Thorn.	R12	61
Crossloan Pl. G51	K12	33
Crossloan Rd. G51	K12	33
Crossloan Ter. G51	K12	33
Crossmill Av., Barr.	Q 8	59
Crossmyloof Gdns.	N14	50
G41		
Crosspoint Dr. G23	E15	9
Invershiel Rd.		
Crosstobs Rd. G53	N10	48
Crovie Rd. G53	O10	48
Crow Ct., The, Bish.	E18	10
Kenmure Av.		
Crow La. G13	G12	19
Crow Rd. G11	H12	19
Crow Wood Rd., Chr.	F25	26
Crowflats Rd., Udd.	P27	69
Lady Isle Cres.		
Crowhill Rd. G64	F18	22
Crowhill St. G22	G17	22
Crowlin Cres. G33	K22	38
Crown Av., Clyde.	D 7	5
Crown Circuit G12	H13	20
Crown Rd.		
Crown Circus G12	H13	20
Crown Rd. S.		
Crown Ct. G1	K17	36
Virginia St.		
Crown Gdns. G12	H13	20
Crown Rd. N.		
Crown Mansions G11	H13	20
North Gardner St.		
Crown Rd. N. G12	H13	20
Crown Rd. S. G12	H13	20
Crown Rd. S.		
Crown St. G5	M17	52
Crown St., Bail.	M24	55
Crown Ter. G12	H13	20
Crown Rd. S.		
Crownpoint Rd. G40	L18	36
Crowpoint Rd. G40	L19	37
Alma St.		
Crowwood Ter., Chr.	F25	26
Croy Pl. G21	G20	23
Rye Rd.		
Croy Pl. G21	G20	23
Croy Rd.		
Croy Rd. G21	G20	23
Cruachan Av., Renf.	J 8	31
Cruachan Cres., Pais.	O 6	46
Cruachan Dr., Barr.	R 8	59
Cruachan Rd. G73	Q20	65
Cruachan Rd., Bear.	B10	6
Ledi Dr.		
Cruachan St. G46	Q12	61
Cruachan Way, Barr.	R 8	59
Cruden St. G51	L12	33
Crum Av., Thorn.	Q13	62
Crusader Av. G13	E11	7
Cubie St. G40	L18	36
Cuilhill Rd., Bail.	K27	41
Cuillin Way, Barr.	R 8	59
Cuillins Rd. G73	Q20	65
Cuillins, The, Udd.	N26	56
Culbin Dr. G13	F 9	18
Cullen St. G32	M22	54
Cullins, The, Chr.	D28	15
Culloden St. G31	K19	37
Culrain Gdns. G32	L22	38
Culrain St. G32	L22	38
Culross La. G32	M23	55
Culross St. G32	M23	55
Cult Rd., Lenz.	D24	13
Cults St. G51	L12	33
Culzean Cres., Bail.	M25	56
Huntingtower Rd.		
Culzean Dr. G32	M23	39
Cumberland Ct. G1	L17	36
Gallowgate		
Cumberland La. G5	M16	51
Cumberland St.		
Cumberland Pl. G5	M17	52
Cumberland Pl., Pais.	M 6	46
Laigh Kirk La.		
Cumberland St. G5	L16	35
Cumberland St. G5	M17	52
Cumbernauld Rd. G31	K20	37
Cumbrae Ct., Clyde.	E 7	5
Montrose St.		
Cumbrae Rd., Pais.	O 6	46
Cumbrae Rd., Renf.	J 8	31
Cumbrae St. G33	K22	38
Cumlodden Dr. G20	F14	20
Cumming Dr. G42	O16	51
Cumnock Dr., Renf.	R 8	59
Cunard St., Clyde.	F 8	17
Cunningham Dr., Clyde.	C 6	4
Cunningham Dr., Giff.	Q15	63
Cunningham Rd. G73	O20	53
Cambuslang Rd.		
Cunningham Rd., G52	K 9	32
Cunninghame Rd., Kilb.	M07	42
Curfew Rd. G13	E11	7
Curle St. G14	J11	33
Curlew Pl., John.	O08	43
Curling Cres. G44	O17	52
Currie St. G20	G15	21
Curtis Av. G44	O17	52
Curzon St. G20	G15	21
Cut, The, Udd.	P27	69
Cuthbert St., Udd.	O28	57
Oakdene Av.		
Cuthbertson St. G42	N16	51
Cuthelton Dr. G31	M21	54
Cuthelton St.		
Cuthelton St. G31	M20	53
Cuthelton Ter. G31	M20	53
Cypress Av., Blan.	S26	68
Cypress Av., Udd.	O28	57
Myrtle Rd.		
Cypress Ct., Lenz.	C22	12
Cypress St. G22	G17	22
Cyprus Av., John.	N 1	44
Cyprus St., Clyde.	F 8	17
Cyril St., Pais.	M 7	47
Daer Av., Renf.	J 9	32
Dairsie Gdns., Bish.	F20	23
Dairsie St. G44	Q15	63
Daisy St. G42	N16	51
Dakota Way, Renf.	J 8	31
Friendship Way		
Dalbeth Rd. G32	N21	54
Dalchurn Path G34	K25	40
Dalchurn Pl.		
Dalchurn Pl. G34	K25	40
Dalcraig Cres., Blan.	R26	68
Byres Rd.		
Dalcross La. G11	J14	34
Dalcross St. G11	J14	34
Dalcruin Gdns. G69	D28	15
Daldowie Av. G32	M23	55

Name	Ref		Name	Ref		Name	Ref
Dale Path G40	M18 52		Darvel Cres., Pais.	M 8 47		Devonshire Gdns. G12	H13 20
Dale St. G40	M18 52		Darvel St. G53	P 9 60		Devonshire Gdns. La.	H13 20
Dale Way G73	Q19 65		Darwin Pl., Dalm.	D 5 4		G12	
Daleview Av. G12	G13 20		Dava St. G51	K13 34		*Hyndland Rd.*	
Dalfoil Ct. G52	M 9 48		Davaar Rd., Pais.	O 6 46		Devonshire Ter. G12	H13 20
Dalgarroch Av. G13	F 9 18		Davaar St. G40	M19 53		Devonshire Ter. La. G12	H13 20
Dalgleish Av., Clyde.	C 6 4		Daventry Dr. G12	G13 20		*Hughenden Rd.*	
Dalhousie Gdns., Bish.	E18 10		David Pl., Bail.	M24 55		Diana Av. G13	F10 18
Dalhousie La. G3	J16 35		David Pl., Pais.	K 7 31		Dick St. G20	H15 21
Scott St.			*Killarn Way*			*Henderson St.*	
Dalhousie La. W. G3	J16 35		David St. G40	L19 37		Dickens Av., Clyde.	D 6 4
Buccleuch St.			David Way, Pais.	K 7 31		Dilwara Av. G14	J12 33
Dalhousie Rd., Kilb.	N07 42		*Killarn Way*			Dimity St., John.	N09 43
Dalhousie St. G3	J16 35		Davidson Gdns. G14	H11 19		Dinard Dr., Giff.	Q14 62
Dalilea Dr. G34	J26 40		*Westland Dr.*			Dinart St. G33	J20 37
Dalilea Path G34	J26 40		Davidson Quad., Clyde.	B 6 4		Dinduff St. G34	J26 40
Dalilea Dr.			Davidson St. G40	N19 53		Dingwall St. G3	K14 34
Dalilea Pl. G34	J26 40		Davidson St., Clyde.	F 9 18		*Kelvinhaugh St.*	
Dalintober St. G5	L16 35		Davidston Pl., Lenz.	D24 13		Dinmont Pl. G41	N15 51
Dalkeith Av. G41	M13 50		Davieland Rd., Giff.	R13 62		*Norham St.*	
Dalkeith Av., Bish.	D19 11		Daviot St. G51	L11 33		Dinmont Rd. G41	N14 50
Dalkeith Rd., Bish.	D19 11		Dawes La. N. G14	H11 19		Dinwiddie St. G21	J20 37
Dalmahoy St. G32	K21 38		*Upland Dr.*			Dipple Pl. G15	E10 6
Dalmally St. G20	H15 21		Dawson Pl. G4	H16 21		Dirleton Av. G41	O15 51
Dalmarnock Ct. G40	M19 53		*Dawson Rd.*			Dirleton Dr., Pais.	N 4 45
Baltic St.			Dawson Rd. G4	H16 21		Dirleton Gate, Bear.	E11 7
Dalmary Dr., Pais.	L 7 31		Dealston Rd., Barr.	Q 7 59		Divernia Way, Barr.	S 8 59
Dalmeny Av., Giff.	Q14 62		Dean Park Dr. G72	Q23 67		Dixon Av. G42	N16 51
Dalmeny Dr., Barr.	R 7 59		Dean Park Rd., Renf.	J 9 32		Dixon Rd. G42	N17 52
Dalmeny St. G5	N18 52		Dean St., Clyde.	E 8 5		Dixon St. G1	L16 35
Dalmuir Ct., Dalm.	D 6 4		Deanbrae St., Udd.	P27 69		Dixon St., Pais.	M 6 46
Stewart St.			Deanfield Quad. G52	L 9 32		Dobbies Loan G4	J16 35
Dalnair St. G3	J14 34		Deanpark Av., Udd.	Q28 69		Dobbies Loan Pl. G4	K17 36
Dalness Pass. G32	M22 54		Deans Av. G72	Q23 67		Dochart Av., Renf.	J 9 32
Ochil St.			Deanside La. G4	K17 36		Dochart St. G33	J21 38
Dalness St. G32	M22 54		*Rotton Row*			Dock St., Clyde.	F 8 17
Dalnottar Hill Rd.,	C 4 4		Deanside Rd., Renf.	K10 32		Dodhill Pl. G13	G10 18
Old.K.			Deanston Dr. G41	O15 51		Dodside Gdns. G32	M23 55
Dalreoch Av., Bail.	L26 40		Deanwood Av. G44	Q15 63		Dodside Pl. G32	M23 55
Dalriada St. G40	M20 53		Deanwood Rd. G44	Q15 63		Dodside St. G32	M23 55
Dalry Rd., Udd.	O28 57		Debdale Cotts. G13	G12 19		Dolan St., Bail.	L25 40
Myrtle Rd.			*Whittingehame Dr.*			Dollar Ter. G20	F14 20
Dalry St. G32	M22 54		Dechmont Av. G72	Q23 67		*Crosbie St.*	
Dalserf Cres., Giff.	R13 62		Dechmont Gdns., Blan.	R26 68		Dolphin Rd. G41	N14 50
Dalserf St. G31	L19 37		Dechmont Gdns., Udd.	N27 57		Don Av., Renf.	J 9 32
Dalsetter Av. G15	E 9 6		Dechmont Pl. G72	Q23 67		Don Dr., Pais.	N 3 45
Dalsetter Pl. G15	E10 6		Dechmont Rd., Udd.	N27 57		Don Pl., John.	O08 43
Dalsholm Rd. G20	F13 20		Dechmont St. G31	M20 53		Don St. G33	K20 37
Dalskeith Av., Pais.	L 4 29		Dechmont Vw., Udd.	O28 57		Donald Way, Udd.	O28 57
Dalskeith Cres., Pais.	L 4 29		*Hamilton Vw.*			Donaldson Dr., Renf.	H 8 17
Dalskeith Rd., Pais.	M 4 45		Dee Av. G78	N 3 45		*Ferguson St.*	
Dalswinton Pl. G34	K26 40		Dee Av., Renf.	H 9 18		Donaldswood Rd., Pais.	O 5 46
Dalswinton St.			Dee Dr., Pais.	N 3 45		Doncaster St. G20	H16 21
Dalswinton St. G34	K26 40		Dee Pl., John.	O08 43		Doon Cres., Bear.	D11 7
Dalton Av., Clyde.	E 9 6		Dee St. G33	J20 37		Doon Side, Cumb.	C 3 71
Dalton St. G31	L21 38		Deepdene Rd., Bear.	E11 7		Doon St., Clyde.	D 8 5
Dalveen Av., Udd.	O27 57		Deepdene Rd., Chr.	E28 15		Doonfoot Rd. G43	P14 62
Dalveen Ct., Barr.	R 8 59		Delburn St. G31	M20 53		Dora St. G40	M19 53
Dalveen St. G32	L21 38		Delhi Av., Dalm.	D 5 4		Dorchester Av., G12	G13 20
Dalveen Way G73	Q20 65		Delhmont Vw., Udd.	O28 57		Dorchester Ct. G12	G13 20
Dalwhinnie Av., Blan.	R26 68		*Hamilton Vw.*			*Dorchester Av.*	
Daly Gdns., Blan.	R27 69		Delny Pl. G33	K24 39		Dorchester Pl. G12	G13 20
Dalziel Dr. G41	M14 50		Delvin Rd., G44	P16 63		Dorian Dr., Clark.	S14 62
Dalziel Quadrant G41	M14 50		Denbeck St. G32	L21 38		Dorlin Rd. G33	G24 25
Dalziel Dr.			Denbrae St. G32	L21 38		Dormanside Rd. G53	M10 48
Dalziel Rd. G52	K 9 32		Dene Wk., Bish.	F20 23		Dornal Av. G13	F 9 18
Damshot Cres. G53	N11 49		Denewood Av., Pais.	O 5 46		Dornford Av. G32	N23 55
Damshot Rd. G53	O11 49		Denham St. G22	H16 21		Dornford Rd. G32	N23 55
Danes Cres. G14	G10 18		Denholme Dr., Giff.	R14 62		Dornie Dr. G32	O23 55
Danes Dr. G14	G10 18		Denkenny Sq. G15	D 9 6		Dornie Dr. G46	Q12 61
Danes La. S. G14	H11 19		Denmark St. G22	H17 22		Dornoch Av., Giff.	R14 62
Dunglass Av.			Denmilne Path G34	K26 40		Dornoch Pl., Bish.	E20 11
Dargarvel Av. G41	M13 50		Denmilne Pl. G34	K26 40		Dornoch Pl., Chr.	E26 14
Darkwood Cres., Pais.	L 4 29		Denmilne St. G34	K26 40		Dornoch Rd., Bear.	E11 7
Darleith St. G32	L21 38		Derby St. G3	K15 35		Dornoch St. G40	L18 36
Darluith Rd., Linw.	L 1 28		Derby Terrace La. G3	K15 35		Dorset Sq. G3	K15 35
Darnaway Av. G33	J23 39		*Derby St.*			*Dorset St.*	
Darnaway St. G33	J23 39		Derwent St. G22	H16 21		Dorset St. G3	K15 35
Darnick St. G21	H19 23		Despard Av. G32	M24 55		Dosk Av. G13	F 9 18
Hobden St.			Despard Gdns. G32	M24 55		Dosk Pl. G13	F 9 18
Darnley Cres., Bish.	D18 10		Deveron Av., Giff.	R14 62		Douglas Av. G32	N22 54
Darnley Gdns. G41	N15 51		Deveron Rd., Bear.	E11 7		Douglas Av. G73	P20 65
Darnley Pl. G41	N15 51		Deveron St. G33	J20 37		Douglas Av., Giff.	R14 62
Darnley Rd.			Devol Cres. G53	O10 48		Douglas Av., John.	N 1 44
Darnley Rd. G41	N15 51		Devon Gdns. G12	H13 20		Douglas Av., Lenz.	C23 13
Darnley Rd., Barr.	Q 9 60		*Hyndland Rd.*			Douglas Ct., Lenz.	C23 13
Darnley St. G41	N15 51		Devon Gdns., Bish.	D18 10		Douglas Dr. G15	E 9 6
Darroch Way, Cumb.	B 3 71		Devon Pl. G42	M16 51		Douglas Dr. G72	P21 66
Dartford St. G22	H16 21		Devon St. G5	M16 51		Douglas Dr., Bail.	L24 39
Darvaar Rd., Renf.	J 8 31		Devondale Av., Blan.	R26 68		Douglas Dr., Both.	R28 69

Street	Ref	Pg
Douglas Gdns., Bear.	D12	7
Douglas Gdns., Giff.	R14	62
Douglas Gdns., Lenz.	C23	13
Douglas Gdns., Udd.	P27	69
Douglas La. G2	K16	35
West George St.		
Douglas Park Cres.,	C13	8
Bear.		
Douglas Pl., Bear.	C12	7
Douglas Pl., Lenz.	C23	13
Douglas Rd.,	K 7	31
Pais. & Renf.		
Douglas St. G2	K16	35
Douglas St., Pais.	L 5	30
Douglas St., Udd.	O28	57
Douglas Ter. G41	M15	51
Shields Rd.		
Douglas Ter., Pais.	J 6	30
Douglaston Rd. G23	E15	9
Dougray Pl., Barr.	R 8	59
Dougrie Dr. G45	Q17	64
Dougrie Pl. G45	Q18	64
Dougrie Rd. G45	R17	64
Dougrie St. G45	Q18	64
Dougrie Ter. G45	Q17	64
Doune Cres., Bish.	D19	11
Doune Gdns. G20	H15	21
Doune Quad. G20	H15	21
Dove St. G53	P10	60
Dovecot G43	O14	50
Shawhill Rd.		
Dovecothall St., Barr.	Q 8	59
Dowanfield Rd., Cumb.	C 2	70
Dowanhill Pl. G11	J14	34
Old Dumbarton Rd.		
Dowanhill St. G11	J14	34
Dowanside La. G12	H14	20
Byres Rd.		
Dowanside Rd. G12	H14	20
Dowanvale Ter. G11	J13	34
White St.		
Down St. G21	H18	22
Downcraig Dr. G45	R17	64
Downcraig Rd. G45	R17	64
Downcraig Ter. G45	R17	64
Downfield Gdns., Both.	R27	69
Downfield St. G32	M21	54
Downiebrae Rd. G73	N19	53
Dowrie Cres. G53	N10	48
Dows Pl. G4	H16	21
Possil Rd.		
Drainie St. G34	K25	40
Westerhouse Rd.		
Drake St. G40	L18	36
Drakemire Av. G45	Q17	64
Drakemire Dr. G45	Q17	64
Dreghorn St. G31	K20	37
Drem Pl. G11	J13	34
Merkland St.		
Drimnin Rd. G33	G24	25
Drive Gdns., John.	M 3	45
Drive Rd. G51	K12	33
Drochil St. G34	J25	40
Drumbeg Dr. G53	P10	60
Drumbeg Pl. G53	P10	60
Drumbottie Rd. G21	G19	23
Drumby Cres., Clark.	S14	62
Drumby Dr., Clark.	S14	62
Drumcavel Rd.,	F26	26
Chr. & Gart.		
Drumchapel Gdns. G15	E10	6
Drumchapel Pl. G15	E10	6
Drumchapel Rd. G15	E10	6
Drumclog Gdns. G33	G21	24
Auchinleck Av.		
Drumclutha Dr., Both.	R28	69
Drumcross Rd. G53	N11	49
Drumhead Pl. G32	N21	54
Drumhead Rd. G32	N21	54
Drumilaw Rd. G73	P19	65
Drumilaw Way G73	P19	65
Drumlaken Av. G23	E14	8
Drumlaken Ct. G23	E14	8
Drumlaken St. G23	E14	8
Drumlanrig Av. G34	J26	40
Drumlanrig Pl. G34	J26	40
Drumlanrig Quad. G34	J26	40
Drumlochy Rd. G33	J22	38
Drummond Av. G73	O18	52
Drummond Dr., Pais.	M 8	47
Drummond Gdns. G13	G12	19
Crow Rd.		
Drummore Rd. G15	D10	6
Drummyne Pl. G51	L12	33
Drumoyne Circus		
Drumover Dr. G31	M21	54
Drumoyne Av. G51	K12	33
Drumoyne Circus G51	L12	33
Drumoyne Dr. G51	K12	33
Drumoyne Quad. G51	L12	33
Drumoyne Rd. G51	L12	33
Drumoyne Sq. G51	K12	33
Drumpark St. G46	Q12	61
Drumpark St., Coat.	M28	57
Dunnachie Dr.		
Drumpeller Rd., Bail.	M25	56
Drumpellier Av., Bail.	M25	56
Drumpellier Pl., Bail.	M25	56
Drumpellier St. G33	J20	37
Drumreoch Dr. G42	O18	52
Drumreoch Pl. G42	O18	52
Drumry Pl. G15	E 9	6
Drumry Rd. E. G15	E 9	6
Drumry Rd., Clyde.	D 7	5
Drums Av., Pais.	L 5	30
Drums Cres., Pais.	L 5	30
Drums Rd. G53	M10	48
Drumsack Av., Chr.	F26	26
Drumsargard Rd. G73	P20	65
Drumshaw Dr. G32	O23	55
Drumvale Dr., Chr.	E27	15
Drury St. G2	K16	35
Dryad St. G46	P12	61
Dryborough Av., John.	N 4	45
Dryburgh Av. G73	O19	53
Dryburgh Gdns. G20	H15	21
Dryburgh Rd., Bear.	C11	7
Dryburn Av. G52	L10	32
Drygate G4	K18	36
Drygrange Rd. G33	J23	39
Drymen Pl., Lenz.	D23	13
Drymen Rd., Bear.	C11	7
Drymen St. G52	L12	33
Morven St.		
Drymen Wynd, Bear.	D12	7
Drynoch Pl. G22	F16	21
Duart Dr., John.	N 1	44
Duart St. G20	F14	20
Dubs Rd., Barr.	Q 9	60
Dubton Path G34	J25	40
Dubton St. G34	J25	40
Duchall Pl. G14	H10	18
Duchess Pl. G73	O20	53
Duchess Rd. G73	N20	53
Duchray Dr., Pais.	M 9	48
Duchray La. G31	J20	37
Duchray St.		
Duchray St. G31	J20	37
Ducraig St. G32	L22	38
Dudhope St. G33	J23	39
Dudley Dr. G12	H13	20
Duffus Pl. G32	O23	55
Duffus St. G34	J25	40
Duffus Ter. G32	O23	55
Duisdale Rd. G32	O23	55
Duke St., G4	K18	36
Duke St., Linw.	L 2	28
Duke St., Pais.	N 6	46
Dukes Gate, Both.	Q27	69
Dukes Rd. G72 & G73	P20	65
Dukes Rd., Bail.	L28	41
Dulnain St. G72	P24	67
Dulsie Rd. G21	G20	23
Dumbarton Rd. G11	G 9	18
Dumbarton Rd., Clyde.	C 6	4
Dumbarton Rd., Old.K.	D 5	4
Dalm. & Clyde.		
Dumbreck Av. G41	M13	50
Dumbreck Ct. G41	M13	50
Dumbreck Pl., Lenz.	D24	13
Dumbreck Rd. G41	M13	50
Dumbreck Sq. G41	M13	50
Dumbreck Av.		
Dunagoil Rd. G45	R17	64
Dunagoil St. G45	R18	64
Dunagoil Ter. G45	R18	64
Dunalastair Dr. G33	G22	24
Dunalistair Av. G33	G22	24
Dunan Pl. G33	K24	39
Dunard Rd. G73	O19	53
Dunard St. G20	H15	21
Dunard Way, Pais.	K 5	30
Mosslands Rd.		
Dunaskin St. G11	J14	34
Dunbar Av. G73	O20	53
Dunbar Av., John.	O09	43
Dunbar Rd., Pais.	N 4	45
Dunbeith Pl. G20	G14	20
Dunblane St. G4	J16	35
Dunbrach Rd., Cumb.	B 1	70
Duncan Av. G14	H11	19
Duncan La. G14	H11	19
Duncan Av.		
Duncan La. N. G14	H11	19
Ormiston Av.		
Duncan St., Clyde.	D 7	5
Duncansby Rd. G33	L23	39
Dunchatt St. G31	K18	36
Dunchattan Pl. G31	K18	36
Duke St.		
Dunchurch Rd., Pais.	L 8	31
Dunclutha Dr., Both.	R28	69
Dunclutha St. G40	N19	53
Duncombe St. G20	F14	20
Duncombe Vw., Clyde.	D 8	5
Kirkoswald Dr.		
Duncraig Cres., John.	O08	43
Duncrub Dr., Bish.	E18	10
Duncruin St. G20	F14	20
Duncryne Av. G32	M23	55
Duncryne Gdns. G32	M24	55
Duncryne Pl., Bish.	F18	22
Dundas La. G1	K17	36
Dundas St. G1	K17	36
Dundasvale Ct. G4	J16	35
Maitland St.		
Dundasvale Rd. G4	J16	35
Maitland St.		
Dundee Dr. G52	M10	48
Dundonald Av., John.	N08	43
Dundonald Rd. G12	H14	20
Dundonald Rd., Pais.	K 7	31
Dundrennan Rd. G42	O15	51
Dunearn Pl., Pais.	M 7	47
Dunearn St. G4	J15	35
Dunegoin St. G51	K13	34
Sharp St.		
Dunellan Dr., Clyde.	B 7	5
Dunellan St. G52	L12	33
Dungeonhill Rd. G34	K26	40
Dunglass Av. G14	H11	19
Dunglass La. N. G14	H11	19
Verona Av.		
Dungoil Av., Cumb.	B 1	70
Dungoil Rd., Lenz.	D24	13
Dungoyne St. G20	F14	20
Dunira St. G32	M21	54
Dunivaig St. G33	K24	39
Dunkeld Av. G73	O19	53
Dunkeld Dr., Bear.	D13	8
Dunkeld Gdns., Bish.	E19	11
Dunkeld La., Chr.	E28	15
Burnbrae Av.		
Dunkeld St. G31	M20	53
Dunkenny Pl. G15	D 9	6
Dunkenny Rd. G15	D 9	6
Dunlop Cres., Both.	R28	69
Dunlop Cres., Renf.	H 8	17
Hairst St.		
Dunlop St. G1	L17	36
Dunlop St. G72	P24	67
Dunlop St., Linw.	L 2	28
Dunlop St., Renf.	H 8	17
Hairst St.		
Dunmore La. G5	L16	35
Norfolk St.		
Dunmore St. G5	L16	35
Dunmore St., Clyde.	F 8	17
Dunn St. G40	M19	53
Dunn St., Clyde.	C 6	4
Dunn St., Dalm.	D 6	4
Dunn St., Pais.	M 7	47
Dunnachie Dr., Coat.	M28	57
Dunnichen Pl., Bish.	E20	11
Dunning St. G31	M20	53
Dunolly St. G21	J19	37
Dunottar St. G33	J22	38
Dunottar St., Bish.	E20	11
Dunphail Dr. G34	K26	40
Dunphail Rd. G34	K26	40

Elliston Dr. G53 P11 61
Elliston Pl. G53 P11 61
Ravenscraig Dr.
Elm Av., Lenz. C23 13
Elm Av., Renf. H 8 17
Elm Bank, Bish. E19 11
Elm Dr., John. O09 43
Elm Gdns., Bear. C12 7
Elm Rd. G73 Q19 65
Elm Rd., Dalm. C 7 5
Elm Rd., Pais. N 7 47
Elm St. G14 H11 19
Elm Wk., Bear. C12 7
Elmbank Av., Udd. O28 57
Elmbank Cres. G2 K16 35
Elmbank La. G3 K15 35
North St.
Elmbank St. G2 K16 35
Elmbank Street La. G3 K15 35
North St.
Elmfoot St. G5 N17 52
Elmore Av. G44 P16 63
Elmore La. G44 P16 63
Elmslie Ct., Bail. M25 56
Elmvale Row E. G21 H18 22
Elmvale Row
Elmvale Row G21 H18 22
Elmvale Row W. G21 H18 22
Elmvale Row
Elmvale St. G21 G18 22
Elmwood Av. G11 H12 19
Elmwood Ct., Both. R28 69
Blantyre Mill Rd.
Elmwood Gdns. G11 H12 19
Randolph Rd.
Elmwood Gdns., Kirk. C22 12
Elmwood La. G11 H11 19
Elmwood Av.
Elmwood Ter. G11 H12 19
Crow Rd.
Elphin St. G23 E14 8
Invershiel Rd.
Elphinstone Pl. G51 K14 34
Elrig Rd. G44 P16 63
Elspeth Gdns., Bish. E19 11
Eltham St. G22 H16 21
Elvan Ct. G32 L21 38
Edrom St.
Elvan St. G32 L21 38
Embo Dr. G13 G10 18
Emerson Rd., Bish. E19 11
Emerson St. G20 G16 21
Emily Pl. G31 L18 36
Endfield Av. G12 G13 20
Endrick Bank, Bish. D19 11
Endrick Dr., Bear. D12 7
Endrick Dr., Pais. L 7 31
Endrick St. G21 H17 22
Endsleigh Gdns. G11 H13 20
Partickhill Rd.
Ennerdale St. G32 L21 38
Ensay St. G22 F17 22
Enterkin St. G32 M21 54
Ericht Rd. G43 P14 62
Eriska Av. G14 G10 18
Erradale St. G22 F16 21
Erriboll Pl. G22 F16 21
Erriboll St. G22 F16 21
Errogie St. G34 K25 40
Erskine Av. G41 M13 50
Erskine Sq. G52 K 9 32
Erskine Vw., Clyde. D 7 5
Singer St.
Erskinefauld Rd., Linw. L 1 28
Ervie St. G34 K26 40
Esk Av., Renf. J 9 32
Esk Dr., Pais. N 3 45
Esk St. G14 G 9 18
Esk Way, Pais. N 3 45
Eskbank St. G32 L22 38
Eskdale Dr. G73 O20 53
Eskdale Rd., Bear. E11 7
Eskdale St. G42 N16 51
Esmond St. G3 J14 34
Espedair St., Pais. M 6 46
Essenside Av. G15 E11 7
Essex Dr. G14 H12 19
Essex La. G14 H12 19
Esslemont Av. G14 G10 18
Estate Quad. G32 O23 55
Estate Rd. G32 O23 55
Etive Av., Bear. D13 8
Etive Cres., Bish. E19 11
Etive Ct., Clyde. C 8 5
Etive Dr., Giff. R14 62
Etive St. G32 L22 38
Eton Gdns. G12 J15 35
Oakfield Av.
Eton La. G12 J15 35
Great George St.
Eton Pl. G12 J15 35
Oakfield Av.
Eton Ter. G12 J15 35
Oakfield Av.
Ettrick Av., Renf. J 9 32
Ettrick Cres. G73 O20 53
Ettrick Ct. G72 Q24 67
Gateside Av.
Ettrick Oval, Pais. O 3 45
Ettrick Pl. G43 O14 50
Ettrick Ter., John. O08 43
Ettrick Way, Renf. J 9 32
Evan Cres., Giff. R14 62
Evan Dr., Giff. R14 62
Evanton Dr. G46 R12 61
Evanton Pl. G46 Q12 61
Evanton Dr.
Everard Dr. G21 F18 22
Everard Pl. G21 F18 22
Everard Quad. G21 F18 22
Everglades, The, Chr. F25 26
Eversley St. G32 M22 54
Everton Rd. G53 N11 49
Ewart Pl. G3 K14 34
Kelvinhaugh St.
Ewing Pl. G31 L20 37
Ewing St. G73 O19 53
Ewing St., Kilb. M07 42
Exchange Pl. G1 K17 36
Buchanan St.
Exeter Dr. G11 J13 34
Exeter La. G11 J13 34
Exeter Dr.
Eynort St. G22 F16 21
Fagan Ct., Blan. R27 69
Faifley Rd., Clyde. C 7 5
Fairbairn Cres., Thorn. R13 62
Fairbairn Path G40 M19 53
Ruby St.
Fairbairn St. G40 M19 53
Dalmarnock Rd.
Fairburn St. G32 M21 54
Fairfax Av. G44 P17 64
Fairfield Gdns. G51 K12 33
Fairfield Pl. G51 K12 33
Fairfield Pl. G71 R28 69
Fairfield St. G51 K12 33
Fairhaven Dr. G23 F14 20
Fairhill Av. G53 O11 49
Fairholm St. G32 M21 54
Fairley St. G51 L13 34
Fairlie Park Dr. G11 J13 34
Fairway Av., Pais. O 5 46
Fairways, Bear. C10 6
Fairyknowe Gdns. G71 R28 69
Falcon Cres., Pais. L 4 29
Falcon Rd., John. O08 43
Falcon Ter. G20 F14 20
Falfield St. G5 M16 51
Falkland Cres., Bish. F20 23
Falkland Mansions G12 H13 20
Clarence Dr.
Falkland St. G12 H13 20
Falloch Rd., Bear. E11 7
Fallside Rd., Both. R28 69
Falside Av., Pais. N 6 46
Falside Rd. G32 M22 54
Falside Rd., Pais. N 5 46
Fara St. G23 F15 21
Farie St. G73 O19 53
Farm Ct., Both. Q28 69
Fallside Rd.
Farm La., Udd. P28 69
Myers Cres.
Farm Pk., Lenz. D23 13
Farm Rd. G41 M13 50
Farm Rd., Blan. R26 68
Farm Rd., Clyde. C 7 5
Farm Rd., Dalm. D 5 4
Farme Cross G73 N19 53
Farmeloan Rd. G73 O19 53
Farmington Av. G32 L23 39
Farmington Gate G32 L23 39
Farmington Gdns. G32 L23 39
Farmington Gro. G32 L23 39
Farne Dr. G44 Q16 63
Farnell St. G4 J16 35
Farrier Ct., John. M09 43
Faskally Av., Bish. D18 10
Faskin Cres. G53 O 9 48
Faskin Pl. G53 O 9 48
Faskin Rd. G53 O 9 48
Fasque Pl. G15 D 9 6
Fastnet St. G33 K22 38
Faulbswood Cres., Pais. N 4 45
Fauldhouse St. G5 M17 52
Faulds Gdns., Bail. L26 40
Faulds, Bail. L26 40
Fauldshead Rd., Renf. H 8 17
Fauldspark Cres., Bail. L26 40
Fauldswood Cres., Pais. N 4 45
Fauldswood Dr., Pais. N 4 45
Fearnmore Rd. G20 F14 20
Fendoch St. G32 M22 54
Fenella St. G32 L22 38
Fennsbank Av. G73 Q20 65
Fenwick Dr., Barr. R 8 59
Fenwick Pl., Giff. R13 62
Fenwick Rd., Giff. R14 62
Fereneze Av., Barr. Q 7 59
Fereneze Av., Pais. K 7 31
Fereneze Cres. G13 F10 18
Fereneze Dr., Pais. O 5 46
Fergus Ct. G20 H15 21
Fergus Dr. G20 H15 21
Ferguslie Park Av., L 4 29
Pais.
Ferguslie Park Cres., M 4 45
Pais.
Ferguslie Pk. L 3 29
Ferguslie Wk., Pais. M 4 45
Ferguslie, Pais. M 4 45
Ferguson Av., Renf. H 8 17
Ferguson St., John. M09 43
Ferguson St., Renf. H 8 17
Fergusson Rd., Cumb. C 2 70
Ferguston Rd., Bear. D12 7
Fern Av., Bish. F19 23
Fern Av., Lenz. C23 13
Fern Dr., Barr. Q 7 59
Fern Hill Grange G71 R28 69
Fernan St. G32 L21 38
Fernbank Av. G72 Q23 67
Fernbank St. G22 G18 22
Fernbrae Rd. G46 Q20 65
Fernbrae Way G73 Q19 65
Ferncroft Dr. G44 P17 64
Ferndale Ct. G23 F14 20
Rothes Dr.
Ferndale Dr. G23 F14 20
Ferndale Gdns. G23 F14 20
Ferndale Pl. G23 F14 20
Rothes Drive
Ferness Oval G21 F20 23
Ferness Pl. G21 F20 23
Ferness Rd. G21 G20 23
Ferngrove Av. G12 G13 20
Fernhill Rd. G73 Q19 65
Fernleigh Pl., Chr. E27 15
Fernleigh Rd. G43 P14 62
Fernslea Av. G72 S26 68
Ferry Rd. G3 K13 34
Ferry Rd., Both. R28 69
Ferry Rd., Renf. H 8 17
Ferry Rd., Udd. P26 68
Ferryden St. G14 J12 33
Fersit St. G43 P14 62
Fetlar Dr. G44 P17 64
Fettercairn Av. G15 D 9 6
Fettercairn Gdns., Bish. E20 11
Fettes St. G33 K21 38
Fidra St. G33 K21 38
Fielden Pl. G40 L19 37
Fielden St. G40 L19 37
Fieldhead Dr. G43 P13 62
Fieldhead Sq. G43 P13 62
Fife Av. G52 M10 48
Fife Cres., Both. R28 69
Fifeway, Bish. F20 23

Name	Ref
Fifth Av. G12	G12 19
Fifth Av. G33	G22 24
Fifth Av., Lenz.	E23 13
Fifth Av., Renf.	J 8 31
Finart Dr., Pais.	N 7 47
Finch Pl., John.	O08 43
Findhorn Av., Renf.	H 9 18
Findhorn Cres., Pais.	N 3 45
Findhorn St. G33	K20 37
Findochty St. G33	J23 39
Fingal La. G20	F14 20
Fingal St.	
Fingal St. G20	F14 20
Fingask St. G32	M23 55
Finglas Av., Pais.	N 7 47
Fingleton Av., Barr.	R 8 59
Finhaven St. G32	M21 54
Finlarig St. G34	K26 40
Finlas St. G22	H17 22
Finlay Dr. G31	K19 37
Finlay Dr., Linw.	L 1 28
Finnart Sq. G40	M18 52
Finnart St. G40	M18 52
Finnieston Pl. G3	K15 35
Finnieston St.	
Finnieston St. G3	K15 35
Finsbay St. G51	L12 33
Fintry Av., Pais.	O 6 46
Fintry Cres., Barr.	R 8 59
Fintry Cres., Bish.	E20 11
Fintry Dr. G44	O17 52
Fir Pl. G72	P23 67
Caledonian Circuit	
Fir Pl., Bail.	M25 56
Fir Pl., John.	N 1 44
Firbank Ter., Barr.	R 9 60
Firdon Cres. G15	E10 6
Firhill Rd. G20	H16 21
Firhill St. G20	H16 21
Firpark Pl. G31	K18 36
Firpark St.	
Firpark Rd., Bish.	F19 23
Firpark St. G31	K18 36
Firpark Ter. G31	K18 36
Ark La.	
First Av. G33	H22 24
First Av. G44	R15 63
First Av., Bear.	D13 8
First Av., Lenz.	E23 13
First Av., Renf.	J 8 31
First Av., Udd.	O27 57
First Gdns. G41	M13 50
First St., Udd.	O27 57
First Ter., Clyde.	D 7 5
Firwood Dr. G44	P17 64
Fisher Cres., Clyde.	C 7 5
Fisher Ct. G31	K18 36
Fishers Rd., Renf.	G 8 17
Fishescoates Av. G73	Q20 65
Fishescoates Gdns. G73	P20 65
Fishescoates Rd.	
Fishescoates Rd. G73	P20 65
Fitzalan Dr., Pais.	L 7 31
Fitzalan Rd., Renf.	J 7 31
Fitzroy La. G3	K15 35
Claremont St.	
Fitzroy Pl. G3	K15 35
Claremont St.	
Fitzroy Pl. G3	K15 35
Sauchiehall St.	
Flax Rd., Udd.	P28 69
Fleet Av., Renf.	J 9 32
Fleet St. G32	M22 54
Fleming Av., Chr.	F26 26
Fleming Av., Clyde.	F 8 17
Fleming Rd., Cumb.	C 2 70
Fleming St. G31	L19 37
Fleming St., Pais.	K 6 30
Flemington Rd. G72	R24 67
Flemington St. G21	H18 22
Fleurs Av. G41	M13 50
Fleurs Rd. G41	M13 50
Floors St., John.	N09 43
Floorsburn Cres., John.	N09 43
Flora Gdns., Bish.	E20 11
Florence Dr., Giff.	R14 62
Florence Gdns. G73	Q20 65
Florence St. G5	L17 36
Florence St. G73	M17 52
Florentine Pl. G12	J15 35
Gibson St.	
Florentine Ter. G12	J15 35
Southpark Av.	
Florida Av. G42	O16 51
Florida Cres. G42	O16 51
Florida Dr. G42	O16 51
Florida Gdns., Bail.	L25 40
Florida Sq. G42	O16 51
Florida St. G42	O16 51
Fochabers Dr. G52	L11 33
Fogo Pl. G20	G14 20
Forbes Dr. G40	L18 36
Forbes Pl., Pais.	M 6 46
Forbes St. G40	L18 36
Ford Rd. G12	H14 20
Fordneuk St. G40	L19 37
Fordoun St. G34	K26 40
Fordyce St. G11	J13 34
Fore St. G14	H11 19
Forehouse Rd., Kilb.	MO6 42
Forest Dr., Udd.	Q28 69
Forest Gdns., Lenz.	D22 12
Forest Pl., Lenz.	D22 12
Forest Pl., Pais.	N 6 46
Brodie Park Av.	
Forest Rd., Cumb.	C 4 71
Forest Vw., Cumb.	B 4 71
Forfar Av. G52	M10 48
Forfar Cres., Bish.	F20 23
Forgan Gdns., Bish.	F20 23
Forge St. G21	J19 37
Forglen St. G34	J25 40
Formby Dr. G23	E14 8
Forres Av. G46	Q14 62
Forres Gate, Giff.	R14 62
Forres Av.	
Forres St. G23	E15 9
Tolsta St.	
Forrest St. G40	L19 37
Forrestfield St. G21	J19 37
Fortevoit Av., Bail.	L26 40
Fortevoit Pl., Bail.	L26 40
Forth Av., Pais.	N 3 45
Forth Av., Renf.	J 8 31
Third Av.	
Forth Pl., John.	O08 43
Forth Rd. G61	C11 7
Forth Rd., Bear.	E11 7
Forth St. G41	M15 51
Fortingall Av. G12	G14 20
Grandtully Dr.	
Fortingall Pl. G12	G14 20
Fortrose St. G11	J13 34
Foswell Pl. G15	C 9 6
Fotheringay La. G41	N15 51
Beaton Rd.	
Fotheringay Rd. G41	N14 50
Foulis La. G13	G12 19
Foulis St. G13	G12 19
Foundry La., Barr.	R 7 59
Main St.	
Foundry Open G31	L19 37
Fountain St. G31	L18 36
Fountainwell Av. G.21	J17 36
Fountainwell Dr. G21	J17 36
Fountainwell Pl. G21	J17 36
Fountainwell Rd. G21	J17 36
Fountainwell Sq. G21	J18 36
Fountainwell Ter. G21	J18 36
Fourth Av., G33	G22 24
Fourth Av., Lenz.	E23 13
Fourth Av., Renf.	J 8 31
Third Av.	
Fourth Gdns. G41	M13 50
Fourth St., Udd.	N27 57
Fox La. G1	L17 36
Fox St. G1	L16 35
Foxbar Cres., Pais.	O 3 45
Foxbar Dr. G13.	G10 18
Foxbar Dr. G78	O 3 45
Foxbar Rd., Pais.	O 3 45
Foxes Gro. G66	C24 13
Foxhills Pl. G23	E15 9
Foxley St. G.32	N23 55
Foyers Ct. G13	G10 18
Kirkton Av.	
Foyers Ter. G21	H19 23
Francis St. G5	M16 51
Frankfield Rd. G33	G24 25
Frankfield St. G33	J20 37
Frankfort St. G41	N15 51
Franklin St. G40	M18 52
Fraser Av. G73	O20 53
Fraser Av., John.	N 1 44
Fraser St. G72	P21 66
Fraserbank St. G21	H17 22
Keppochill Rd.	
Frazer St. G31	L20 37
Freeland Dr. G53	P10 60
Freeland Dr., Renf.	G 5 16
Freelands Cres., Old K	C 5 4
Freelands Ct., Old K.	C 5 4
Freelands Pl., Old K.	D 5 4
Freelands Rd., Old K.	C 5 4
French St. G40	M18 52
French St., Dalm.	D 6 4
French St., Renf.	J 7 31
Freuchie St. G34	K25 40
Friar Av., Bish.	D19 11
Friars Court Rd., Chr.	E25 14
Friars Pl. G13	F11 19
Friarscourt Av. G13	E11 7
Friarscourt La. G13	F11 19
Arrowsmith Av.	
Friarton Rd. G43	P15 63
Friendship Way, Renf.	J 8 31
Fruin Pl. G22	H17 22
Fruin Rd. G15	E 9 6
Fruin St. G22	H17 22
Fulbar Av., Renf.	H 8 17
Fulbar Ct., Renf.	H 8 17
Fulbar Av.	
Fulbar La., Renf.	H 8 17
Fulbar Rd. G51	K11 33
Fulbar Rd., Pais.	M 3 45
Fulbar St., Renf.	H 8 17
Fullarton Av. G32	N22 54
Fullarton Rd. G32	O21 54
Fullerton St., Pais	K 5 30
Fullerton Ter., Pais.	K 6 30
Fulmar Ct., Bish.	F18 22
Fulmar Pl., John.	O08 43
Fulton Cres., Kilb.	M07 42
Fulton St. G13	F11 19
Fulwood Av. G13	F 9 18
Fulwood Av., Linw.	L 1 28
Fulwood Pl. G13	F 9 18
Fynloch Pl., Clyde.	B 6 4
Fyvie Av. G43	P13 62
Gadie Av., Renf.	J 9 32
Gadie St. G33	K20 37
Gadloch Av., Lenz.	E23 13
Gadloch Gdns., Lenz.	D23 13
Gadloch St. G22	G17 22
Gadloch Vw. G66	E23 13
Gadsburn Ct. G21	G20 23
Wallacewell Quadrant	
Gadshill St. G21	J18 36
Gailes Pk., Both.	R27 69
Gailes St. G40	M19 53
Gairbraid Av. G20	G14 20
Gairbraid Ct. G20	G14 20
Gairbraid Pl. G20	G14 20
Gairbraid Ter., Bail.	L28 41
Gairn St. G11	J13 34
Castlebank St.	
Gala Av., Renf.	J 9 32
Gala St. G33	J21 38
Galbraith Av. G51	K12 33
Burghead Dr.	
Galbraith Dr. G51	K11 33
Galbraith St. G51	K11 33
Moss Rd.	
Galdenoch St. G33	J22 38
Gallacher Av., Pais.	N 4 45
Gallan Av. G23	E15 9
Galloway Dr. G73	Q19 65
Galloway St. G21	G18 22
Gallowflat St. G73	O19 53
Gallowgate G1	L17 36
Gallowhill Av., Lenz.	C23 13
Gallowhill Gro., Lenz.	C23 13
Gallowhill Rd., Lenz.	C23 13
Gallowhill Rd., Pais.	L 6 30
Galston St. G53	P 9 60
Gamrie Dr. G53	O10 48
Gamrie Gdns. G53	O10 48
Gamrie Rd. G53	O10 48

Name	Ref	Pg
Gannochy Dr., Bish.	E20	11
Gantock Cres. G33	K22	38
Gardenside Av. G32	O22	54
Gardenside Av., Udd.	P27	69
Gardenside Cres. G32	O22	54
Gardenside Pl. G32	O22	54
Gardenside St., Udd.	P27	69
Gardner La., Bail.	M26	56
Church St.		
Gardner St. G11	J13	34
Gardyne St. G34	J25	40
Garfield St. G31	L19	37
Garforth Rd., Bail.	M24	55
Gargrave Av., Bail.	M24	55
Garion Dr. G13	G10	18
Garion Dr. G13	G10	18
Talbot Dr.		
Garlieston Rd. G33	L24	39
Garmouth Ct. G51	K12	33
Garmouth St.		
Garmouth Gdns. G51	K12	33
Garmouth St. G51	K12	33
Garnet La. G3	J16	35
Garnet St.		
Garnet St. G3	J16	35
Garnethill St. G3	J16	35
Garngaber Av., Lenz.	C23	13
Garngaber Ct. G66	C24	13
Woodleigh Rd.		
Garnie Av., Renf.	F 5	16
Garnie Cres., Renf.	E 5	4
Garnie La., Renf.	E 5	4
Garnie Oval, Renf.	E 5	4
Garnie Pl., Renf.	E 5	4
Garnieland Rd., Renf.	E 5	4
Garnkirk La. G33	G24	25
Garnkirk St. G21	J18	36
Garnock St. G21	J18	36
Garrell Way, Cumb.	C 2	70
Garrioch Cres. G20	G14	20
Garrioch Dr. G20	G14	20
Garrioch Gate G20	G14	20
Garrioch Quad. G20	G14	20
Garrioch Rd. G20	H14	20
Garriochmill Rd. G20	H15	21
Raeberry St.		
Garriochmill Way G20	H15	21
Woodside Rd.		
Garrowhill Dr., Bail.	M24	55
Garry Av., Bear.	E13	8
Garry Dr., Pais.	N 4	45
Garry St. G44	O16	51
Garscadden G13	F10	18
Garscadden Rd. G15	E10	6
Garscadden Vw., Clyde.	D 8	5
Kirkoswald Dr.		
Garscube Rd. G20	H16	21
Gartcarron Hill, Cumb.	B 1	70
Dunbrach Rd.		
Gartconnel Dr., Bear.	C12	7
Gartconnel Gdns., Bear.	C12	7
Gartconnel Rd., Bear.	C12	7
Gartcosh Rd., Bail. & Gart.	K28	41
Gartcraig Rd. G33	K21	38
Gartferry Av., Chr.	E27	15
Gartferry Rd., Chr.	E27	15
Gartferry St. G21	H19	23
Garth St. G1	K17	36
Garthamlock Rd. G33	J24	39
Garthland Dr. G31	K19	37
Garthland La., Pais.	L 6	30
Gartliston Ter., Bail.	L28	41
Gartloch Cotts., Chr.	G25	26
Gartloch Cotts., Gart.	H27	27
Gartloch Rd. G33	J21	38
Gartly St. G44	Q15	63
Clarkston Rd.		
Gartmore Gdns., Udd.	O27	57
Gartmore La., Chr.	E28	15
Gartmore Rd., Pais.	M 8	47
Gartmore Ter. G72	Q21	66
Gartness St. G31	K19	37
Gartocher Rd. G32	L23	39
Gartochmill Rd. G20	H15	21
Gartons Rd. G21	H20	23
Gartshore Rd., Drumbreck	C27	15
Garturk St. G42	N16	51
Garvald Ct. G40	M19	53
Baltic St.		
Garvald St. G40	M19	53
Garve Av. G44	Q16	63
Garvel Cres. G33	L24	39
Garvel Rd. G33	L24	39
Garvock Dr. G43	P13	62
Gas St., John.	M 1	44
Gask Pl. G13	F 9	18
Gatehouse St. G32	L22	38
Gateside Av. G72	P23	67
Gateside Cres., Barr.	R 7	59
Gateside Pl., Kilb.	MO7	42
Gateside Rd., Barr.	R 7	59
Gateside St. G31	L19	37
Gauldry Av. G52	M11	49
Gauze St., Pais.	L 6	30
Gavins Rd., Clyde.	C 7	5
Gavinton St. G44	Q15	63
Gear Ter. G40	N19	53
Geary St. G23	E14	8
Torrin Rd,		
Geddes Rd. G21	F20	23
Gelston St. G32	M22	54
General Terminus Quay G51	L15	35
Generals Gate, Udd.	P27	69
Cobbleriggs Way		
Gentle Row, Clyde.	C 6	4
George Av., Clyde.	D 8	5
Robert Burns Av.		
George Cres., Clyde.	D 8	5
George Gray St. G73	O20	53
George Mann Ter. G73	P19	65
George Pl., Pais.	M 6	46
George Reith Av. G12	G12	19
George Sq. G2	K17	36
George St. G1	K17	36
George St., Bail.	M25	56
George St., Barr.	Q 7	59
George St., John.	MO9	43
George St., Pais.	M 5	46
Gertrude Pl., Barr.	R 7	59
Gibb St. G21	J18	36
Royston Rd.		
Gibson Cres., John.	NO9	43
Gibson Rd., Renf.	J 7	31
Gibson St. G12	J15	35
Gibson St. G40	L18	36
Giffnock Park Av., Giff.	Q14	62
Gifford Dr. G52	L10	32
Gilbert St. G3	K14	34
Gilbertfield Pl. G33	J22	38
Gilbertfield Rd. G72	Q23	67
Gilbertfield St. G33	J22	38
Gilfillan Way, Pais.	O 3	45
Ashton Way		
Gilhill St. G20	F14	20
Gilia St. G72	P21	66
Gillies La., Bail.	M26	56
Bredisholm Rd.		
Gills Ct. G31	L19	37
Gilmarton Rd., Linw.	L 1	28
Gilmerton St. G32	M22	54
Gilmour Av., Clyde.	C 7	5
Gilmour Cres. G73	O18	52
Gilmour Pl. G5	M17	52
Gilmour St., Clyde.	D 8	5
Gilmour St., Pais.	L 6	30
Girthon St. G32	M23	55
Girvan St. G33	J20	37
Gladney Av. G13	F 9	18
Gladsmuir Rd. G52	L10	32
Gladstone Av., Barr.	R 7	59
Gladstone St. G4	J16	35
Gladstone St., Dalm.	E 6	4
Glaive Rd. G13	E11	7
Glamis Av., John.	N 1	44
Glamis Gdns., Bish.	D19	11
Glamis Pl. G31	M20	53
Glamis Rd.		
Glamis Rd. G31	M20	53
Glanderston Av., Barr.	R 9	60
Glanderston Dr. G13	F10	18
Glaselune St. G34	K26	40
Lochdochart Rd.		
Glasgow Bridge	B21	12
Glasgow Rd. G72	P21	66
Glasgow Rd. G72 & E.K.	R21	66
Glasgow Rd. G73	N18	52
Glasgow Rd., Bail.	M24	55
Glasgow Rd., Barr.	Q 8	59
Glasgow Rd., Blan.	R26	68
Glasgow Rd., Clyde.	C 7	5
Glasgow Rd., Clyde.	F 7	17
Glasgow Rd., Cumb.	B 3	71
Glasgow Rd., Cumb.	D 1	70
Glasgow Rd., Pais.	L 7	31
Glasgow Rd., Renf.	H 9	18
Glasgow Rd., Udd.	O26	56
Glasgow St. G12	H15	21
Glassel Rd. G34	J26	40
Glasserton Pl. G43	P15	63
Glasserton Rd. G43	P15	63
Glassford St. G1	K17	36
Glebe Av. G71	R28	69
Green St.		
Glebe Ct. G4	K17	36
Glebe Hollow G71	R28	69
Glebe Wynd		
Glebe Pl. G72	P22	66
Glebe Pl. G73	O18	52
Glebe St. G4	J17	36
Glebe St., Renf.	H 8	17
Glebe Wynd G71	R28	69
Glebe, The, Both.	R28	69
Gleddoch Rd. G52	L 9	32
Glen Affric Av. G53	Q11	61
Glen Affric Dr. G53	Q11	61
Glen Affric Pl. G53	Q11	61
Glen Alby Pl. G53	Q11	61
Glen Av. G32	L22	38
Glen Av., Chr.	E27	15
Glen Clunie Av. G53	Q11	61
Glen Clunie Dr. G53	Q11	61
Glen Clunie Pl. G53	Q11	61
Glen Cona Dr. G53	P11	61
Glen Cres. G13	F 9	18
Glen Esk Dr. G53	Q11	61
Glen Gdns., John.	M 2	44
Glen La., Pais.	L 6	30
Glen Livet Pl. G53	Q11	61
Glen Loy Pl. G53	Q11	61
Glen Mallie Dr. G53	Q11	61
Glen Markie Dr. G53	Q11	61
Glen Moriston Rd., Thorn. G53	Q11	61
Glen Nevis Pl. G73	R20	65
Glen Ogle St. G32	M23	55
Glen Orchy Dr. G53	Q11	61
Glen Orchy Pl. G53	Q11	61
Glen Park Av., Thorn.	R12	61
Glen Rd. G32	K22	38
Glen Sax Dr., Renf.	J 9	32
Glen Sq. G33	H22	24
Glen St. G72	Q23	67
Glen St., Barr.	O 8	59
Glen St., Pais.	L 6	30
Glen Vw., Cumb.	B 4	71
Glenacre Cres., Udd.	O27	57
Glenacre Dr. G45	Q17	64
Glenacre Quad. G45	Q17	64
Glenacre Rd., Cumb.	D 2	70
Glenacre St. G45	Q17	64
Glenacre Ter. G45	Q17	64
Glenallan Way, Pais.	O 3	45
Glenalmond Rd. G73	Q20	65
Glenalmond St. G32	M22	54
Glenapp Av., Pais.	N 7	47
Glenapp Rd., Pais.	N 7	47
Glenapp St. G41	M15	51
Glenarklet Dr., Pais.	N 7	47
Glenartney Row, Chr.	E26	14
Glenashdale Way, Pais.	N 7	47
Glenbrittle Dr.		
Glenavon Av. G73	Q20	65
Glenavon Rd. G20	F14	20
Thornton St.		
Glenavon Ter. G11	J13	34
Crow Rd.		
Glenbank Av., Lenz.	D23	13
Glenbank Dr., Thorn.	R12	61
Glenbank Rd., Lenz.	D23	13
Glenbarr St. G21	J18	36
Glenbervie Pl. G23	E14	8
Glenbrittle Dr., Pais.	N 7	47
Glenbrittle Way, Pais.	N 6	46
Glenbuck Av. G33	G21	24
Glenbuck Dr. G33	G21	24
Glenburn Av. G73	P20	65

Glenburn Av., Bail.	L26	40
Glenburn Av., Chr.	E27	15
Glenburn Cres., Pais.	O 5	46
Glenburn Gdns., Bish.	E18	10
Glenburn Rd., Bear.	C11	7
Glenburn Rd., Giff.	R13	62
Glenburn Rd., Pais.	O 4	45
Glenburn St. G20	F15	21
Glenburnie Pl. G34	K25	40
Glencairn Dr. G41	N14	50
Glencairn Dr. G73	O18	52
Glencairn Dr., Chr.	E27	15
Glencairn Gdns. G41	N15	51
Glencairn Dr.		
Glencairn Rd., Cumb.	C 4	71
Glencairn Rd., Pais.	K 7	31
Glencally Av., Pais.	N 7	47
Glencart Gro., John.	N08	43
Milliken Park Rd.		
Glenclora Dr., Pais.	N 7	47
Glencloy St. G20	F14	20
Glencoe Pl. G13	F12	19
Glencoe Rd. G73	Q20	65
Glencoe St. G13	F12	19
Glencorse Rd., Pais.	N 5	46
Glencorse St. G32	K21	38
Glencroft Av., Udd.	O27	57
Glencroft Rd. G44	P17	64
Glencryan Rd., Cumb.	D 3	71
Glendale Cres., Bish.	F20	23
Glendale Dr., Bish.	F20	23
Glendale Pl. G31	L19	37
Glendale St.		
Glendale Pl. G64	F20	23
Glendale St. G31	L19	37
Glendaruel Av., Bear.	D13	8
Glendaruel Rd. G73	R21	66
Glendee Gdns., Renf.	J 8	31
Glendee Rd., Renf.	J 8	31
Glendenning Rd. G13	E12	7
Glendevon Pl., Dalm.	D 6	4
Glendevon Sq. G33	J22	38
Glendore St. G14	J12	33
Glendower Way	O 3	45
Spencer Dr.		
Glenduffhill Rd., Bail.	L24	39
Muirfield Rd.		
Gleneagles Av., Cumb.	A 3	71
Gleneagles Cotts. G14	H11	19
Dumbarton Rd.		
Gleneagles Dr., Bish.	D19	11
Gleneagles Gdns., Bish.	D19	11
Gleneagles La. N. G14	H11	19
Dunglass Av.		
Gleneagles Pk., Both.	R27	69
Gleneagles Ter. G14	H11	19
Dumbarton Rd.		
Glenelg Quad. G34	J26	40
Glenetive Pl. G73	R21	66
Glenfarg Cres., Bear.	D13	8
Glenfarg Rd. G73	Q19	65
Glenfarg St. G20	J16	35
Glenfield Cres., Pais.	P 5	58
Glenfield Rd., Pais.	P 5	58
Glenfinnan Dr. G20	G14	20
Glenfinnan Dr., Bear.	D14	8
Glenfinnan Pl. G20	G14	20
Glenfinnan Rd. G20	G14	20
Glenfruin Dr., Pais.	N 7	47
Glengarry Dr. G52	L10	33
Wedderlea Dr.		
Glengavel Cres. G33	G21	24
Glengyre St. G34	J26	40
Glenhead Cres. G22	G17	22
Glenhead Rd., Dalm.	C 7	5
Glenhead Rd., Lenz.	D23	13
Glenhead St. G22	G17	22
Glenholme, Pais.	N 4	45
Glenhove Rd., Cumb.	C 3	71
Gleniffer Av. G13	G10	18
Gleniffer Cres., John.	N 2	44
Gleniffer Dr., Barr.	P 7	59
Gleniffer Rd., Pais.	O 4	45
Gleniffer Rd., Renf.	J 7	31
Gleniffer Vw., Clyde.	D 8	5
Kirkoswald Dr.		
Glenisa Av., Chr.	D28	15
Glenisla St. G31	M20	53
Glenkirk Dr. G15	E10	6
Glenlee Cres. G52	M 9	48
Glenlora Dr. G53	O10	48
Glenlora Ter. G53	O10	48
Glenluce Dr. G32	M23	55
Glenlui Av. G73	P19	65
Glenlyon Pl. G73	Q20	65
Glenmalloch Pl., John.	M 2	44
Glenmanor Av., Chr.	E27	15
Glenmore Av. G42	O18	52
Glenmuir Dr. G53	P10	60
Glenpark Rd. G31	L19	37
Glenpark St. G31	L19	37
Glenpark Ter. G72	O21	54
Glenpatrick Bldgs.,	N 2	44
John.		
Floors St.		
Glenpatrick Rd., John.	N 2	44
Glenraith Rd. G33	H22	24
Glenraith Sq. G33	H22	24
Glenraith Wk. G33	H23	25
Glenshee St. G31	M20	53
Glenshiel Av., Pais.	N 7	47
Glenside Av. G53	N10	48
Glenside Dr. G73	P20	65
Glenspean Pl. G43	P14	62
Glenspean St.		
Glenspean St. G43	P14	62
Glentanar Pl. G22	F16	21
Glentarbert Rd. G73	Q20	65
Glenturret St. G32	M22	54
Glentyan Av., Kilb.	M07	42
Glentyan Dr. G53	P10	60
Glentyan Ter. G53	O10	48
Glenview Cres., Chr.	D28	15
Glenview Pl., Blan.	R26	68
Glenville Av., Giff. ✓	Q13	62
Glenwood Ct., Kirk.	C22	12
Glenwood Dr., Thorn.	R12	61
Glenwood Gdns., Kirk.	C22	12
Glenwood Pl., Kirk.	C22	12
Glenwood Rd., Kirk.	C22	12
Gloucester Av. G73	P20	65
Gloucester St. G5	L16	35
Gockston Rd., Pais.	K 5	30
Gogar Pl. G33	K21	38
Gogar St. G33	K21	38
Goldberry Av. G14	G10	18
Goldie Rd., Udd.	Q28	69
Golf Ct. G44	R15	63
Golf Dr. G15	E 9	6
Golf Dr., Pais.	M 8	47
Golf Rd. G73	Q19	65
Golf Vw., Bear.	C10	6
Golf Vw., Dalm.	D 6	4
Golfhill Dr. G31	K19	37
Golfhill La. G31	K19	37
Whitehill St.		
Golfhill Ter. G31	K18	36
Firpark St.		
Golspie St. G51	K13	34
Goosedubbs G1	L17	36
Stockwell St.		
Gopher Av., Udd.	O28	57
Myrtle Rd.		
Gorbals Cross G5	L17	36
Gorbals La. G5	L16	35
Oxford St.		
Gorbals St. G5	L16	35
Gordon Av. G44	R15	63
Gordon Av., Bail.	L24	39
Gordon Dr. G44	Q15	63
Gordon La. G1	K16	35
Gordon St.		
Gordon Rd. G44	R15	63
Gordon St. G1	K16	35
Gordon St., Pais.	M 6	46
Gordon Ter., Blan.	R26	68
Gorebridge St. G32	K21	38
Gorget Av. G13	E11	7
Gorget Pl. G13	E11	7
Gorget Quad. G15	E10	6
Gorget Av.		
Gorse Dr., Barr.	Q 7	59
Gorse Pl., Udd.	O28	57
Myrtle Rd.		
Gorsewood, Bish.	E18	10
Gorstan Pl. G20	G14	20
Wyndford Rd.		
Gorstan St. G23	F14	20
Gosford La. G14	G 9	18
Dumbarton Rd.		
Goudie St., Pais.	K 5	30
Gough St. G33	K20	37
Gourlay Path G21	H17	22
Endrick St.		
Gourlay St. G21	H17	22
Gourlay St. G21	H18	22
Millarbank St.		
Gourock St. G5	M16	51
Govan Cross G51	K13	34
Govan Rd. G51 ✓	K12	33
Govanhill St. G42	N16	51
Gowanbank Gdns.,	N09	43
John.		
Floors St.		
Gowanbrae, Lenz.	C23	13
Gallowhill Rd.		
Gowanlea Av. G15	E10	6
Gowanlea Dr., Giff.	Q14	62
Gowanlea Ter., Udd.	O28	57
Gower La. G51	L14	34
Gower St.		
Gower St. G43	M14	50
Gower Ter. G41	L14	34
Goyle Av. G15	D11	7
Grace Av., Bail.	L27	41
Grace St. G3	K15	35
Graffham Av., Giff.	Q14	62
Grafton Pl. G4	K17	36
Graham Av. G72	P23	67
Graham Av., Clyde.	D 7	5
Graham Sq. G31	L18	36
Graham St., Barr.	Q 7	59
Graham St., John.	N09	43
Graham Ter., Bish.	F19	23
Grahamston Cres., Pais.	O 8	47
Grahamston Ct., Pais.	O 8	47
Grahamston Pl., Pais.	O 8	47
Grahamston Rd.		
Grahamston Rd., Barr.	P 7	59
Graighead Av. G33	H20	23
Grainger Rd., Bish.	E20	11
Grampian Av., Pais.	O 5	46
Grampian Cres. G32	M22	54
Grampian Pl. G32	M22	54
Grampian St. G32	M22	54
Grampian Way, Barr.	R 8	59
Gran St., Clyde.	F 9	18
Granby La. G12	H14	20
Great George St.		
Granby Pl. G12	H14	20
Great George St.		
Grandtully Dr. G12	G14	20
Grange Gdns. G71	R28	69
Blairston Av.		
Grange Rd. G42	O16	51
Grange Rd., Bear.	C12	7
Grangeneuk Gdnd.,	C 1	70
Cumb.		
Grant St. G3	J15	35
Grantlea Gro. G32	M23	55
Grantlea Ter. G32	M23	55
Grantley Gdns. G41	O14	50
Grantley St. G41	O14	50
Granton St. G5	N18	52
Granville St. G3	K15	35
Granville St., Clyde.	D 7	5
Gray Dr., Bear.	D12	7
Gray St. G3	J14	34
Great Dovehill G1	L17	36
Great George La. G12	H14	20
Great George St.		
Great George St. G12	H14	20
Great Hamilton St., Pais.	N 6	46
Great Kelvin La. G12	H15	21
Glasgow St.		
Great Western Rd. G12	H14	20
Great Western Ter. G12	H14	20
Great Western Terrace	H14	20
La. G12		
Westbourne Gdns. W.		
Green Av., Lenz.	B23	13
Green Farm Rd., Linw.	L 1	28
Green Lodge Ter. G40	M18	52
Greenhead St.		
Green Pk., Both.	R28	69
Green St.		
Green Rd. G73	O19	53
Green Rd., Pais.	M 4	45
Green St. G40	L18	36
Green St., Both.	R28	69
Green St., Clyde.	D 7	5

Green, The, G40 — L18 36
Greenan Av. G42 — O18 52
Greenbank Dr., Pais. — O 5 46
Greenbank Rd., Cumb. — C 1 70
Greenbank St. G43 — P13 62
Harriet St.
Greenbank St. G73 — O19 53
Greendyke St. G1 — L17 36
Greenend Av., John. — N08 43
Greenend Pl. G32 — K23 39
Greenfaulds Cres., — D 3 71
Cumb.
Greenfaulds Rd., Cumb. — D 2 70
Greenfield Av. G32 — K22 38
Greenfield Pl. G32 — L22 38
Budhill Av.
Greenfield Rd. G32 — L23 39
Greenfield St. G51 — K12 33
Greengairs Av. G51 — K11 33
Greenhaugh St. G51 — K13 34
Greenhead Rd., Bear. — D12 7
Greenhead Rd., Renf. — F 5 16
Greenhead St. G40 — M18 52
Greenhill Av., Gart. — F27 27
Greenhill Av., Giff. — R13 62
Greenhill Cres., John. — N 2 44
Greenhill Cres., Linw. — L 2 28
Greenhill Ct. G73 — O19 53
Greenhill Dr., Linw. — L 2 28
Greenhill Rd. G73 — O19 53
Greenhill Rd., Pais. — L 5 30
Greenhill St. G73 — O19 53
Greenhill, Bish. — E19 11
Greenholm Av., Udd. — O27 57
Greenholme St. G40 — P16 63
Holmlea Rd.
Greenknowe Rd. G43 — P13 62
Greenlaw Av., Pais. — L 7 31
Greenlaw Dr., Pais. — L 7 31
Greenlaw Rd. G14 — G 9 18
Greenlaw Ter., Pais. — L 7 31
Greenlaw Av.
Greenlea Rd., Chr. — F25 26
Greenlea St. G13 — G12 19
Greenlees Gdns. G72 — Q21 66
Greenlees Pk. G72 — Q22 66
Greenlees Rd. G72 — P22 66
Greenloan Av. G51 — K11 33
Greenmount G22 — F16 21
Greenock Av. G44 — P16 63
Greenock Rd., Pais. — K 5 30
Greenock Rd., Renf. — G 5 16
Greenrig St. G33 — H20 23
Greenrig St., Udd. — P27 69
Greenrigg Rd., Cumb. — C 3 71
Greenshields Rd., Bail. — L25 40
Greenside Cres. G33 — H21 24
Greenside St. G33 — H21 24
Greentree Dr., Bail. — M24 55
Greenview St. G43 — O14 50
Greenways Av., Pais. — N 4 45
Greenways Ct., John. — N 4 45
Greenwell Pl. G51 — K13 34
Greenwell St. G51 — K13 34
Govan Rd.
Greenwood Av. G72 — P24 67
Greenwood Av., Chr. — E27 57
Greenwood Dr., Bear. — D13 8
Greenwood Quad., — E 8 5
Clyde.
Greer Quad., Clyde. — D 7 5
Grenville Dr. G72 — Q21 66
Greran Dr., Renf. — H 7 17
Gretna St. G40 — M19 53
Greyfriars St. G32 — K21 38
Greystone Av. G73 — P20 65
Greywood St. G13 — F12 19
Grier Path G31 — L20 37
Grierson La. G33 — K20 37
Lomak St.
Grierson St. G33 — K20 37
Grieve Rd., Cumb. — B 3 71
Griqua Ter. G71 — R28 69
Grogary Rd. G15 — D10 6
Springside Pl.
Grosvenor Cres. G12 — H14 20
Observatory Rd.
Grosvenor Cres. La. — H14 20
G12
Byers Rd.

Grosvenor La. G12 — H14 20
Byers Rd.
Grosvenor Mansions — H14 20
G12
Observatory Rd.
Grosvenor Ter. G12 — H14 20
Grove Pk., Lenz. — D23 13
Grove, The, Giff. — S13 62
Grove, The, Kilb. — M07 42
Groveburn Av., Thorn. — Q13 62
Grovepark Pl. G20 — H16 21
Grovepark St. G20 — H16 21
Groves, The, Bish. — F20 23
Woodhill Rd.
Grudie St. G34 — K25 40
Gryffe Av., Renf. — H 7 17
Gryffe Cres., Pais. — N 3 45
Gryffe St. G44 — P16 63
Guildford St. G33 — J23 39
Gullane Cres., Cumb. — A 2 70
Gullane St. G11 — J13 34
Purdon St.
Guthrie St. G20 — G14 20

Hagg Cres., John. — M09 43
Hagg Pl., John. — M09 43
Hagg Rd., John. — N09 43
Haggs Rd. G41 — N14 50
Haggs Wood Av. G41 — N14 50
Haghill Rd. G31 — K20 37
Haig Dr., Bail. — M24 55
Haig St. G21 — H19 23
Hailes Av. G32 — L23 39
Haining Rd., Renf. — H 8 17
Hairmyres St. G42 — N16 51
Govanhill St.
Hairst St., Renf. — H 8 17
Halbeath Av. G15 — D 9 6
Halbert St. G41 — N15 51
Haldane La. G14 — H11 19
Haldane St.
Haldane St. G14 — H11 19
Halgreen Av. G15 — D 9 6
Halifax Way, Renf. — J 8 31
Britannia Way
Hall St., Clyde. — E 7 5
Hallbrae St. G33 — J21 38
Halley Dr. G13 — F 9 18
Halley Pl. G13 — G 9 18
Halley Sq. G13 — F 9 18
Halley St. G13 — F 9 18
Hallhill Cres. G33 — L24 39
Hallhill Rd. G32 — L22 38
Hallhill Rd., John. — O08 43
Hallidale Cres., Renf. — J 9 32
Hallrule Dr. G52 — L11 33
Hallside Av. G72 — P24 67
Hallside Cres. G72 — P24 67
Hallside Dr. G72 — P24 67
Hallside Rd. G72 — Q24 67
Hallside St. G5 — M17 52
Hallydown Dr. G13 — G11 19
Halton Gdns., Bail. — M24 55
Hamilton Av. G41 — M13 50
Hamilton Cres. G72 — Q23 67
Hamilton Cres., Bear. — B12 7
Hamilton Cres., Renf. — G 8 17
Hamilton Dr. G12 — H15 21
Hamilton Dr. G72 — P22 66
Hamilton Dr., Both. — R28 69
Hamilton Dr., Giff. — R14 62
Hamilton Park Av. — H15 21
G12
Hamilton Rd. G32 — N24 55
Hamilton Rd. G72 & — P22 66
Blan.
Hamilton Rd. G73 — O19 53
Hamilton Rd., Both. — R28 69
Hamilton Rd. G42 — N17 52
Hamilton St., Clyde. — F 8 17
Hamilton St., Pais. — L 6 30
Hamilton Ter., Clyde. — F 8 17
Hamilton Vw., Udd. — O28 57
Hamiltonhill Rd. G22 — H16 21
Hampden Dr. G42 — O16 51
Cathcart Rd.
Hampden La. G42 — O16 51
Cathcart Rd.
Hampden Ter. G42 — O16 51
Cathcart Rd.

Hampden Way, Renf. — J 8 31
Lewis Av.
Hangingshaw Pl. G42 — O17 52
Haning, The, Renf. — J 8 31
Hanover St. G1 — K17 36
Hanson St. G31 — K18 36
Hapland Av. G53 — N11 49
Hapland Rd. G53 — N11 49
Harbour La., Pais. — L 6 30
Harbour Rd., Pais. — K 6 30
Harburn Pl. G23 — E15 9
Harbury Pl. G14 — G 9 18
Harcourt Dr. G31 — K19 37
Hardgate Dr. G51 — K11 33
Hardgate Gdns. G51 — K11 33
Hardgate Pl. G51 — K11 33
Hardgate Rd. G51 — K11 33
Hardie Av. G73 — O20 53
Hardridge Av. G52 — N11 49
Hardridge Rd.
Hardridge Pl. G52 — N12 49
Hardridge Rd. G52 — N11 49
Harefield Dr. G14 — G10 18
Harelaw Av. G44 — Q15 63
Harelaw Av., Barr. — R 8 59
Harelaw Cres., Pais. — O 5 46
Harhill St. G51 — K12 33
Harland Cotts. G14 — J11 33
South St.
Harland St. G14 — H11 19
Harlaw Gdns. G64 — E20 11
Harley St. G51 — L14 34
Harmetray St. G22 — G17 22
Harmony Pl. G51 — K13 34
Harmony Row G51 — K13 34
Harmony Sq. G51 — K13 34
Harmsworth St. G11 — J12 33
Harport St. G46 — Q12 61
Harriet St. G73 — O19 53
Harrington St. G20 — G15 21
Maryhill Rd.
Harris Rd. G23 — E15 9
Harrison Dr. G51 — L13 34
Harrow Ct. G15 — D 9 6
Linkwood Dr.
Harrow Pl. G15 — D 9 6
Hart St. G31 — L21 38
Hart St., Linw. — L 1 28
Hartfield Ter., Pais. — N 7 47
Hartlaw Cres. G52 — L10 32
Hartree Av. G13 — F 9 18
Hartstone Pl. G53 — O10 48
Hartstone Rd. G53 — O10 48
Hartstone Ter. G53 — O10 48
Harvey St. G4 — J17 36
Harvie St. G51 — L14 34
Harwood St. G32 — K21 38
Hastie St. G3 — J14 34
Old Dumbarton Rd.
Hatfield Dr. G12 — G12 19
Hathaway Dr., Giff. — R13 62
Hathaway La. G20 — G15 21
Avenuepark St.
Hathaway St. G20 — G15 21
Hathersage Av., Bail. — L25 40
Hathersage Dr., Bail. — L25 40
Hathersage Gdns., Bail. — L25 40
Hatters Row G40 — M18 52
Dalmarnock Rd.
Hatton Dr. G52 — M10 48
Hatton Gdns. G52 — M10 48
Haugh Rd. G3 — K14 34
Haughburn Pl. G53 — O10 48
Haughburn Rd. G53 — O10 48
Haughburn Ter. G53 — O11 49
Havelock La. G11 — J14 34
Dowanhill St.
Havelock St. G11 — J14 34
Hawick Av. G78 — N 4 45
Hawick St. G13 — F 9 18
Hawkhead Av., Pais. — N 7 47
Hawkhead Rd., Pais. — M 7 47
Hawthorn Av., Bish. — F19 23
Hawthorn Av., Lenz. — C23 13
Hawthorn Av., Renf. — F 6 16
Hawthorn Cres., Renf. — E 5 4
Hawthorn Cres., Renf. — F 5 16
Hawthorn Dr., Barr. — S 8 59
Hawthorn Quad. G22 — G17 22
Hawthorn Rd., Renf. — F 6 16

Street	Ref	Pg
Hawthorn St. G22	G17	22
Hawthorn St., Clyde.	D 7	5
Hawthorn Wk. G72	P20	65
Hawthorn Wk., Bish.	F20	23
Letham Dr.		
Hawthornden Gdns. G23	E15	9
Hawthorne Av., Bear.	B13	8
Hawthorne Av., John.	N 1	44
Hawthorne Ter., Udd.	O28	57
Douglas St.		
Hay Dr., John.	M 1	44
Hayburn Cres. G11	H13	20
Hayburn Ct. G11	J13	34
Hayburn La. G12	H13	20
Queensborough Gdns.		
Hayburn St. G11	J13	34
Hayfield St. G5	M17	52
Hayhill Cotts., Gart.	G28	27
Hayle Gdns., Chr.	D27	15
Haylynn St. G14	J12	33
Haymarket St. G32	K21	38
Haystack Pl., Lenz.	D23	13
Hayston Cres. G22	G16	21
Hayston St. G22	G16	21
Haywood St. G22	G16	21
Hazel Av. G44	Q15	63
Clarkston Rd.		
Hazel Av., John.	N 1	44
Hazel Av., Lenz.	C23	13
Hazel Dene, Bish.	E19	11
Hazel Gro., Lenz.	C23	13
Hazel Rd., Cumb.	B 4	71
Hazel Ter., Udd.	O28	57
Douglas St.		
Hazelden Gdns. G44	Q15	63
Hazellea Dr., Giff.	O14	62
Hazelwood Av. G78	O 3	45
Hazelwood Dr., Blan.	S26	68
Hazelwood Gdns. G73	Q20	65
Hazelwood Rd. G41	M14	50
Hazlitt St. G20	G16	21
Heath Av., Bish.	F19	23
Heath Av., Lenz.	D23	13
Heathcliffe Av., Blan.	R26	68
Heathcot Av. G15	E 9	6
Heathcot Pl. G15	E 9	6
Heathcot Av.		
Heather Av., Barr.	P 7	59
Heather Dr., Lenz.	D22	12
Heather Gdns., Lenz.	D22	12
Heather Pl., John.	N 1	44
Heather Pl., Lenz.	C22	12
Heather St. G41	L15	35
Scotland St.		
Heatherbrae, Bish.	E18	10
Heatheryknowe Rd., Bail.	K27	41
Heathfield Av., Chr.	E27	15
Heathfield St. G33	K23	39
Heathfield Ter. G21	G18	22
Broomfield Rd.		
Heathside Rd., Giff.	Q14	62
Heathwood Dr., Thorn.	Q13	62
Hecla Av. G15	D 9	6
Hecla Pl. G15	D 9	6
Hector Rd. G41	O14	50
Heggie Ter. G14	H11	19
Dumbarton Rd.		
Helen St. G52	L12	33
Helenburgh Dr. G13	G11	19
Helenslea G72	Q23	67
Helenvale Ct. G31	L20	37
Helenvale St.		
Helenvale St. G31	M20	53
Helmsdale Av., Blan.	Q26	68
Helmsdale Ct. G72	P23	67
Hemlock St. G13	F12	19
Henderland Rd., Bear.	E12	7
Henderson Av. G72	P23	67
Henderson St. G20	H15	21
Henderson St., Clyde.	F 9	18
Henderson St., Pais.	L 5	30
Henrietta St. G14	H11	19
Henry St., Barr.	Q 7	59
Hepburn Rd. G52	K10	32
Herald Av. G13	E11	7
Herald Way, Renf.	J 8	31
Viscount Av.		
Herbert St. G20	H15	21
Herbertson St. G5	L16	35
Eglinton St.		
Hercules Way, Renf.	J 8	31
Friendship Way		
Herichell St. G13	G12	19
Foulis La.		
Heriot Av., Pais.	O 3	45
Heriot Cres., Bish.	D19	11
Heriot Rd., Lenz.	D23	13
Herma St. G23	F15	21
Hermiston Av. G32	L23	39
Hermiston Pl. G32	L23	39
Hermiston Rd. G32	K22	38
Hermitage Av. G13	G11	19
Heron Ct., Clyde.	C 7	5
Heron Pl., John.	O08	43
Heron St. G40	M18	52
Heron Way, Renf.	J 8	31
Britannia Way		
Herries Rd. G41	N14	50
Herriet St. G41	M15	51
Herschell St. G13	G12	19
Foulis La.		
Hertford Av. G12	G13	20
Hexham Gdns. G41	N14	50
Heys St., Barr.	R 8	59
Hickman St. G42	N16	51
Hickory St. G42	G18	22
High Barholm, Kilb.	M07	42
High Calside, Pais.	M 5	46
High Craighall Rd. G4	J16	35
High Parksail, Renf.	F 5	16
High Rd., Pais.	M 5	46
High St. G1	L17	36
High St. G73	O19	53
High St., John.	M09	43
High St., Pais.	M 5	46
High St., Renf.	H 8	17
Highburgh Dr. G73	P19	65
Highburgh Rd. G12	J14	34
Highburgh Ter. G12	J14	34
Highburgh Rd.		
Highcraig Av., John.	N08	43
Highcroft Av. G44	P17	64
Highfield Av., Pais.	O 5	46
Highfield Cres., Pais.	O 5	46
Highfield Dr. G12	G13	20
Highfield Dr. G73	Q20	65
Highfield Pl. G12	G13	20
Highkirk Vw., John.	N09	43
Hilary Av. G73	P20	65
Hilary Dr., Bail.	L24	39
Hilda Cres. G33	H21	24
Hill Path G52	L10	32
Hill Pl. G52	L10	32
Hill St. G3	J16	35
Hillcrest Av. G32	O22	54
Hillcrest Av. G44	Q15	63
Hillcrest Av., Clyde.	B 7	5
Hillcrest Av., Cumb.	C 2	70
Hillcrest Av., Pais.	P 5	58
Hillcrest Ct., Cumb.	C 2	70
Hillcrest Rd. G32	O23	55
Hillcrest Rd., Bear.	D12	7
Hillcrest Rd., Udd.	O28	57
Hillcrest Ter., Both.	Q28	69
Churchill Cres.		
Hillcrest, Chr.	F26	26
Hillcroft Ter., Bish.	F18	22
Hillend Cres., Clyde.	B 6	4
Hillend Rd. G22	F16	21
Hillend Rd. G73	P19	65
Hillfoot Av. G73	O19	53
Hillfoot Av., Bear.	C12	7
Hillfoot Dr., Bear.	C12	7
Hillfoot Gdns., Udd.	O27	57
Hillfoot St. G31	K19	37
Hillfoot Ter., Bear.	C13	8
Milngavie Rd.		
Hillhead Av. G73	Q19	65
Hillhead Av., Chr.	E27	15
Hillhead Gdns. G12	J14	34
Hillhead St.		
Hillhead Pl. G12	J15	35
Bank St.		
Hillhead St. G12	J14	34
Hillhouse St. G21	H19	23
Hillington Gdns. G52	M11	49
Hillington Ind. Est. G52	K 9	32
Hillington Pk. Cres. G52	L11	33
Hillington Quad. G52	L10	32
Hillington Rd. G52	J 9	32
Hillington Rd. S., Renf.	L10	32
Hillington Ter. G52	L10	32
Hillkirk Pl. G21	H18	22
Hillkirk St. G21	H18	22
Hillkirk Street La. G21	H18	22
Hillkirk St.		
Hillneuk Av., Bear.	C12	7
Hillneuk Dr., Bear.	C13	8
Hillpark Av., Pais.	N 5	46
Hillpark Dr. G43	P14	62
Hillsborough Rd., Bail.	L24	39
Hillsborough Sq. G12	J14	34
Hillhead St.		
Hillsborough Ter. G12	H15	21
Bower St.		
Hillside Av., Bear.	C12	7
Hillside Ct., Thorn.	Q12	61
Hillside Dr., Barr.	Q 7	59
Hillside Dr., Bear.	C13	8
Hillside Dr., Bish.	E19	11
Hillside Gardens La. G11	H13	20
North Gardner St.		
Hillside Gdns. G11	H13	20
Turnberry Rd.		
Hillside Gro., Barr.	Q 7	59
Hillside Quad. G43	P13	62
Hillside Rd. G43	P13	62
Hillside Rd., Barr.	Q 7	59
Hillside Rd., Pais.	N 7	47
Hillswick Cres. G22	F16	21
Hilltop Rd., Chr.	E27	15
Eastwood Rd.		
Hillview Cres., Udd.	O27	57
Hillview Dr., Blan.	R26	68
Hillview Rd., John.	N 2	44
Hillview St. G32	L21	38
Hilton Gardens La. G13	F12	19
Fulton St.		
Hilton Gdns. G13	F12	19
Hilton Pk., Bish.	D18	10
Hilton Rd., Bish.	D18	10
Hilton Ter. G13	F12	19
Hilton Ter. G72	Q21	66
Hilton Ter., Bish.	D18	10
Hinshaw St. G20	H16	21
Hinshelwood Dr. G51	L13	34
Hinshelwood Pl. G51	L13	34
Edmiston Dr.		
Hirsel Pl., Bush.	R28	69
Lomond Dr.		
Hobart Cres., Dalm.	C 5	4
Hobart St. G22	H16	21
Hobden St. G21	H19	23
Hoddam Av. G45	Q19	65
Hoddam Av. G45	Q19	65
Ardencraig Rd.		
Hoddam Ter. G45	Q19	65
Hoey St. G51	K14	34
Hogan Ct., Clyde.	C 6	4
Dalgleish Av.		
Hogarth Av. G32	K20	37
Hogarth Cres. G32	K20	37
Hogarth Dr. G32	K20	37
Hogarth Gdns. G32	K20	37
Hogg Av., John.	N09	43
Hogganfield St. G33	J20	37
Holburn Av., Pais.	L 4	29
Hole Brae, Cumb.	B 3	71
Holeburn Rd. G43	P14	62
Holehouse Dr. G13	G10	18
Holland St. G2	K16	35
Hollinwell Rd. G23	F15	21
Hollowglen Rd. G32	L22	38
Hollows Av., Pais.	O 3	45
Hollows Cres., Pais.	O 3	45
Holly Pl., John.	O 1	44
Holly St., Clyde.	D 7	5
Hollybank Pl. G72	Q22	66
Hollybank St. G21	J19	37
Hollybrook St. G42	N16	51
Hollybush Av., Pais.	O 4	45
Hollybush Rd. G52	L 9	32
Hollymount, Bear.	E12	7
Holm Av., Pais.	N 6	46
Holm Av., Udd.	O26	57
Holm Pl., Linw.	K 1	28
Holm St. G2	K16	35

Name	Ref	Page
Holmbank Av. G41	O14	50
Holmbrae Av., Udd.	O27	57
Holmbrae Rd., Udd.	O27	57
Holmbyre Rd. G45	R17	64
Holmbyre Ter. G45	R17	64
Holmes Av., Renf.	J 8	31
Holmfauldhead Dr. G51	K12	33
Holmhead Cres. G44	P16	63
Holmhead Pl. G44	P16	63
Holmhead Rd. G44	P16	63
Holmhill Av. G72	Q22	66
Holmhills Dr. G72	Q21	66
Holmhills Gdns. G72	Q21	66
Holmhills Gro. G72	Q21	66
Holmhills Pl. G72	Q21	66
Holmhills Rd. G72	Q21	66
Holmhills Ter. G72	Q21	66
Holmlea Rd. G44	O16	51
Holms Pl., Gart.	F27	27
Holmswood Av., Blan.	R26	68
Holmwood Av., Udd.	O27	57
Holmwood Gdns., Udd.	P27	69
Holyrood Cres. G20	J15	35
Holyrood Quad. G20	J15	35
Holywell St. G31	L19	37
Homeston Av., Udd.	Q28	69
Honeybog Rd. G52	L 9	32
Hood St., Clyde.	E 8	5
Hope St. G2	K16	35
Hopefield Av. G12	G14	20
Hopehill Pl. G20	H16	21
Hopehill Rd		
Hopehill Rd. G20	H16	21
Hopeman Av. G46	Q12	61
Hopeman Dr. G46	Q12	61
Hopeman Rd. G46	Q12	61
Hopeman St. G46	Q12	61
Hopetoun Pl. G23	E15	9
Hornal Rd., Udd.	Q28	69
Hornbeam Dr., Dalm.	D 7	5
Hornbeam Rd., Udd.	O28	57
Myrtle Rd.		
Horndean Cres. G33	J23	39
Horndean Ct., Bish.	D19	11
Horne St. G22	G18	22
Hawthorn St.		
Hornshill Rd. G33	F24	25
Hornshill St. G21	H19	23
Horsburgh St. G33	J23	39
Horse Shoe La., Bear.	D12	7
Horse Shoe Rd., Bear.	C12	7
Horslethill Rd. G12	H14	20
Hospital St. G5	M16	51
Hotspur St. G20	H15	21
Houldsworth La. G3	K15	35
Finnieston St.		
Houldsworth St. G3	K15	35
Househillmuir Cres. G53	O11	49
Househillmuir La. G53	O11	49
Househillmuir Pl. G53	O11	49
Househillmuir Rd. G53	P10	60
Househillwood Cres. G53	O10	48
Househillwood Rd. G53	P10	60
Housel Av. G13	F10	18
Houston Pl. G5	L15	35
Houston Pl., John.	N 2	44
Houston Rd., Loanhead	H 1	28
Houston Sq., John.	M09	43
Houston St. G5	L15	35
Houston St., Renf.	H 8	17
Howard St. G1	L16	35
Howard St., Pais.	M 7	47
Howat St. G51	K13	34
Howden Dr., Linw.	L 1	28
Howe St., Pais.	M 3	45
Howford Rd. G52	M10	48
Howgate Av. G15	D 9	6
Howieshill Av. G72	P22	66
Howieshill Rd. G72	Q22	66
Howth Dr. G13	F12	19
Howth Ter. G13	F12	19
Howwood St. G41	L15	35
Hoylake Pk., Both.	R27	69
Hoylake Pl. G23	E15	9
Hozier Cres., Udd.	O27	57
Hozier St. G40	M18	52
Hubbard Dr. G11	J12	33
Hugh Murray Gro. G72	P23	67
Hughenden Dr. G12	H13	20
Hughenden Gdns. G12	H13	20
Hughenden La. G12	H13	20
Hughenden Rd. G12	H13	20
Hughenden Ter. G12	H13	20
Hughenden Rd.		
Hugo St. G20	G15	21
Hume Dr., Both.	Q28	69
Hume Dr., Udd.	O27	57
Hume Rd., Cumb.	B 3	71
Hume St., Clyde.	E 7	5
Hunter Pl. G78	NO7	42
Hunter Rd. G73	N20	53
Hunter St. G4	L18	36
Hunter St., Pais.	L 6	30
Hunterfield Dr. G72	P21	66
Hunterhill Av., Pais.	M 6	46
Hunterhill Rd.		
Hunterhill Rd., Pais.	M 6	46
Huntersfield Rd., John.	NO8	43
Huntershill Rd., Bish.	F18	22
Huntershill St. G21	G18	22
Huntershill Way, Bish.	F18	22
Crowhill Rd.		
Huntingdon Sq. G21	J18	36
Huntingdon Rd.		
Huntington Rd. G21	J18	36
Huntingtower Rd., Bail.	M25	56
Huntley Dr., Bear.	B12	7
Tweedsmuir Dr.		
Huntley Rd. G52	K 9	32
Huntly Av., Giff.	R14	62
Huntly Dr. G72	Q22	66
Huntly Gdns. G12	H14	20
Huntly Path, Chr.	E28	15
Burnbrae Av.		
Huntly Rd. G12	H14	20
Huntly Ter., Pais.	N 7	47
Hurlet Rd., Pais.& G53	N 8	47
Hurley Hawkin, Bish.	F20	23
Hurlford Av. G13	F 9	18
Hutcheson Rd., Thorn.	R13	62
Hutcheson St. G1	K17	36
Hutchinson Ct. G2	K16	35
Hope St.		
Hutchinson Pl. G72	Q24	67
Hutchison Ct., Giff.	Q13	62
Berryhill Rd.		
Hutchison Dr., Bear.	E13	8
Hutton Dr. G51	K12	33
Huxley St. G20	G15	21
Hydepark Pl. G21	G18	22
Springburn Rd.		
Hydepark St. G3	K15	35
Hyndal Av. G53	N11	49
Hyndford St. G51	K13	34
Hyndland Av. G11	J13	34
Hyndland Rd. G12	H13	20
Hyndland St. G11	J14	34
Hyndlee Dr. G52	L11	33
Hyslop Pl., Clyde.	D 7	5
Albert Rd.		
Iain Dr., Bear.	C11	7
Iain Rd., Bear.	C11	7
Ibrox St. G51	L14	34
Ibrox Ter. G51	L13	34
Ibrox Terrace La. G51	L13	34
Ibroxholm La. G51	L14	34
Paisley Rd. W.		
Ibroxholm Oval G51	L13	34
Ibroxholm Pl. G51	L14	34
Ilay Av., Bear.	F12	19
Ilay Ct., Bear.	F13	20
Ilay Rd., Bear.	F13	20
Inchbrae Rd. G52	M11	49
Inchfad Dr. G15	D 9	6
Inchholm St. G11	J12	33
Inchinnan Rd., Pais.	K 6	30
Inchinnan Rd., Renf.	H 7	17
Inchkeith Pl. G32	K22	38
Inchlee St. G14	J12	33
Inchmurrin Dr. G73	R20	65
Inchmurrin Gdns. G73	R20	65
Inchmurrin Pl. G73	R20	65
Inchoch St. G33	J24	39
Inchrory Pl. G15	D 9	6
Incle St., Pais.	L 6	30
India Dr., Renf.	G 5	16
India St. G2	K16	35
India St. G73	O19	53
Inga St. G20	F15	21
Ingerbreck Av. G73	Q20	65
Ingleby Dr. G31	K19	37
Inglefield St. G42	N16	51
Ingleneuk Av. G33	G22	24
Inglestone Av., Thorn.	R13	62
Inglis St. G31	L19	37
Ingram St. G1	K17	36
Inishail Rd. G33	J23	39
Inkerman Rd. G52	L 9	32
Innerwick Dr. G52	L10	32
Inver Rd. G33	K24	39
Inverary Dr., Bish.	D19	11
Invercanny Dr. G15	D 9	6
Invercanny Pl. G15	D10	6
Inverclyde Gdns. G11	H12	19
Broomhill Dr.		
Inverclyde Gdns. G73	Q21	66
Inveresk Cres. G32	L22	38
Inveresk St. G32	L22	38
Inverewe Av. G46	Q11	61
Inverewe Dr. G46	R11	61
Inverewe Gdns. G46	R11	61
Inverewe Pl. G46	Q11	61
Invergarry Av. G46	R11	61
Invergarry Ct. G46	R11	61
Invergarry Dr. G46	R11	61
Invergarry Gdns. G46	R11	61
Invergarry Gro. G46	R11	61
Invergarry Pl. G46	R11	61
Invergarry Quad. G46	R12	61
Invergarry Vw. G46	R12	61
Inverglas Av., Renf.	J 9	32
Morriston Cres.		
Invergordon Av. G43	O15	51
Invergyle Dr. G52	L10	32
Inverkar Dr., Pais.	N 4	45
Inverkip St. G5	L17	36
Inverlair Av. G43	P15	63
Inverleith St. G32	L20	37
Inverlochy St. G33	J23	39
Inverness St. G51	L11	33
Inveroran Dr., Bear.	D13	8
Invershiel Rd. G23	E14	8
Invershin Dr. G20	G14	20
Wyndford Rd.		
Inverurie St. G21	H17	22
Inzievar Ter. G32	N22	54
Iona Ct. G51	K13	34
Iona Dr., Pais.	O 5	46
Iona La., Chr.	E28	15
Heathfield Av.		
Iona Rd. G73	Q21	66
Iona Rd., Renf.	J 8	31
Iona St. G51	K13	34
Irongray St. G31	K20	37
Irvine Dr., Linw.	L 1	28
Irvine St. G40	M19	53
Irving Av., Clyde.	C 7	5
Stewart Dr.		
Irving Quad., Clyde.	C 7	5
Stewart Dr.		
Iser La. G41	O15	51
Island Rd., Cumb.	D 1	70
Islay Av. G73	Q21	66
Islay Cres., Pais.	O 5	46
Ivanhoe Rd. G13	F11	19
Ivanhoe Rd., Cumb.	D 2	70
Ivanhoe Rd., Pais.	N 3	45
Ivanhoe Way, Pais.	N 3	45
Ivanhoe Rd.		
Ivybank Ave. G72	Q23	67
Jacks Rd., Udd.	P28	69
Jagger Gdns., Bail.	M24	55
Jamaica St. G1	L16	35
James Dunlop Gdns., Bish.	F19	23
Graham Ter.		
James Gray St. G41	O15	51
James Morrison St. G1	L17	36
St. Andrews Sq.		
James Nisbet St. G21	K18	36
James St. G40	M18	52
James Watt La. G2	K16	35
James Watt St.		
James Watt St. G2	K16	35
Jamieson Ct. G42	N16	51
Jamieson Ct., Clyde.	B 7	5

Name	Ref	Page
Jamieson Path G42	N16	51
Jamieson St.		
Jamieson St. G42	N16	51
Janebank Av. G72	Q23	67
Janefield Av., John.	N 9	43
Janefield St. G31	L19	37
Janes Brae, Cumb.	D 2	70
Janetta St., Clyde.	D 7	5
Jardine St. G20	H15	21
Jardine Ter., Gart.	G27	27
Jasgray St. G42	N15	51
Jean Armour Dr., Clyde.	D 8	5
Jedburgh Av. G73	O19	53
Jedburgh Dr., Pais.	N 4	45
Jedburgh Gdns. G20	H15	21
Jedworth Av. G15	D10	6
Jellicoe St. Dalm.	D 6	4
Jennys Well Rd., Pais.	N 7	47
Jerviston Rd. G33	J23	39
Jessie St. G42	N17	52
Jessiman Sq., Renf.	J 7	31
John Brown Pl., Chr.	F26	26
John Knox La. G4	K18	36
Drygate		
John Knox St. G4	K18	36
John Knox St., Clyde.	F 8	17
John Lang St., John.	M 1	44
John St. G1	K17	36
John St., Barr.	Q 7	59
John St., Pais.	M 5	46
Johnshaven St. G43	O14	50
Bengal St.		
Johnston Rd., Gart.	G28	27
Johnston St., Pais.	M 6	46
Gordon St.		
Johnstone Av. G52	L10	32
Johnstone Av., Clyde.	F 8	17
Johnstone Cotts., Kirk.	B21	12
Johnstone Dr. G72	P22	66
Johnstone Dr. G73	O19	53
Joppa St. G33	K21	38
Jordan St. G14	J11	33
Jordanhill Cres. G13	G11	19
Jordanhill Dr. G13	G11	19
Jordanhill La. G13	G12	19
Austen Rd.		
Jordanvale Av. G14	J11	33
Jowitt Av., Clyde.	E 8	5
Joycelyn Sq. G1	L17	36
Jubilee Bank, Lenz.	D23	13
Heriot Rd.		
Jubilee Path, Bear.	D12	7
Jubilee Ter., John.	N08	43
Julian Av. G12	H14	20
Julian La. G12	H14	20
Julian Av.		
Juniper Ct., Lenz.	C22	12
Juniper Pl., John.	O 1	44
Juniper Pl. G32	M24	55
Juniper Ter. G32	M24	55
Jura Av., Renf.	J 8	31
Jura Ct. G52	L12	33
Jura Dr., Blan.	Q26	68
Jura Rd., Pais.	O 5	46
Jura St. G52	L12	33
Kaim Dr. G53	P11	61
Kames St. G5	M16	51
Karol Path G4	J16	35
St. Peters St.		
Katewell Av. G15	D 9	6
Katrine Av., Bish.	E19	11
Katrine Dr., Pais.	N 3	45
Kay St. G21	H18	22
Kaystone Rd. G15	E10	6
Keal Av. G15	F10	18
Keal Cres. G15	F10	18
Keal Dr. G15	F10	18
Keal Pl. G15	F10	18
Kearn Av. G15	E10	6
Kearn Pl. G15	E10	6
Keats Pk., Udd.	Q28	69
Keir Dr., Bish.	E18	10
Keir St. G41	M15	51
Keirhill Rd, Cumb.	C 1	70
Woodburn Rd.		
Keirs Wk. G72	P22	66
Keith Av., Giff.	Q14	62
Keith Ct. G11	J14	34
Keith St.		
Keith St. G11	J14	34
Kelbourne St. G20	H15	21
Kelburn St., Barr.	R 7	59
Kelburne Dr., Pais.	L 7	31
Kelburne Gdns., Bail.	M25	56
Kelburne Gdns., Pais.	L 7	31
Kelburne Oval, Pais.	L 7	31
Kelhead Av. G52	L 9	32
Kelhead Dr. G52	L 9	32
Kelhead Path G52	L10	32
Kelhead Pl. G52	L 9	32
Kellas St. G51	L13	34
Kells Pl. G15	D 9	6
Kelso Av. G73	O19	53
Kelso Av., Pais.	N 4	45
Kelso St. G13	G 9	18
Kelton St. G32	M22	54
Kelty Pl. G5	L16	35
Bedford St.		
Kelty St. G5	M16	51
Eglinton St.		
Kelvin Av. G52	J 9	32
Kelvin Cres., Bear.	E12	7
Kelvin Ct. G12	G12	19
Kelvin Dr. G20	H14	20
Kelvin Dr., Barr.	R 8	59
Kelvin Dr., Bish.	E19	11
Kelvin Dr., Chr.	E27	15
Kelvin Rd., Cumb.	D 3	71
Kelvin Rd., Udd.	O27	57
Kelvin Way G3	J14	34
Kelvin Way, Udd.	Q28	69
Bracken Ter.		
Kelvindale Bldgs. G12	G14	20
Kelvindale Rd.		
Kelvindale Cotts. G12	G14	20
Kelvindale Rd.		
Kelvindale Glen G12	G14	20
Kelvindale Rd.		
Kelvindale Pl. G20	G14	20
Kelvindale Rd. G12	G14	20
Kelvingrove St. G3	K15	35
Kelvingrove Ter. G3	K15	35
Kelvingrove St.		
Kelvinhaugh Pl. G3	K14	34
Kelvinhaugh St.		
Kelvinhaugh St. G3	K14	34
Kelvinside Av. G20	H15	21
Queen Margaret Dr.		
Kelvinside Dr. G20	H15	21
Kelvinside Gdns. E. G20	H15	21
Kelvinside Gdns. G20	H15	21
Kelvinside Ter. S. G20	H15	21
Kelvinside Ter. W. G20	H15	21
Kemp Av., Renf.	J 7	31
Kemp St. G21	H18	22
Kempock St. G31	M20	53
Kempsthorn Cres. G53	N10	48
Kempsthorn Path G53	N10	48
Kempsthorn Rd. G53	N10	48
Kendal Av., Giff.	Q14	62
Kendal Dr. G12	G13	20
Kendal Ter. G12	G13	20
Kendoon Av. G15	D 9	6
Kenilworth Av. G41	O14	50
Kenilworth Cres., Bear.	C11	7
Kenilworth Way, Pais.	O 3	45
Kenmar Gdns., Udd.	O26	56
Kenmore Gdns., Bear.	C13	8
Kenmore Rd., Cumb.	C 3	71
Kenmore St. G32	L22	38
Kenmuir Av. G32	M24	55
Kenmuir Rd. G32	O23	55
Kenmuirhill Rd. G32	N23	55
Kenmure Av., Bish.	E18	10
Kenmure Cres., Bish.	E18	10
Kenmure Dr., Bish.	E18	10
Kenmure Gdns., Bish.	E18	10
Kenmure Row G22	E16	9
Kenmure St. G41	M15	51
Kenmure Way G73	Q19	65
Kennedar Dr. G51	K12	33
Kennedy Ct., Giff.	Q14	62
Braidholm Cres.		
Kennedy St. G4	K17	36
Kennet St. G21	J19	37
Kennishead Av. G46	P12	61
Kennishead Pl. G46	P12	61
Kennishead Rd. G46	P12	61
Kennishead Rd. G53	Q11	61
Kennisholm Av. G46	P12	61
Kennisholm Pl. G46	P12	61
Kennoway Dr. G11	J12	33
Kennoway La. G11	J12	33
Thornwood Dr.		
Kennyhill Sq. G31	K19	37
Kensington Dr., Giff.	R14	62
Kensington Gate G12	H14	20
Kensington Rd.		
Kensington Rd. G12	H14	20
Kent Dr. G73	P20	65
Kent Rd. G3	K15	35
Kent St. G40	L18	36
Kentallen Rd. G33	L24	39
Kentigern Ter., Bish.	F19	23
Keppel Dr. G44	O18	52
Keppoch St. G21	H17	22
Keppochhill Rd. G22	H17	22
Kerfield Pl. G15	D 9	6
Kerr St. G40	L18	36
Kerr St., Barr.	R 7	59
Kerr St., Blan.	S27	69
Kerr St., Pais.	L 5	30
Kerrera Pl. G33	L23	39
Kerrera Rd. G33	L23	39
Kerry Pl. G15	D 9	6
Kerrycroy Av. G42	O17	52
Kerrycroy Pl. G42	O17	52
Kerrycroy Av.		
Kerrycroy St. G42	O17	52
Kerrydale St. G40	M19	53
Kerrylamont Av. G42	O18	52
Kersland La. G12	H14	20
Kersland St.		
Kersland St. G12	H14	20
Kessington Dr., Bear.	D13	8
Kessington Rd., Bear.	D13	8
Kestral Ct., Clyde.	C 7	5
Kestrel Pl., John.	O08	43
Kestrel Rd. G13	G11	19
Kew Gdns. G12	H14	20
Ruthven St.		
Kew Gdns., Udd.	O28	57
Kew La. G12	H14	20
Saltoun St.		
Kew Ter. G12	H14	20
Keyden St. G41	L15	35
Kibbleston Rd., Kilb.	M07	42
Kidston St. G5	M17	52
Kierhill Rd., Cumb.	C 1	70
Kilbarchan Rd., John.	N08	43
Kilbarchan St. G5	L16	35
Bedford St.		
Kilbeg Ter. G46	Q11	61
Kilberry St. G21	J19	37
Kilbirnie St. G5	M16	51
Kilbowie Ct., Clyde.	D 7	5
Crown Av.		
Kilbowie Rd., Clyde.	C 7	5
Kilbowie Rd., Cumb.	C 3	71
Kilbrennan Rd., Linw.	L 1	28
Kilbride St. G5	N17	52
Kilbride Vw., Udd.	O28	57
Hamilton Vw.		
Kilburn Gro., Blan.	R26	68
Kilburn Pl. G13	G10	18
Kilchattan Dr. G44	O17	52
Kilchoan Rd. G33	J23	39
Kilcloy Av. G15	D10	6
Kildale Way G73	O18	52
Kildary Av. G44	P16	63
Kildary Rd. G44	P16	63
Kildermorie Rd. G34	K25	40
Kildonan Dr. G11	J13	34
Kildonan Ter. G51	L13	34
Copland Rd.		
Kildrostan St. G41	N15	51
Terregles Av.		
Kildrum Rd., Cumb.	B 3	71
Kilearn Rd., Pais.	K 7	31
Kilfinan St. G22	F16	21
Kilkerran Dr. G33	G21	24
Killarn Way, Pais.	K 7	31
Killearn Dr., Pais.	M 9	48
Killearn St. G22	H16	21
Killermont Av., Bear.	E13	8
Killermont Ct., Bear.	D13	8
Killermont Meadows, Both.	R27	69

Name	Grid	Page
Killermont Rd., Bear.	D13	8
Killermont St. G1	K17	36
Killermont Vw. G20	E13	8
Killiegrew Rd. G41	N14	50
Killin Dr., Linw.	L 1	28
Killin St. G32	M22	54
Killoch Av., Pais.	L 4	29
Killoch Dr. G13	F10	18
Killoch Dr., Barr.	R 8	59
Killoch Rd., Pais.	L 4	29
Kilmailing Rd. G44	P16	63
Kilmair Pl. G20	G14	20
Wyndford Rd.		
Kilmaluag Ter. G46	Q11	61
Kilmany Dr. G32	L21	38
Kilmardinny Av., Bear.	C12	7
Kilmardinny Cres., Bear.	C12	7
Kilmardinny Dr., Bear.	C12	7
Kilmardinny Gate, Bear.	C12	7
Kilmardinny Av.		
Kilmardinny Gro., Bear.	C12	7
Kilmarnock Rd. G43	P14	62
Kilmartin Pl., Thorn.	Q12	61
Kilmaurs Dr., Giff.	Q15	63
Kilmaurs St. G51	L12	33
Kilmorie Dr. G73	O18	52
Kilmory Av., Udd.	O28	57
Spindlehow Rd.		
Kilmuir Cres. G46	Q11	61
Kilmuir Dr. G46	Q12	61
Kilmuir Rd. G46	Q12	61
Kilmuir Rd., Udd.	N27	57
Kilmun La. G20	F14	20
Kilmun St.		
Kilmun Pl. G20	F14	20
Kilmun St.		
Kilmun St. G20	F14	20
Kilnside Rd., Pais.	L 6	30
Kiloran St. G46	Q12	61
Kilpatrick Av., Pais.	N 4	45
Kilpatrick Cres., Pais.	N 5	46
Kiltearn Rd. G33	K24	39
Kilvaxter Dr. G46	Q12	61
Kilwynet Way, Pais.	K 7	31
Kimberley St., Dalm.	C 5	4
Kinalty Rd. G44	P16	63
Kinarvie Cres. G53	O 9	48
Kinarvie Gdns. G53	O 9	48
Kinarvie Rd.		
Kinarvie Pl. G53	O 9	48
Kinarvie Rd. G53	O 9	48
Kinarvie Ter. G53	O 9	48
Kinbuck St. G22	H17	22
Kincardine Cres., Bish.	F19	23
Graham Ter.		
Kincardine Dr., Bish.	F19	23
Kincardine Pl., Bish.	F20	23
Kincardine Sq. G33	J23	39
Kincath Av. G73	Q20	65
Kinclaven Av. G15	D10	6
Kincraig St. G51	L11	33
Kinellan Rd., Bear.	E12	7
Kinellar Dr. G14	G10	18
Kinfauns Dr. G15	D 9	6
Kinfauns Ter. G51	L13	34
Copland Rd.		
King Edward Rd. G13	G12	19
King George V Bridge G5	L16	35
King St. G1	L17	36
King St. G73	O19	53
King St., Clyde.	F 8	17
King St., Pais.	L 5	30
Kingarth St. G42	N16	51
Kinghorn Dr. G44	O17	52
Kinglas Rd., Bear.	E11	7
Kings Cres. G72	P22	66
Kings Cres., John.	M 2	44
Kings Cross G31	K18	36
Kings Dr. G40	M18	52
Kings Dr., Cumb.	A 2	70
Kings Inch Rd., Renf.	G 8	17
Kings La. W., Renf.	H 8	17
Bell St.		
Kings Park Av. G44	P17	64
Kings Park Rd. G44	O16	51
Kings Pl. G22	F16	21
Kings Rd., John.	N 1	44
Kingsacre Rd. G44	O17	52
Kingsbarns Dr. G44	O16	51
Kingsborough Gate G12	H13	20
Prince Albert Rd.		
Kingsborough Gdns. G12	H13	20
Kingsborough Ter. G12	H13	20
Hyndland Rd.		
Kingsbrae Dr. G44	O17	52
Kingsbridge Cres. G44	P17	64
Kingsbridge Dr. G44	P17	64
Kingsburgh Dr., Pais.	L 7	31
Kingsburn Dr. G73	P19	65
Kingsburn Gro. G73	P19	65
Kingscliffe Av. G44	P17	64
Kingscourt Av. G44	P17	64
Kingsdale Av. G44	O17	52
Kingsdyke Av. G44	O17	52
Kingsford Av. G44	Q15	63
Kingshall Cotts., Gart.	H28	27
Kingsheath Av. G73	P18	64
Kingshill Dr. G44	P17	64
Kingshouse Av. G44	P17	64
Kingshurst Av. G44	O17	52
Kingsknowe Dr. G73	P18	64
Kingsland Cres. G52	L10	32
Kingsland Dr. G52	L10	32
Kingsley Av. G42	N16	51
Kingsley Ct., Udd.	O28	57
Kingslynn Dr. G44	P17	64
Kingslynn La. G44	P17	64
Kingslynn Dr.		
Kingsmuir Dr. G73	P18	64
Kingston Bri. G3	L15	34
Kingston Pl., Dalm.	D 5	4
Kingston St. G5	L16	35
Kingsway Ct. G14	G10	18
Kingsway G14	G10	18
Kingswood Dr. G44	P17	64
Kingussie Dr. G44	P17	64
Kiniver Dr. G15	E10	6
Kinloch Av. G72	Q22	66
Kinloch Av., Linw.	L 1	28
Pentland Dr.		
Kinloch Rd., Renf.	J 7	31
Kinloch St. G40	M20	53
Kinmount Av. G44	O16	51
Kinmount La. G44	O16	51
Kinmount Av.		
Kinnaird Cres., Bear.	D13	8
Kinnaird Dr., Linw.	L 1	28
Kinnaird Pl. G64	F19	23
Kinnear Rd. G40	M19	53
Kinnell Av. G52	M11	49
Kinnell Cres. G52	M11	49
Kinnell Pl. G52	N12	49
Mosspark Dr.		
Kinnell Sq. G52	M11	49
Kinning St. G5	L15	35
Kinnoul Pl. G12	H13	20
Crown Rd.		
Kinpurnie Rd., Pais.	L 8	31
Kinross Av. G52	M10	48
Kinsail Dr. G52	L 9	32
Kinstone Av. G14	G10	18
Kintessack Pl., Bish.	E20	11
Kintillo Dr. G13	G10	18
Kintore Rd. G43	P15	63
Kintra St. G51	L13	34
Kintyre Av., Linw.	L 1	28
Kintyre St. G21	J19	37
Kippen St. G22	G17	22
Kippford St. G32	M23	55
Kirk La. G43	O14	50
Riverbank St.		
Kirk Pl., Udd.	P27	69
Kirk Rd., Bear.	C12	7
Kirkaig Av., Renf.	J 9	32
Kirkbean Av. G73	Q19	65
Kirkburn Av. G72	Q22	66
Kirkcaldy Rd. G41	N14	58
Kirkconnel Av. G13	G 9	18
Kirkconnel Dr. G73	P18	64
Kirkdale Dr. G52	M12	49
Kirkfield Rd., Udd.	Q28	69
Kirkford Rd., Chr.	E27	15
Bridgeburn Dr.		
Kirkhill Av. G72	Q22	66
Kirkhill Dr. G20	G14	20
Kirkhill Gdns. G72	Q22	66
Kirkhill Gro. G72	Q22	66
Kirkhill Pl. G20	G14	20
Kirkhill Rd., Gart.	G27	27
Kirkhill Rd., Udd.	O27	57
Kirkhill Ter. G72	Q22	66
Kirkhope Dr. G15	E10	6
Kirkinner Rd. G32	M23	55
Kirkintilloch Rd., Bish.	F18	22
Kirkintilloch Rd., Lenz.	C23	13
Kirkland St. G20	H15	21
Kirklandneuk Rd., Renf.	H 7	17
Kirklands Cres., Udd.	Q28	69
Kirklea Av., Pais.	L 4	29
Kirklee Circus G12	H14	20
Kirklee Gardens La. G12	G14	20
Bellshaugh Rd.		
Kirklee Gdns. G12	G14	20
Bellshaugh Rd.		
Kirklee Pl. G12	H14	20
Kirklee Quad. G12	H14	20
Kirklee Quad. La. G12	H14	20
Kirklee Quad.		
Kirklee Rd. G12	H14	20
Kirklee Ter. G12	H14	20
Kirklee Terrace La. G12	H14	20
Kirklee Ter.		
Kirkliston St. G32	L21	38
Kirkmuir Av., Renf.	J 7	31
Kirkmuir Dr. G73	Q19	65
Kirknewton St. G32	L22	38
Kirkoswald Dr., Clyde.	D 8	5
Kirkoswald Rd. G43	P14	62
Kirkpatrick St. G40	L19	37
Kirkriggs Av. G73	P19	65
Kirkriggs Gdns. G73	P19	65
Kirkriggs Way, Ruth.	P19	65
Kirkstall Gdns., Bish.	D19	11
Kirkstonside, Barr.	R 7	59
Kirkton Av. G13	G10	18
Kirkton Cres. G13	G10	18
Kirkton Rd. G72	P22	66
Kirkview Gdns., Udd.	O27	57
Glencroft Av.		
Kirkville Pl. G15	E10	6
Kirkwall Av., Blan.	Q26	68
Kirkwall, Cumb.	A 3	71
Kirkwell Rd. G44	P16	63
Kirkwood Av., Clyde.	E 8	5
Kirkwood Quad., Clyde.	E 8	5
Kirkwood Av.		
Kirkwood Rd., Udd.	N27	57
Newlands Rd.		
Kirkwood St. G51	L14	34
Kirkwood St. G73	O19	53
Kirn St. G20	F14	20
Kilmun St.		
Kirriemuir Av. G52	M11	49
Kirriemuir Gdns., Bish.	E20	11
Kirriemuir Rd., Bish.	E20	11
Kirtle Dr., Renf.	J 9	32
Kirton Av., Barr.	R 7	59
Kishorn Pl. G33	J23	39
Knapdale St. G22	F16	21
Knightsbridge Rd. G13	G11	19
Knightscliffe Av. G13	F11	19
Knightswood Cross G13	F11	19
Knightswood Rd. G13	E11	7
Knightswood Ter., Blan.	R27	69
Knock Way, Pais.	K 7	31
Knockburnie Rd., Udd.	Q28	69
Knockhall St. G33	J23	39
Knockhill Dr. G44	O16	51
Knockhill La. G44	O16	51
Mount Annan Dr.		
Knockhill Rd., Renf.	J 7	31
Knockside Av., Pais.	O 5	46
Knowe Rd., Chr.	F26	26
Knowe Rd., Pais.	K 7	31
Knowe Ter. G22	F16	21
Hillend Rd.		
Knowehead Dr., Udd.	P27	69
Knowehead Gdns. G41	M15	51
Knowehead Ter.		
Knowehead Gdns., Udd.	P27	69
Knowehead Ter. G41	M15	51
Knowetap St. G20	F15	21
Knox St., Pais.	M 4	45
Kyle Dr., Giff.	Q14	62
Kyle Rd., Cumb.	B 3	71
Kyle Sq. G73	P19	65
Kyle St. G4	J17	36

Name	Ref.
Lochy Gdns., Bish.	E19 11
Lockhart Av. G72	P23 67
Lockhart Dr. G72	P23 67
Lockhart St. G21	J19 37
Locksley Av. G13	F11 19
Locksley Rd., Pais.	N 3 45
Logan Dr., Cumb.	B 1 70
Logan Dr., Pais.	L 5 30
Logan St. G5	N17 52
Logan Tower G72	Q24 67
Claude Av.	
Loganswell Dr. G46	R11 61
Loganswell Gdns. G46	R12 61
Loganswell Pl. G46	R12 61
Loganswell Rd. G46	R12 61
Logie St. G51	K13 34
Lomax St. G33	K20 37
Lomond Av., Renf.	J 7 31
Lomond Cres., Pais.	O 5 46
Lomond Ct., Barr.	R 8 59
Lomond Dr., Barr.	Q 7 59
Lomond Dr., Udd.	Q28 69
Lomond Gdns., John.	N 2 44
Lomond Pl. G33	H23 25
Lomond Rd., Bear.	E12 7
Lomond Rd., Bish.	D18 10
Lomond Rd., Lenz.	C23 13
Lomond Rd., Udd.	N27 57
Lomond St. G22	G16 21
Lomond Vw., Clyde.	D 7 5
Granville St.	
London Arcade G1	L17 36
London Rd.	
London La. G1	L17 36
London Rd.	
London Rd. G1	L17 36
London St., Renf.	G 8 17
Long Row, Bail.	L26 40
Longay Pl. G22	F17 22
Longay St. G22	F17 22
Longcroft Dr., Renf.	H 8 17
Longdale Rd., Chr.	E27 15
Longden St., Clyde.	F 8 17
Longford St. G33	K20 37
Longlee, Bail.	M25 56
Longmeadow, John.	N08 43
Longstone Rd. G33	K22 38
Longwill Ter., Cumb.	B 3 71
Lonmay Rd. G33	K23 39
Lonsdale Av., Giff.	Q14 62
Loom St. G40	L18 36
Stevenson St.	
Loom Wk., Kilb.	M07 42
Shuttle St.	
Lora Dr. G52	M12 49
Loretto Pl. G33	K21 38
Loretto St. G33	K21 38
Lorne Av., Chr.	F26 26
Lorne Cres., Bish.	E20 11
Lorne Dr., Linw.	L 1 28
Lorne Pl. G42	O16 51
Cathcart Rd.	
Lorne Rd. G52	K 9 32
Lorne St. G51	L14 34
Lorne Ter. G72	Q21 66
Lorraine Gdns. G12	H14 20
Kensington Rd.	
Lorraine Rd. G12	H14 20
Loskin Dr. G22	F16 21
Lossie Cres., Renf.	J 9 32
Lossie St. G33	J20 37
Lothian Cres., Pais.	N 5 46
Lothian Dr., Clark.	R14 62
Lothian Gdns. G20	H15 21
Lothian St. G52	K 9 32
Loudon Gdns.	M 1 44
Loudon Rd. G33	G22 24
Loudon Ter. G12	H14 20
Observatory Rd.	
Lounsdale Cres., Pais.	N 4 45
Lounsdale Dr., Pais.	N 4 45
Lounsdale Pl. G14	H10 18
Lounsdale Rd., Pais.	N 4 45
Lourdes Av. G52	M11 49
Lovat Pl. G73	Q20 65
Lovat St. G4	J17 36
Love St., Pais.	L 6 30
Low Barholm, Kilb.	N07 42
Low Cres., Clyde.	F 9 18
Low Parksail, Renf.	F 5 16
Low Rd., Pais.	M 5 46
Lower Bourtree Dr. G73	Q20 65
Lower English Bldgs. G42	M16 51
Lower Millgate, Udd.	O27 57
Lowndes La., Pais.	L 6 30
New Sneddon St.	
Lowndes St., Barr.	R 8 59
Lowther Ter. G12	H14 20
Loyne Dr., Renf.	J 9 32
Morriston Cres.	
Luath St. G51	K13 34
Lubas Av. G42	O17 52
Lubas Pl. G42	O17 52
Lubnaig Rd. G43	P15 63
Luckingsford Av., Renf.	F 5 16
Luckingsford Dr., Renf.	F 5 16
Luckingsford Rd., Renf.	F 5 16
Lucy Brae, Udd.	O27 57
Ludovic Sq., John.	M09 43
Luffness Gdns. G32	N22 54
Lugar Dr. G52	M12 49
Lugar Pl. G44	P18 64
Luggiebank Pl., Bail.	M28 57
Luing Rd. G52	L12 33
Lumloch St. G21	H19 23
Lumsden La. G3	K14 34
Lumsden St.	
Lumsden St. G3	K14 34
Lunan Dr., Bish.	F20 23
Lunan Pl. G51	K12 33
Luncarty Pl. G32	M22 54
Luncarty St. G32	M22 54
Lunderston Dr. G53	O10 48
Lundie Gdns., Bish.	F20 23
Lundie St. G32	M21 54
Lunn Brae, John.	N09 43
Luss Rd. G51	K12 33
Lusset Vw., Clyde.	D 7 5
Radnor St.	
Lusshill Ter., Udd.	N25 56
Lyall Pl. G21	H17 22
Keppochhill Rd.	
Lyall St. G21	H17 22
Lybster Cres. G73	Q20 65
Lye Brae, Cumb.	C 3 71
Lyle Ter., Pais.	N 6 46
Lymburn St. G3	K14 34
Lyndale Pl. G20	F14 20
Lyndale Rd. G20	F14 20
Lyndhurst Gdns. G20	H15 21
Lyne Croft, Bish.	D19 11
Lyne Dr. G23	E15 9
Lynedoch Cres. G3	J15 35
Lynedoch Pl. G3	J15 35
Lynedoch St. G3	J15 35
Lynedoch Ter. G3	J15 35
Lynn Gdns. G12	H14 20
Great George St.	
Lynn Wk., Udd.	P28 69
Flax Rd.	
Lynnhurst, Udd.	O27 57
Lynton Av., Giff.	R13 62
Lyon Cross Av., Barr.	R 8 59
Lyon Rd., Pais.	N 3 45
Lyoncross Cres., Barr.	Q 8 59
Lyoncross Rd. G53	N10 48
Lytham Dr. G23	E15 9
Lytham Meadows, Both.	R27 69
Macbeth Pl. G31	M20 53
Macbeth St.	
Macbeth St. G31	M20 53
Macdougal St. G43	O14 50
Macdowall St., John.	M09 43
Macdowall St., Pais.	L 5 30
Macduff Pl. G31	M20 53
Macduff St. G31	M20 53
Mace Rd. G13	E11 7
Macfarlane Rd., Bear.	E12 7
Machrie Dr. G45	Q18 64
Machrie Rd. G45	Q18 64
Machrie St. G45	Q18 64
Mackean St., Pais.	L 5 30
Mackeith St. G40	M18 52
Mackenchnie St. G51	K13 34
Mackenzie Dr. John.	O07 42
Mackie St. G4	H17 22
Borron St.	
Mackiesmill Rd., John.	O 2 44
Mackinlay St. G5	M16 51
Maclay Av., Kilb.	N07 42
Maclean St. G41	L15 35
Maclean St. G51	L14 34
Maclean St., Clyde.	F 9 18
Wood Quadrant	
Maclehose Rd., Cumb.	B 4 71
Maclellan St. G41	L14 34
Madison Av. G44	P16 63
Madison La. G44	P16 63
Carmunnock Rd.	
Madras Pl. G40	M18 52
Madras St.	
Madras St. G40	M18 52
Mafeking St. G51	L13 34
Magdalen Way, Pais.	O 2 44
Magnus Cres. G44	Q16 63
Mahon Ct., Chr.	E27 15
Maida St. G43	O13 50
Maidland Rd. G53	O11 49
Mailerbeg Gdns., Chr.	D27 15
Mailing Av., Bish.	E19 11
Main Rd., John.	M 2 44
Main Rd., Pais.	M 5 46
Main St. G40	M18 52
Main St. G72	P22 66
Main St. G73	O19 53
Main St., Bail.	M25 56
Main St., Barr.	R 7 59
Main St., Both.	R28 69
Main St., Chr.	E26 14
Main St., Cumb.	A 3 71
Main St., Thorn.	Q12 61
Main St., Udd.	P27 69
Mainhead Ter., Cumb.	A 3 71
Roadside	
Mainhill Av., Bail.	L26 40
Mainhill Pl., Bail.	L26 40
Mainhill Rd., Bail.	L27 41
Mains Av., Giff.	R13 62
Mains Dr., Renf.	E 5 4
Mains Hill, Renf.	E 5 4
Mains Holm, Renf.	E 5 4
Mains River, Renf.	E 5 4
Mains Wood, Renf.	E 5 4
Mainscroft, Renf.	E 5 4
Mair St. G51	L15 35
Maitland Pl., Renf.	J 7 31
Maitland St. G4	J16 35
Malcolm St. G31	L20 37
Malin Pl. G33	K21 38
Mallaig Path G51	K11 33
Mallaig Pl. G51	K11 33
Mallaig Rd. G51	K11 33
Mallard Rd., Clyde.	C 7 5
Malloch Cres., John.	N 1 44
Malloch St. G20	G15 21
Malta St., Clyde.	F 8 17
Maltbarns St. G20	H16 21
Malvern Ct. G31	L19 37
Malvern Way, Pais.	K 5 30
Mambeg Dr. G51	K12 33
Mamore Pl. G43	P14 62
Mamore St. G43	P14 62
Manchester Dr. G12	G13 20
Manitoba Pl. G31	L19 37
Janefield St.	
Mannering Ct. G41	O14 50
Pollokshaws Rd.	
Mannering Rd. G31	O14 50
Mannering Rd., Pais.	O 3 45
Mannofield, Bear.	D11 7
Chesters Rd.	
Manor Rd. G14	H12 19
Manor Rd. G15	E 9 6
Manor Rd., Gart.	G27 27
Manor Rd., Pais.	N 3 45
Manor Way G73	Q19 65
Manse Av., Bear.	C12 7
Manse Brae G44	P16 63
Manse Ct., Barr.	Q 8 59
Manse Rd. G32	M23 55
Manse Rd., Bail.	L27 41
Manse Rd., Bear.	C12 7
Manse St., Renf.	H 8 17
Mansefield Av. G72	Q22 66
Mansefield Dr., Udd.	P28 69
Mansefield St. G11	J14 34
Mansel St. G21	G18 22
Mansewood Rd. G43	P13 62

Name	Grid	Page
Mansfield Rd. G52	K 9	32
Mansion Ct. G72	P22	66
Mansion St. G22	G17	22
Mansion St. G72	P22	66
Mansionhouse Av. G32	O23	55
Mansionhouse Dr. G32	L23	39
Mansionhouse Gdns.	O15	51
G41		
Mansionhouse Rd.		
Mansionhouse Rd. G32	M24	55
Mansionhouse Rd. G42	O15	51
Mansionhouse Rd., Pais.	L 7	31
Maple Ct., Barr.	S 8	59
Oakbank Dr.		
Maple Dr., Dalm.	C 6	4
Maple Dr., John.	O 1	44
Maple Dr., Lenz.	C22	12
Maple Rd. G41	M13	50
Mar Gdns. G73	Q20	65
March La. G41	N15	51
Nithsdale Dr.		
March St. G41	N15	51
Marchfield Av., Pais.	K 5	30
Marchfield, Bish.	D18	10
Marchfield, Bish.	D18	10
Westlands		
Marchglen Pl. G51	K11	33
Mallaig Rd.		
Marchmont Gdns., Bish.	D18	10
Marchmont Ter. G12	H14	20
Observatory Rd.		
Maree Dr. G52	M12	49
Maree Gdns., Bish.	E19	11
Maree Rd., Pais.	N 4	45
Marfield St. G32	L21	38
Margaret St. G41	K17	36
Martha St.		
Margarette Bldgs. G44	P16	63
Clarkston Rd.		
Marguerite Av., Lenz.	C23	13
Marguerite Dr., Lenz.	C23	13
Marguerite Gdns., Lenz.	C23	13
Marguerite Gdns., Udd.	Q28	69
Marguerite Gro., Lenz.	C23	13
Mariscat Rd. G41	N15	51
Marjory Dr., Pais.	K 7	31
Marjory Rd., Renf.	J 7	31
Market Rd., Lenz.	B25	14
Market St. G40	L18	36
Markinch St. G5	L16	35
West St.		
Marlborough Av. G11	H12	19
Marlinford Rd., Renf.	H10	18
Marlow St. G41	M15	51
Marlow Ter. G41	L15	35
Seaward St.		
Marmion Pl., Cumb.	D 2	70
Marmion Rd., Cumb.	D 2	70
Marmion Rd., Pais.	O 3	45
Marmion St. G20	H15	21
Marne St. G31	K19	37
Marnock Ter., Pais.	N 7	47
Marnock Way, Chr.	E27	15
Braeside Av.		
Marr St. G51	K13	34
Marshalls La., Pais.	M 6	46
Mart St. G1	L17	36
Martha St. G1	K17	36
Martin Cres., Bail.	L26	40
Martin St. G40	M18	52
Martlet Dr., John.	O08	43
Martyr St. G4	K18	36
Martyrs Pl. G64	F19	23
Marwick St. G31	K19	37
Marwood Av., Chr. &	C25	14
Waterside		
Mary St. G4	J16	35
Mary St., John.	M 1	44
Mary St., Pais.	N 6	46
Maryhill Rd.,	E13	8
Bear.& G20		
Maryland Dr. G52	L12	33
Maryland Gdns. G52	L12	33
Marys La., Renf.	H 8	17
Maryston Pl. G33	J20	37
Maryston St. G33	J20	37
Maryview Gdns., Udd.	N26	56
Edinburgh Rd.		
Maryville Av., Giff.	R14	62
Maryville Vw., Udd.	N26	56
Marywood Sq. G41	N15	51
Masonfield Av., Cumb.	C 1	70
Masterton St. G21	H17	22
Mathieson La. G5	M17	52
Mathieson St.		
Mathieson Rd. G73	N20	53
Mathieson St. G5	M17	52
Mathieson St., Pais.	L 7	31
Matilda Rd. G41	M15	51
Mauchline St. G5	M16	51
Maukinfauld Ct. G31	M21	54
Maukinfauld Rd. G32	M21	54
Mauldslie St. G40	M19	53
Maule Dr. G11	J13	34
Mause Av., Both.	R28	69
Mavis Bank, Bish.	F18	22
Mavisbank Rd. G51	K13	34
Govan Rd.		
Mavisbank Ter., Pais.	M 6	46
Maxton Av., Barr.	Q 7	59
Maxton Gro., Barr.	Q 7	59
Maxton Ter. G72	Q21	66
Maxwell Av. G41	M15	51
Maxwell Av., Bail.	M25	56
Maxwell Av., Bear.	E12	7
Maxwell Dr. G41	M14	50
Maxwell Dr., Bail.	L25	40
Maxwell Gdns. G41	M14	50
Maxwell Gro. G41	M14	50
Maxwell Oval G41	M15	51
Maxwell Pl. G41	M16	51
Maxwell Rd. G41	M15	51
Maxwell Sq. G41	M15	51
Maxwell St. G18	L17	36
Maxwell St., Bail.	M25	56
Maxwell St., Dalm.	D 6	4
Maxwell St., Pais.	L 6	30
Maxwellton Rd. G78	M 4	45
Maxwellton St., Pais.	M 5	46
Maxwelton Rd. G33	J20	37
May Rd., Pais.	O 6	46
May Ter. G42	O16	51
Prospecthill Rd.		
May Ter., Giff.	Q14	62
Maybank La. G42	N16	51
Victoria Rd.		
Maybank St. G42	N16	51
Mayberry Cres. G32	L23	39
Mayberry Gdns. G32	L23	39
Maybole St. G53	P 9	60
Mayfield St. G20	G15	21
McAlpine St. G2	L16	35
McArthur St. G43	O14	50
Pleasance St.		
McAslin Ct. G4	K17	36
McAslin St. G4	K18	36
McCallum Av. G73	O19	53
McClue Rd., Renf.	H 7	17
McClue Rd., Renf.	H 7	17
McCracken Av., Renf.	J 7	31
McCreery St., Clyde.	F 8	17
McCulloch St. G41	M15	51
McDonald Av., John.	N09	43
McDonald Cres., Clyde.	F 8	17
McEwan St. G31	L20	37
McFarlane St. G4	L18	36
McFarlane St., Pais.	K 5	30
McGhee St., Clyde.	D 7	5
McGown St., Pais.	L 5	30
McGregor Av., Renf.	J 7	31
Porterfield Rd.		
McGregor Rd., Cumb.	C 2	70
McGregor St. G51	L12	33
McGregor St., Clyde.	F 8	17
McIntosh Ct. G31	K18	36
McIntosh St.		
McIntosh St. G31	K18	36
McIntyre Pl., Pais.	N 5	46
McIntyre St. G72	K15	35
McIntyre Ter. G72	P22	66
McIver St. G72	P23	67
McKay Cres., John.	N 1	44
McKenzie Av., Clyde.	D 7	5
McKenzie St., Pais.	L 5	30
McKerrel St., Pais.	L 7	31
McLaren Av., Renf.	J 8	31
Newmains Rd.		
McLaurin Cres., John.	N08	43
McLean Pl., Pais.	K 5	30
McLean Sq. G51	L14	34
McLean St., Clyde.	F 9	18
Wood Quad.		
McLennan St. G42	O16	51
McNair St. G32	L22	38
McNeil St. G5	M17	52
McNeill Av., Clyde.	E 9	6
McPhail St. G40	M18	52
McPhater St. G4	J16	35
Dunblane St.		
McPherson Dr., Udd.	Q28	69
Wordsworth Way		
McPherson St. G1	L17	36
High St.		
McTaggart Rd., Cumb.	D 2	70
Meadow La., Renf.	G 8	17
Meadow Rd. G11	J13	34
Meadow Vw., Cumb.	B 4	71
Meadowbank La., Udd.	P27	69
Meadowburn Av. G66	C24	13
Meadowburn, Bish.	D19	11
Meadowhead Av., Chr.	E27	15
Meadowpark St. G31	K19	37
Meadowside Av., John.	N 2	44
Meadowside St. G11	J13	34
Meadowside St., Renf.	G 8	17
Meadowwell St. G32	L22	38
Meadside Av. G78	M07	42
Meadside Rd., Kilb.	M07	42
Mears Way, Bish.	E20	11
Medlar Rd., Cumb.	C 4	71
Medwin St. G72	P24	67
Mill Rd.		
Medwyn St. G14	H11	19
Meek Pl. G72	P22	66
Meetinghouse La., Pais.	L 6	30
Moss St.		
Megan Gate G40	M18	52
Megan St.		
Megan St. G40	M18	52
Meikle Av., Renf.	J 8	31
Meikle Rd. G53	O11	49
Meiklerig Cres. G53	N11	49
Meikleriggs Dr., Pais.	N 4	45
Meiklewood Rd. G51	L11	33
Melbourne Av., Dalm.	C 5	4
Melbourne Ct., Giff.	Q14	62
Melbourne St. G31	L18	36
Meldon Pl. G51	K12	33
Meldrum Gdns. G41	N14	50
Meldrum St., Clyde.	F 9	18
Melford Av., Giff.	R14	62
Melford Way, Pais.	K 7	31
Knock Way		
Melfort Av., Clyde.	D 7	5
Melfort Av., Linw.	L 1	28
Melfort Gdns., John.	N08	43
Milliken Park Rd.		
Mellerstain Dr. G14	G 9	18
Melness Pl. G51	K11	33
Mallaig Rd.		
Melrose Av. G73	O19	53
Melrose Av., Bail.	L27	41
Melrose Av., Linw.	L 1	28
Melrose Av., Pais.	N 4	45
Melrose Gdns. G20	H15	21
Melrose Gdns., Udd.	N27	57
Lincoln Av.		
Melrose Pl., Blan.	R26	68
Melrose St. G4	J16	35
Queens Cres.		
Melvaig Pl. G20	G14	20
Melvick Pl. G51	K11	33
Mallaig Rd.		
Melville Ct. G1	K17	36
Brunswick St.		
Melville Gdns., Bish.	E19	11
Melville St. G41	M15	51
Memel St. G21	G18	22
Memus Av. G52	M11	49
Mennock Dr., Bish.	D19	11
Menock Rd. G44	P16	63
Menteith Av., Bish.	E19	11
Menteith Dr. G73	R20	65
Menteith Pl. G73	R20	65
Menzies Dr. G21	G19	23
Menzies Pl. G21	G19	23
Menzies Rd. G21	G19	23
Merchant La. G1	L17	36
Clyde St.		

Street	Grid	Page
Merchants Clo., Pais.	M07	42
Church St.		
Merchiston Av., Linw.	L 1	28
Merchiston St. G32	K21	38
Merkland Ct. G11	J13	34
Vine St.		
Merkland St. G11	J13	34
Merksworth Way, Pais.	K 5	30
Mosslands Rd.		
Merlewood Av. G71	Q28	69
Merlin Way, Pais.	K 7	31
Merrick Gdns. G51	L13	34
Merrick Ter., Udd.	O28	57
Merrick Way G73	Q19	65
Merryburn Av., Giff.	P14	62
Merrycrest Av., Giff.	Q14	62
Merrycroft Av., Giff.	Q14	62
Merryland Pl. G51	K14	34
Merryland St. G51	K13	34
Merrylee Cres., Giff.	P14	62
Merrylee Park Av., Giff.	Q14	62
Merrylee Park La., Giff.	Q14	62
Merrylee Park Ms., Giff.	Q14	62
Merrylee Rd. G43	P14	62
Merryton Av. G15	D10	6
Merryton Av., Giff.	Q14	62
Merryton Pl. G15	D10	6
Merryvale Av., Giff.	Q14	62
Merryvale Pl., Giff.	P14	62
Merton Dr. G52	L10	32
Meryon Gdns. G32	N23	55
Meryon Rd. G32	N23	55
Methil St. G14	H11	19
Methuen Rd., Renf.	J 7	31
Methven Av., Bear.	C13	8
Methven St. G31	M20	53
Methven St., Dalm.	D 6	4
Metropole La. G1	L16	35
Howard St.		
Michillen Rd., Bear.& G23	C14	8
Mid Cotts, Gart.	H26	26
Midcroft Av. G44	P17	64
Midcroft, Bish.	D18	10
Middle Hard St., Clyde.	B 8	5
Middlemuir Av., Lenz.	C23	13
Middlemuir Rd., Lenz.	C23	13
Middlerigg Rd., Cumb.	C 1	70
Middlesex St. G41	L15	35
Middleton Cres., Pais.	L 5	30
Middleton Rd., Linw.	K 2	28
Middleton St. G51	L14	34
Midland St. G1	L16	35
Midlem Dr. G52	L11	33
Midlem Oval G52	L11	33
Midlock St. G51	L14	34
Midlothian Dr. G41	N14	50
Midton Cotts., Chr.	E28	15
Midton St. G21	H18	22
Midwharf St. G4	J17	36
Migvie Pl. G20	G14	20
Wyndford Rd.		
Milan St. G41	M16	51
Milford St. G33	K22	38
Mill Cres. G40	M18	52
Mill Ct. G73	O19	53
Mill Pl., Linw.	L 1	28
Mill Rd. G72	Q23	67
Mill Rd., Barr.	Q 7	59
Mill Rd., Both.	R28	69
Mill Rd., Clyde.	F 8	17
Mill River, Lenz.	D23	13
Mill Road Gdns. G40	L18	36
Mill St. G40	M18	52
Mill St. G73	O19	53
Mill St., Pais.	M 6	46
Mill Vennel, Renf.	H 9	18
High St.		
Mill Way, Lenz.	C25	14
Millands Av., Blan.	R26	68
Millar St., Pais.	L 6	30
Millar Ter. G73	N19	53
Millarbank St. G21	H18	22
Millarston Av., Pais.	M 4	45
Millarston Dr., Pais.	M 4	45
Millbeg Cres. G33	L24	39
Millbeg Pl. G33	L24	39
Millbrae Cres. G13	F 8	17
Millbrae Cres. G42	O15	51
Millbrae Ct. G42	O15	51
Millbrae Rd.		
Millbrae Rd. G42	O15	51
Millbrix Av. G14	G10	18
Millburn Av. G73	P19	65
Millburn Av., Clyde.	F 9	18
Millburn Av., Renf.	H 9	18
Millburn Dr., Renf.	H 8	17
Millburn Rd., Renf.	H 8	17
Millburn St. G21	J19	37
Millburn Way, Renf.	H 9	18
Millcroft Rd. G73	N18	52
Millcroft Rd., Cumb.	C 3	71
Miller St. G1	K17	36
Miller St., Bail.	M25	56
Miller St., Clyde.	E 7	5
Miller St., John.	M 1	44
Millerfield Pl. G40	M19	53
Millerfield Rd. G40	M19	53
Millers Pl., Lenz.	D23	13
Millersneuk Av., Lenz.	D23	13
Millersneuk Cres. G33	G22	24
Millersneuk Dr., Lenz.	D23	13
Millerston St. G31	L19	37
Millford Dr., Linw.	L 1	28
Millgate Av., Udd.	O27	57
Millgate, Udd.	O27	57
Millholm Rd. G44	Q16	63
Millhouse Cres. G20	F14	20
Millhouse Dr. G20	F14	20
Milliken Dr., Kilb.	N08	43
Milliken Park Rd., Kilb.	N08	42
Millpond Dr. G40	L18	36
Millport Av. G44	O17	52
Millroad Dr. G40	L18	36
Millroad St. G40	L18	36
Millwood St. G41	O15	51
Milnbank St. G31	K19	37
Milncroft Rd. G33	J22	38
Milner Rd. G13	G12	19
Milngavie Rd., Bear.	D12	7
Milnpark Gdns. G41	L15	35
Milnpark St. G41	L15	35
Milovaig St. G23	E14	8
Milrig Rd. G73	O18	52
Milton Av. G72	P21	66
Milton Douglas Rd., Clyde.	C 7	5
Milton Dr., Bish.	F18	22
Milton Gdns., Udd.	O27	57
Milton Mains Rd., Dalm.	C 7	5
Milton St. G4	J17	35
Milverton Av., Bear.	C11	7
Milverton Rd., Giff. ✗	R13	62
Minard Rd. G41	N15	51
Minard Way, Udd.	O28	57
Newton Dr.		
Minerva St. G3	K15	35
Minerva Way G3	K15	35
Mingarry La. G20	H14	20
Clouston St.		
Mingary St. G20	H15	21
Mingulay Cres. G22	F17	22
Mingulay Pl. G22	F18	22
Mingulay St. G22	F17	22
Minmoir Rd. G53	O 9	48
Minstrel Rd. G13	E11	7
Minto Av. G73	Q20	65
Minto Cres. G52	L12	33
Minto St. G52	L12	33
Mireton St. G22	G16	21
Mirrlees Dr. G12	H14	20
Mirrlees La. G12	H14	20
Redlands Rd.		
Mitchell Av. G72	P24	67
Mitchell Av., Renf.	J 7	31
Mitchell Dr. G73	P19	65
Mitchell La. G1	K16	35
Buchanan St.		
Mitchell Rd., Cumb.	C 3	71
Mitchell St. G1	K16	35
Mitchell St., Coat.	M28	57
Mitchellhill Rd. G42	R18	64
Mitchison Rd., Cumb.	B 3	71
Mitre Ct. G14	H11	19
Mitre Rd.		
Mitre La. G14	H12	19
Mitre La. W. G14	H12	19
Mitre La.		
Mitre Rd. G14	H12	19
Moat Av. G13	F11	19
Mochrum Rd. G43	P15	63
Moffat Pl., Blan.	R26	68
Moffat St. G5	M17	52
Mogarth Av., Pais.	O 4	45
Amochrie Rd.		
Moidart Av., Renf.	H 7	17
Moidart Cres. G52	L12	33
Moidart Rd.		
Moidart Ct., Barr.	P 8	59
Moidart Pl. G52	L12	33
Moidart Rd.		
Moidart Rd. G52	L12	33
Moir La. G1	L17	36
Moir St.		
Moir St. G1	L17	36
Molendinar St. G1	L17	36
Mollinsburn St. G21	H18	22
Monach Rd. G33	K23	39
Monachie Gdns.	E20	11
Muirhead Way		
Moncrieff Av., Lenz.	C23	13
Moncrieff Gdns., Lenz.	C23	13
Moncrieff Pl. G4	J16	35
North Woodside Rd.		
Moncrieff St. G4	J16	35
Balnain St.		
Moncur St. G40	L18	36
Moness Dr. G52	M12	49
Monifieth Av. G52	M11	49
Monikie Gdns., Bish.	E20	11
Muirhead Way		
Monkcastle Dr. G73	P22	66
Monkland Av., Lenz.	C23	13
Monkland View Cres., Bail.	L28	41
Monkland Vw, Udd.	N28	57
Lincoln Av.		
Monksbridge Av. G13	E11	7
Monkscroft Av. G11	H13	20
Monkscroft Ct. G11	J13	34
Monkscroft Gdns. G11	H13	20
Monkscroft Av.		
Monkton Dr. G15	E10	6
Monmouth Av. G12	G13	20
Monreith Av., Bear.	E11	7
Monreith Rd. E. G44	P16	63
Monreith Rd. G43	P14	62
Monroe Dr., Udd.	N27	57
Monroe Pl., Udd.	N27	57
Montague La. G12	H13	20
Montague St. G4	J15	35
Montague Ter. G12	H13	20
Hyndland Rd.		
Montclair Pl., Linw.	L 1	28
Monteith Dr., Clark.	S15	63
Monteith Gdns., Clark.	S15	63
Monteith Pl. G40	L18	36
Monteith Pl., Blan.	R27	69
Monteith Row G40	L18	36
Monteith Row La. G40	L18	36
Monteith Pl.		
Montford Av. G44	O17	52
Montgomerie Gdns. G14	H11	19
Lennox Av.		
Montgomery Av., Pais.	K 7	31
Montgomery Dr., Giff.	R14	62
Montgomery Dr., Kilb.	M07	42
Meadside Av.		
Montgomery La. G42	O16	51
Somerville Dr.		
Montgomery Rd., Pais.	K 7	31
Montgomery St. G42	M18	52
London Rd.		
Montgomery St. G72	P24	67
Mill Rd.		
Montrave St. G52	M11	49
Montrave St. G73	N19	53
Montreal Ho., Dalm.	C 5	4
Perth Cres.		
Montron Dr. G15	E10	6
Moraine Av.		
Montrose Av. G32	N22	54
Montrose Av. G52	K 9	32
Montrose Dr., Bear.	B12	7
Montrose Gdns., Blan.	R26	68
Montrose Pl., Linw.	L 1	28
Montrose Rd., Pais.	O 3	45
Montrose St. G4	K17	36
Montrose St., Clyde.	E 7	5

Name	Ref	
Montrose Ter., Bish.	F20	23
Monymusk Gdns., Bish.	E20	11
Monymusk Pl. G15	C 9	6
Moodies Ct. G2	K16	35
Argyle St.		
Moodiesburn St. G33	J20	37
Moorburn Av., Giff.	Q13	62
Moore Dr., Bear.	D12	7
Moore St. G31	L19	37
Gallowgate		
Moorehouse Av. G13	G 9	18
Moorehouse Av., Pais.	N 4	45
Moorfoot Av. G46	Q13	62
Moorfoot Av., Pais.	N 5	46
Moorfoot St. G32	L21	38
Moorfoot, Bish.	E20	11
Moorhouse Av. G13	G 9	18
Moorhouse St., Barr.	R 8	59
Moorpark Av. G52	L 9	32
Moorpark Av., Chr.	F26	26
Moorpark Dr. G52	L10	32
Moorpark Pl. G52	L 9	32
Moorpark Sq., Renf.	J 7	31
Morag Av., Blan.	R26	68
Moraine Av. G15	E10	6
Moraine Circus G15	E10	6
Moraine Dr. G15	E10	6
Moraine Pl. G15	E10	6
Moraine Dr.		
Morar Cres., Bish.	E18	10
Morar Ct., Cumb.	DO	70
Morar Dr. G73	Q19	65
Morar Dr., Bear.	D13	8
Morar Dr., Cumb.	DO	70
Morar Dr., Linw.	L 1	28
Morar Dr., Renf.	H 7	17
Morar Rd. G52	L12	33
Morar Ter., Udd.	O28	57
Moravia Av., Both.	Q28	69
Moray Gate, Both.	Q27	69
Moray Gdns., Udd.	O27	57
Moray Pl. G41	N15	51
Moray Pl., Bish.	E20	11
Moray Pl., Linw.	L 1	28
Mordaunt St. G40	M19	53
Moredun Cres. G32	K23	39
Moredun Dr., Pais.	N 4	45
Moredun Rd., Pais.	N 4	45
Moredun St. G32	K23	39
Morefield Rd. G51	K11	33
Morgan Ms. G42	M16	51
Morion Rd. G13	F11	19
Morley St. G42	O16	51
Morna Pl. G41	J12	33
Victoria Park Dr. S.		
Morningside St. G33	K20	37
Morrin Path G21	H18	22
Crichton St.		
Morrin Sq. G4	K18	36
Collins St.		
Morrin St. G21	H18	22
Morris Pl. G40	L18	36
Morrison Quad., Clyde.	E 9	6
Morrison St. G5	L16	35
Morrison St., Clyde.	C 6	4
Morrisons Ct. G2	K16	35
Argyle St.		
Morriston Cres., Renf.	J 9	32
Morriston St. G72	P22	66
Mortimer St. G20	H15	21
Hotspur St.		
Morton Gdns. G41	N14	50
Morven Av., Bish.	E20	11
Morven Av., Blan.	R26	68
Morven Av., Pais.	O 5	46
Morven Dr., Linw.	L 1	28
Morven Gdns., Udd.	O27	57
Morven Rd. G72	Q21	66
Morven Rd., Bear.	C12	7
Morven St. G52	L12	33
Mosesfield St. G21	G18	22
Mosesfield St. G21	G18	22
Balgray Hill Rd.		
Moss Av., Linw.	L 1	28
Moss Dr., Barr.	P 7	59
Moss Heights Av. G52	L11	33
Moss Knowe, Cumb.	C 4	71
Moss Rd. G51	K11	33
Moss Rd., Chr.	F26	26

Name	Ref	
Moss Rd., Cumb.	B 4	71
Moss Rd., Lenz.	C23	13
Moss Sq. G33	J22	38
Moss St., Pais.	L 6	30
Moss-side Rd. G41	N15	51
Mossbank Dr. G33	H21	24
Mosscastle Rd. G33	J23	39
Mossend La. G33	K23	39
Mossend Rd., Pais.	K 5	30
Mosslands Rd.		
Mossend St. G33	K23	39
Mossgiel Av. G73	P19	65
Mossgiel Dr., Clyde.	D 8	5
Mossgiel Gdns., Udd.	O27	57
Mossgiel Pl. G73	P19	65
Mossgiel Rd. G43	P14	62
Mossgiel Rd., Cumb.	C 3	71
Mossgiel Ter., Blan.	R26	68
Mosshead Rd., Bear.	B13	8
Mossland Rd. G52	K 9	32
Mosslands Rd. G52	J 9	32
Mosslands Rd., Pais.	K 5	30
Mossneuk Dr., Pais.	O 5	46
Mosspark Av. G52	M12	49
Mosspark Boulevard G52	M12	49
Mosspark Dr. G52	M11	49
Mosspark La. G52	N12	49
Mosspark Dr.		
Mosspark Oval G52	M12	49
Mosspark Sq. G52	M12	49
Mossvale Cres. G33	J23	39
Mossvale La., Pais.	L 5	30
Mossvale Path G33	H23	25
Mossvale Rd. G33	H22	24
Mossvale Sq. G33	J23	39
Mossvale St., Pais.	K 5	30
Mossvale Ter., Chr.	D28	15
Mossvale Way G33	J23	39
Mossvale Wk. G33	J23	39
Mossview Cotts., Chr.	G26	26
Mossview Quad. G52	L11	33
Mossview Rd. G33	G24	25
Mote Hill Rd., Pais.	L 7	31
Moulin Circus G52	M10	48
Moulin Pl. G52	M10	48
Moulin Rd. G52	M10	48
Moulin Ter. G52	M10	48
Mount Annan Dr. G44	O16	51
Mount Harriet Av. G33	G24	25
Mount Harriet Dr. G33	G23	25
Mount St. G20	H15	21
Mount Stuart St. G41	O15	51
Mount Vernon Av. G32	M24	55
Mountainblue St. G31	L19	37
Mountblow Ho., Dalm.	C 5	4
Melbourne Av.		
Mountblow Rd., Dalm.	C 6	4
Mountgarrie Path G51	K11	33
Mountgarrie Rd.		
Mountgarrie Rd. G51	K11	33
Mowbray Av., Gart.	G27	27
Mowcraigs Ct., Clyde.	F 8	17
Yokerburn Ter.		
Moy St. G11	J14	34
Church St.		
Moyne Rd. G53	N10	48
Muckcroft Rd., Chr.	D25	14
Muir Park Ter. G64	F18	22
Muir St. G21	H18	22
Muir St., Bish.	E19	11
Muir St., Renf.	H 8	17
Muir Ter., Pais.	K 7	31
Muirbank Av. G73	O18	52
Muirbank Gdns. G73	O18	52
Muirbrae Rd. G73	Q19	65
Muirbrae Way G73	Q19	65
Muirburn Av. G44	Q15	63
Muirdrum Av. G52	M11	49
Muirdykes Av. G52	L10	32
Muirdykes Cres., Pais.	L 4	29
Muirdykes Rd. G52	L10	32
Muirdykes Rd., Pais.	L 4	29
Muiredge Ct., Udd.	P27	69
Watson St.		
Muiredge Ter., Bail.	M25	56
Muirend Av. G44	Q15	63
Muirend Rd. G44	Q15	63
Muirfield Cres. G23	E15	9

Name	Ref	
Muirfield Rd., Cumb.	A 3	71
Muirhead Ct., Bail.	M26	56
Muirhead Dr., Linw.	L 1	28
Muirhead Gdns., Bail.	M26	56
Muirhead Rd., Udd. & Bail.	M25	56
Muirhead St. G11	J13	34
Purdon St.		
Muirhead Way, Bish.	E20	11
Muirhill Av., G44	Q15	63
Muirhill Cres., G13	F10	18
Muirhouse St. G41	N15	51
Pollokshaws Rd.		
Muirkirk Dr. G13	F12	19
Muirpark Av., Renf.	J 8	31
Muirpark Dr., Bish.	F19	23
Muirpark St. G11	J13	34
Muirpark Ter., Bish.	F18	22
Crowhill Rd.		
Muirshiel Av. G53	P11	61
Muirshiel Cres. G53	P11	61
Muirside Av. G32	M24	55
Muirside Rd., Bail.	M25	56
Muirside St., Bail.	M25	56
Muirskeith Cres. G43	P15	63
Muirskeith Pl. G43	P15	63
Muirskeith Rd. G43	P15	63
Muirton Dr., Bish.	D18	10
Muirton Gdns., Bish.	D18	10
Muiryfauld Dr. G31	M21	54
Mulben Cres. G53	O 9	48
Mulben Pl. G53	O 9	48
Mulben Ter. G53	O 9	48
Mulberry Rd. G43	P14	62
Mull Av., Pais.	O 6	46
Mull Av., Renf.	J 8	31
Mull St. G21	J19	37
Mullardoch St. G23	E14	8
Rothes Dr.		
Mungo Pl., Udd.	N28	57
Lincoln Av.		
Munlochy Rd. G51	K11	33
Munro Ct., Clyde.	C 6	4
Gentle Row		
Munro La. G13	G12	19
Munro Pl. G13	G12	19
Munro Pl., Udd.	N28	57
Kirkwood Rd.		
Munro Rd. G13	G12	19
Munro Vw., Udd.	N28	57
Kirkwood Rd.		
Murano St. G20	H15	21
Murdoch St. G21	G18	22
Lenzie St.		
Muriel St., Barr.	Q 8	59
Murray Pl., Barr.	Q 8	59
Murray Rd., Both.	Q28	69
Murray St., Pais.	L 5	30
Murray St., Renf.	H 8	17
Murrayfield Dr., Bear.	E12	7
Murrayfield St. G32	K21	38
Murrayfield, Bish.	D19	11
Ashfield		
Murrin Av., Bish.	E20	11
Murroes Rd. G51	K11	33
Muslin St. G40	M18	52
Mybster Pl. G51	K11	33
Mybster Rd. G51	K11	33
Myers Cres., Udd.	P28	69
Myres Rd. G53	O11	49
Myreside Pl. G32	L20	37
Myreside St. G32	L20	37
Myrie Gdns., Bish.	E19	11
Myroch Pl. G34	J26	40
Myrtle Av., Lenz.	C23	13
Myrtle Hill La. G42	O17	52
Myrtle Hill Vw. G42	O17	52
Myrtle Pk. G42	N17	52
Myrtle Pl. G42	O17	52
Myrtle Rd., Dalm.	D 5	4
Myrtle Rd., Udd.	O28	57
Myrtle Sq., Bish.	F19	23
Myrtle St., Blan.	R26	68
Myrtle Wk. G72	P21	66
Naburn St. G5	M17	52
Nairn Av., Blan.	R26	68
Nairn Gdns., Bear.	D11	7
Nairn Pl., Dalm.	D 6	4
Dumbarton Rd.		

Name	Ref	Page
Nairn St. G3	J14	34
Nairn St., Dalm.	D 6	4
Nairnside Rd. G21	F20	23
Naismith St. G32	O23	55
Nansen St. G20	H16	21
Napier Ct., Old.K.	C 5	4
Freelands Rd.		
Napier Dr. G51	K13	34
Napier Gdns., Linw.	L 2	28
Napier Pl. G51	K13	34
Napier Pl., Old.K.	C 5	4
Old Dalnottar Rd.		
Napier Rd. G52	J 9	32
Napier Rd. G63	K13	34
Napier St. G51	K14	34
Napier St., Clyde.	F 8	17
Napier St., Linw.	L 2	28
Napier Ter. G51	K13	34
Napiershall La. G20	J15	35
Napiershall St.		
Napiershall Pl. G20	J15	35
Napiershall St.		
Napiershall St. G20	J15	35
Naseby Av. G11	H12	19
Nasmyth Rd. G52	K10	32
Nasmyth Rd. N. G52	K10	32
Nasmyth Rd. S. G52	K10	32
National Bank La. G2	K16	35
St. Vincent St.		
Navar Pl., Pais.	N 7	47
Naver St. G33	J21	38
Neilsland Oval G53	O11	49
Neilsland Sq. G53	N11	49
Neilston Av. G53	P11	61
Neilston Rd., Barr.	R 7	59
Neilston Rd., Pais.	M 6	46
Neilvaig Dr. G73	Q20	65
Nelson Mandela Pl. G1	K17	36
Buchanan St.		
Nelson Pl., Bail.	M25	56
Nelson St. G5	L16	35
Nelson St., Bail.	M25	56
Nelson Ter. G12	H15	21
Glasgow St.		
Neptune St. G51	K13	34
Nerston Av. G53	O11	49
Ness Av., John.	O08	43
Ness Dr., Blan.	R27	69
Ness Gdns., Bish.	E19	11
Ness Rd., Renf.	H 7	17
Ness St. G33	J21	38
Netham St. G51	K13	34
Nether Auldhouse Rd. G43	P13	62
Netherburn Av. G44	R15	63
Netherby Dr. G41	M14	50
Nethercairn Rd. G43	Q14	62
Nethercliffe Av. G44	R15	63
Nethercommon Harbour, Pais.	K 6	30
Nethercraig Cotts., Pais.	P 5	58
Glenfield Rd.		
Nethercraigs Dr., Pais.	O 5	46
Nethercraigs Rd., Pais.	O 4	45
Netherdale Dr., Pais.	M 9	48
Netherfield St. G31	L20	37
Netherhill Av. G44	R15	63
Netherhill Cres., Pais.	L 7	31
Netherhill Rd., Chr.	E27	15
Netherhill Rd., Pais.	L 6	30
Netherhouse Av., Lenz.	D24	13
Netherhouse Pl., Bail.	K27	41
Netherhouse Rd.		
Netherhouse Rd., Bail.	K26	40
Netherlee Rd., G44	Q15	63
Netherpark Av. G44	R15	63
Netherplace Cres. G53	O10	48
Netherplace Rd. G53	O10	48
Netherton Ct. G42	R18	64
Netherton Dr., Barr.	R 9	60
Netherton Rd. G13	F12	19
Netherton St. G13	F12	19
Crow Rd.		
Nethervale Av. G44	R15	63
Netherview Rd. G44	R16	63
Netherway G44	R15	63
Nethy Way, Renf.	J 9	32
Teith Av.		
Neuk Way G32	O23	55
Nevis Rd. G43	P13	62
Nevis Rd., Bear.	B10	6
Nevis Rd., Renf.	J 7	31
New City Rd. G4	J16	35
New Edinburgh Rd., Udd.	O27	57
New Inchinnan Rd., Pais.	K 6	30
New Kirk Pl., Bear.	C12	7
New Kirk Rd.		
New Kirk Rd., Bear.	C12	7
New Rd. G72	Q24	67
New Sneddon St., Pais.	L 6	30
New St., Clyde.	C 7	5
New St., Kilb.	M07	42
New St., Pais.	M 6	46
New Wynd G1	L17	36
Newark Dr. G41	M14	50
Newark Dr., Pais.	O 5	46
Newbattle Ct. G32	N22	54
Newbattle Gdns. G32	N22	54
Newbattle Pl. G32	N22	54
Newbattle Rd. G32	N22	54
Newbold Av. G21	F18	22
Newburgh St. G43	O14	50
Newcastleton Dr.	E15	9
Newcroft Dr. G44	P17	64
Newfield Pl. G73	O18	52
Newfield Pl., Thorn.	R12	61
Rouken Glen Rd.		
Newfield Sq. G53	P10	60
Newhall St. G40	M18	52
Newhaven Rd. G33	K22	38
Newhaven St. G32	K22	38
Newhills Rd. G33	K24	39
Newington St. G32	L21	38
Newlands Gdns., John.	N 2	44
Renshaw Rd.		
Newlands Rd. G43	P15	63
Newlands Rd., Udd.	O27	57
Newlandsfield Rd. G43	O14	50
Newluce Dr. G32	M23	55
Newmains Rd., Renf.	J 7	31
Newmill Rd. G21	G20	23
Newnham Rd., Pais.	M 9	48
Newshot Ct., Clyde.	F 8	17
Clydeholm Ter.		
Newshot Dr., Renf.	E 5	4
Newstead Gdns. G23	E15	9
Newton Av. G72	P23	67
Newton Av., Barr.	R 8	59
Newton Av., John.	M 3	45
Newton Brae G72	P24	67
Newton Dr., John.	M 3	45
Newton Dr., Udd.	O28	57
Newton Farm Rd. G72	O24	55
Newton Pl. G3	J15	35
Newton Rd., Lenz.	D24	13
Newton St., Pais.	M 5	46
Newton Station Rd. G72	P24	67
Newton Ter. G3	K15	35
Sauchiehall St.		
Newton Terrace La. G3	J15	35
Elderslie St.		
Newtongrange Av. G32	N22	54
Newtongrange Gdns. G32	N22	54
Newtyle Pl., Bish.	E20	11
Newtyle Rd., Pais.	M 8	47
Nicholas St. G1	K17	36
Nicholson La. G5	L16	35
Nicholson St.		
Nicholson St. G5	L16	35
Niddrie Rd. G42	N15	51
Niddrie Sq. G42	N15	51
Niddry St., Pais.	L 6	30
Nigel Gdns. G41	N14	50
Nigg Pl. G34	K25	40
Nightingale Pl., John.	O08	43
Nimmo Dr. G51	K12	33
Nisbet St. G31	L20	37
Nith Av., Pais.	N 3	45
Nith Dr., Renf.	J 9	32
Nith Pl., John.	O08	43
Nith St. G33	J20	37
Nithsdale Cres., Bear.	C11	7
Nithsdale Pl. G41	M15	51
Sheilds Rd.		
Nithsdale Rd. G41	M13	50
Nithsdale St. G41	N15	51
Nitshill Rd. G53	P 9	60
Niven St. G20	G14	20
Noldrum Av. G32	O23	55
Noldrum Gdns. G32	O23	55
Norbreck Dr., Giff.	Q14	62
Norby Rd. G11	H12	19
Norfield Dr. G44	O16	51
Norfolk Cres., Bish.	D18	10
Norfolk Ct. G5	L16	35
Norfolk La. G5	L16	35
Norfolk St.		
Norfolk St. G5	L16	35
Norham St. G41	N15	51
Norman St. G40	M18	52
Norse La. N. G14	H11	19
Ormiston Av.		
Norse La. S. G14	H11	19
Duncan Av.		
Norse La. S. G14	H11	19
Verona Av.		
Norse Rd. G14	H11	19
North Av. G72	P21	66
North Av., Clyde.	E 7	5
North Bank Pl., Clyde.	F 8	17
North Bank St.		
North Bank St., Clyde.	F 8	17
North Brae Pl., G13	F10	18
North British Rd., Udd.	P27	69
North Canalbank St. G4	J17	36
North Carbrain Rd., Cumb.	D 2	70
North Claremont St. G3	J15	35
North Corsebar Av., Pais.	N 5	46
North Court La. G1	K17	36
Buchanan St.		
North Croft St., Pais.	L 6	30
North Deanpark Av., Udd.	Q28	69
North Douglas St., Clyde.	F 8	17
North Dr. G1	L17	36
North Dr., Linw.	L 1	28
North Elgin St., Clyde.	F 8	17
North Erskine Pk., Bear.	C11	7
North Frederick St. G1	K17	36
North Gardner St. G11	H13	20
North Grange Rd., Bear.	C12	7
North Greenhill Rd., Pais.	K 5	30
North Hanover Pl. G4	J17	36
North Hanover St. G1	K17	36
North Iverton Park Rd., John.	M 1	44
North Lodge Rd., Renf.	H 8	17
North Moraine La. G15	E11	7
Moraine Av.		
North Park Av., Thorn.	Q12	61
North Park St. G20	H15	21
North Pl. G3	K15	35
North St.		
North Portland St. G1	K17	36
North Queen St. G2	K17	36
George Sq.		
North Rd., John.	NO9	43
North Spiers Wf. G4	J16	35
North St. G3	K15	35
North St., Clyde.	E 7	5
Dumbarton Rd.		
North St., Pais	L 6	30
North Vw., Bear.	E11	7
North Wallace St. G4	J17	36
North Way, Blan.	R26	68
North Woodside Rd. G20	H15	21
Northampton Dr. G12	G13	20
Northampton La. G12	G13	20
Northampton Dr.		
Northbank Av. G72	P23	67
Northbank St. G72	P23	67
Northcroft Rd. G21	H18	22
Northcroft Rd., Chr.	E27	15
Northgate Quad. G21	F20	23
Northgate Rd. G21	F20	23
Northinch St. G14	J11	33
Northland Dr. G14	G11	19
Northland La. G14	H11	19
Northland Dr.		
Northmuir Rd. G15	D10	6

Northpark Ter. G12 H15 21
Hamilton Dr.
Northumberland St. H15 21
G20
Norval St. G11 J13 34
Norwich Dr. G12 G13 20
Norwood Dr., Giff. R13 62
Norwood Ter. G12 J15 35
Southpark Av.
Norwood Ter., Udd. O28 57
Norwood, Bear. D12 7
Nottingham Av. G12 G13 20
Nottingham La. G12 G13 20
Northampton Dr.
Novar Dr. G12 H13 20
Novar Gdns., Bish. E18 10
Numrow Ct., Clyde. C 6 4
Nuneaton St. G40 M19 53
Nurseries Rd., Bail. L24 39
Nursery La. G41 N15 51
Nursery St. G41 N15 51
Pollokshaws Rd.
Nursery Street La. G41 N15 51
Nithsdale Dr.
Nutberry Ct. G42 N16 51

Oak Cres., Bail. M25 56
Oak Dr. G72 Q23 67
Oak Dr., Lenz. C22 12
Oak Pl., Bish. E19 11
Oak Rd., Dalm. C 6 4
Oak Rd., Pais. N 7 47
Oakbank Dr., Barr. S 8 59
Oakbank La. G20 H16 21
Oakbank Ter. G20 H16 21
Oakdene Av., Udd. O28 57
Oakfield Av. G12 J15 35
Oakfield Ter. G12 J15 35
Oakfield Av.
Oakhill Av., Bail. M24 55
Oakley Dr. G44 Q15 63
Oakley Ter. G31 K18 36
Oaks, The, John. N08 43
Oakshaw School Brae, L 5 30
Pais.
Oakshaw St., Pais. L 5 30
Oakshawhead, Pais. L 5 30
Oakwood Av., Pais. N 4 45
Oatfield St. G21 H19 23
Oban Ct. G22 H15 21
Oban Dr. G20 H15 21
Observatory La. G12 H14 20
Observatory Rd.
Observatory Rd. G12 H14 20
Ochil Dr., Barr. R 8 59
Ochil Dr., Pais. O 6 46
Ochil Pl. G32 M22 54
Ochil Rd., Bish. E20 11
Ochil Rd., Renf. J 7 31
Ochil St. G32 M22 54
OchiltreeAv. G13 F12 19
Ogilvie Pl. G31 M21 54
Ogilvie St. G31 M20 53
Old Bothwell Rd., Both. R28 69
Old Castle Rd. G44 P16 63
Old Dalmarnock Rd. M18 52
G40
Old Dalnottar Rd., C 5 4
Old K.
Old Dumbarton Rd. G3 J14 34
Old Edinburgh Rd., Udd. N27 57
Old Gartcosh Rd., Gart. G27 27
Old Glasgow Rd., Udd. O26 56
Old Govan Rd., Renf. H 9 18
Old Greenock Rd., Renf. F 5 16
Old Manse Rd. G32 L23 39
Old Mill Rd. G72 P23 67
Old Mill Rd., Both. R28 69
Old Mill Rd., Clyde. C 7 5
Old Mill Rd., Udd. P27 69
Old Rd., John. M 2 44
Old Renfrew Rd., Renf. J10 32
Old Roundknowe Rd., N26 56
Udd.
Old Rutherglen Rd. G5 M17 52
Old Shettleston Rd. G32 L21 38
Old Sneddon St., Pais. L 6 30·
Old St., Clyde. C 6 4
Old Wood Rd., Bail. M25 56
Old Wynd G1 L17 36

Oldhall Rd., Pais. L 8 31
Olifard Av., Udd. Q28 69
Oliphant Cres., Pais. O 3 45
Olive St. G33 H20 23
Olrig Ter. G41 M15 51
Shields Rd.
Olympia St. G40 L18 36
Onslow Dr. G31 K19 37
Onslow Rd., Clyde. E 8 5
Onslow Sq. G31 K19 37
Onslow Dr.
Oran Gate G20 H15 21
Oran Gdns. G20 G15 21
Oran Pl. G20 G15 21
Oran St. G20 G15 21
Oransay Cres., Bear. D13 8
Orcades Dr. G44 Q16 63
Orchard Av. G17 R28 69
Orchard Ct. G32 O22 54
Orchard Ct., Thorn. Q13 62
Orchard Dr. G73 O18 52
Orchard Dr., Giff. Q13 62
Orchard Gro., Giff. Q13 62
Orchard Park Av., Q13 62
Thorn. & Giff.
Orchard Pk., Giff. Q14 62
Orchard Pl., Lenz. B24 13
Orchard Sq., Pais. M 6 46
Orchard St., Pais. M 6 46
Orchard St., Renf. H 8 17
Orchardfield, Lenz. D23 13
Orchy Cres., Bear. E11 7
Orchy Cres., Pais. N 3 45
Orchy Ct., Clyde. C 8 5
Orchy Dr., Clark. R15 63
Orchy Gdns., Clark. R15 63
Orchy St. G44 P16 63
Oregon Pl. G5 M17 52
Orkney Pl. G51 K13 34
Orkney St.
Orkney St. G51 K13 34
Orleans Av. G14 H12 19
Orleans La. G14 H12 19
Ormiston Av. G14 H11 19
Ormiston La. G14 H11 19
Ormiston Av.
Ormiston La. S. G14 H11 19
Ormiston Av.
Ormonde Av. G44 Q15 63
Ormonde Cres. G44 Q15 63
Ormonde Ct. G44 Q15 63
Ormonde Dr. G44 Q15 63
Ornsay St. G22 F17 22
Orr Pl. G40 L18 36
Orr Sq. , Pais. L 6 30
Orr St. G40 L18 36
Orr St., Pais. L 6 30
Orr St., Pais. M 6 46
Orton St. G51 L13 34
Orwell St. G21 H18 22
Osborn Ter. G51 L13 34
Copland Rd.
Osborne St. G1 L17 36
Osborne St., Clyde. D 7 5
Osborne Vill. G44 P16 63
Holmhead Rd.
Osprey Dr., Udd. O28 57
Ossian Av., Pais. L 9 32
Auchmannoch Av.
Ossian Rd. G43 P15 63
Oswald La. G1 L16 35
Oswald St.
Oswald St. G1 L16 35
Otago La. G12 J15 35
Otago St.
Otago La. N. G12 J15 35
Otago St.
Otago St. G12 J15 35
Ottawa Cres., Dalm. D 5 4
Otter La. G11 J13 34
Castlebank St.
Otterburn Dr., Giff. R14 62
Otterswick Pl. G33 J23 39
Oval, The, Clark. R15 63
Overbrae Pl. G15 C 9 6
Overdale Av. G42 O15 51
Overdale Gdns. G42 O15 51
Overdale St. G42 O15 51
Overdale Vills. G42 O15 51
Overdale St.

Overlea Av. G73 P20 65
Overnewton Pl. G3 K14 34
Kelvinhaugh St.
Overnewton Sq. G3 K14 34
Overnewton St. G3 J14 34
Overton Cres., John. M 1 44
Overton Rd. G72 Q23 67
Overton Rd., John. N 1 44
Overton St. G72 Q23 67
Overtoun Ct., Dalm. D 6 4
Dunswin Av.
Overtoun Dr. G73 O19 53
Overtoun Dr., Dalm. D 6 4
Overtoun Rd., D 6 4
Dalm. & Clyde.
Overtown Av. G53 P10 60
Overtown St. G31 L19 37
Overwood Dr. G44 P17 64
Oxford Dr., Linw. L 1 28
Oxford La. G5 L16 35
Oxford Rd., Renf. H 8 17
Oxford St. G5 L16 35 ⚓
Oxgang Pl., Lenz. B24 13
Oxton Dr. G52 L10 32

Paisley Ct., Barr. Q 7 59
Paisley Rd.
Paisley Rd. G5 L15 35
Paisley Rd. W. G5 M10 48
Paisley Rd., Barr. Q 7 59
Paisley Rd., Renf. J 7 31
Palace St. G31 M20 53
Paladin Av. G13 F11 19
Palermo St. G21 H18 22
Palmer Av. G13 E11 7
Palmerston Pl. G3 K14 34
Kelvinhaugh St.
Palmerston Pl., John. O08 43
Pandora Way, Udd. O28 57
Hillcrest Rd.
Panmure St. G20 H16 21
Park Av. G3 J15 35
Park Av., Bar. R 7 59
Park Av., Bish. D19 11
Park Av., John. N 2 44
Park Av., Pais. N 5 46
Park Bank, Renf. E 4 4
Park Brae, Renf. F 5 16
Park Dr.
Park Burn Av., Lenz. B23 13
Park Circus C3 J15 35
Park Circus La. C3 J15 35
Lynedoch Pl.
Park Circus Pl. G3 J15 35
Park Cres., Bear. C10 6
Park Cres., Bish. D19 11
Park Cres., Renf. F 5 16
Park Ct., Bish. D19 11
Park Ct., Dalm. D 6 4
Little Holm
Park Ct., Giff. Q13 62
Belmont Dr.
Park Ct., Giff. R13 62
Park Dr. G3 J15 35
Park Dr. G73 O19 53
Park Dr., Renf. F 5 16
Park Gardens La. G3 J15 35
Park Gate G3 J15 35
Park Gdns. G3 J15 35
Park Gdns., Kilb. M07 42
Park Gro., Renf. F 5 16
Park La. G40 L18 36
Park La., Blan. S26 69
Park La., Pais. L 6 30
Netherhill Rd.
Park Pl. G20 F14 20
Fingal St.
Park Quad. G3 J15 35
Park Rd. G4 J15 35
Park Rd., Bail. L27 41
Park Rd., Bish. E19 11
Park Rd., Chr. F26 26
Park Rd., Dalm. D 6 4
Park Rd., Giff. R14 62
Park Rd., John. N09 43
Park Rd., Pais. N 5 46
Park Rd., Renf. F 5 16
Park Ridge, Renf. F 5 16
Park Dr.

Provand Hall Cres., Bail. M25 56
Provanhill Pl. G21 J18 36
Provanmill Pl. G33 H20 23
Provanmill Rd.
Provanmill Rd. G33 H20 23
Purdon St. G11 J13 34
Pykestone Rd. G33 J23 39

Quadrant Rd. G43 P15 63
Quadrant, The, Clark. S15 63
Quarrelton Rd.; John. N09 43
Quarry Av. G72 Q24 67
Quarry Pl. G72 P21 66
Quarry Rd., Barr. Q 7 59
Quarry Rd., Pais. N 6 46
Quarry St., John. M09 43
Quarrybank, John. N08 43
Quarrybrae St. G31 L21 38
Quarryknowe G73 O18 52
Quarryknowe St. G31 L21 38
Quarrywood Av. G21 H20 23
Quarrywood Rd. G21 H20 23
Quay Rd. G73 N19 53
Quay Rd. N. G73 N19 53
Quebec Ho., Dalm. C 5 4
Perth Cres.
Queen Arc. G2 K16 5
Renfrew St.
Queen Elizabeth Av. K 9 32
G52
Queen Elizabeth Sq. G5 M17 52
Queen Margaret Cres. H15 21
G12
Hamilton Dr.
Queen Margaret Ct. G20 H15 21
Queen Margaret Dr. G12 H14 20
Queen Margaret Dr. G20 H15 21
Queen Margaret Rd. G20 H15 21
Queen Mary Av. G42 N16 51
Queen Mary Av., Clyde. E 8 5
Queen Mary St. G40 M18 52
Queen Sq. G41 N15 51
Queen St. G1 K17 36
Queen St. G73 O19 53
Queen St., Pais. M 5 46
Queen St., Renf. H 8 17
Queen Victoria Dr. G14 H11 19
Queen Victoria Gate G13 G11 19
Queenbank Av., Gart. F27 27
Queens Av. G72 P22 66
Queens Cres. G4 J16 35
Queens Cres., Bail. L27 41
Queens Cross G20 H15 21
Queens Dr. G42 N15 51
Queens Dr., Cumb. A 2 70
Queens Drive La. G42 N16 51
Queens Gdns. G12 H14 20
Victoria Crescent Rd.
Queens Park Av. G42 N16 51
Queens Pl. G12 H14 20
Queens Rd., John. N 2 44
Queensborough Gdns. H13 20
G12
Queensferry St. G5 N18 52
Rosebery St.
Queenshill St. G21 H18 22
Queensland Ct. G52 L11 33
Queensland Dr. G52 L11 33
Queensland Gdns. G52 L11 33
Queensland La. E. G52 L10 32
Kingsland Dr.
Queensland La. W. G52 L11 33
Queensland Dr.
Queenslie Ind. Est. G33 K23 39
Queenslie St. G33 J20 37
Quentin St. G41 N15 51
Quinton Gdns., Bail. L25 40

Raasay Dr., Pais. O 5 46
Raasay Pl. G22 F17 22
Raasay St. G22 F17 22
Rachan St. G34 J26 40
Radnor St. G3 K15 35
Argyle St.
Radnor St., Clyde. D 7 5
Raeberry St. G20 H15 21
Raeswood Dr. G53 O 9 48
Raeswood Gdns. G53 O 9 48
Raeswood Pl. G53 O 9 48
Raeswood Rd. G53 O 9 48

Raglan St. G4 J16 35
Raith Av. G44 Q17 64
Raithburn Av. G45 Q17 64
Raithburn Rd. G45 Q17 64
Ralston Av., Pais. M 9 48
& G52
Ralston Ct. G52 M 9 48
Ralston Dr. G52 M 9 48
Ralston Path G52 M 9 48
Ralston Dr.
Ralston Pl. G52 M 9 48
Ralston Rd., Bear. C12 7
Ralston St., Barr. R 8 59
Ralston St., Pais. M 7 47
Seedhill Rd.
Ram St. G32 L21 38
Rampart Av. G13 F10 18
Ramsay Av., John. N09 43
Ramsay Cres., John. O07 42
Ramsay Pl., John. N09 43
Ramsay St., Dalm. D 6 4
Ranald Gdns. G73 Q20 65
Randolph Av., Clark. R15 63
Randolph Dr., Clark. R15 63
Randolph Gdns., Clark. R15 63
Randolph Rd. G11 H12 19
Randolph Ter. G72 P22 66
Hamilton Rd.
Ranfurley Rd. G52 L 9 32
Rankine Pl., John. M09 43
Rankine St.
Rankine St., John. M09 43
Rankines La., Renf. H 8 17
Manse St.
Rannoch Av., Bish. E19 11
Rannoch Dr., Bear. E13 8
Rannoch Dr., Renf. H 8 17
Rannoch Gdns., Bish. E19 11
Rannoch Pl., Pais. M 7 47
Rannoch Rd., John. N09 43
Rannoch Rd., Udd. N27 57
Rannoch' St. G44 P16 63
Ranza Pl. G33 H20 23
Raploch Av. G14 H10 18
Ratford St. G51 K13 34
Rathlin St. G51 K13 34
Ratho Dr. G21 G18 22
Rattray St. G32 M21 54
Ravel Row G31 L20 37
Ravelston Rd., Bear. E12 7
Ravelston St. G32 L20 37
Ravens Ct., Bish. F18 22
Lennox Cres.
Ravenscliffe Dr., Giff. Q13 62
Ravenscraig Av., Pais. N 5 46
Ravenscraig Dr. G53 P10 60
Ravenscraig Ter. G53 P11 61
Ravenshall Rd. G41 O14 50
Ravenstone Rd., Giff. Q14 62
Ravenswood Dr. G41 N14 50
Ravenswood Rd., Bail. L26 40
Rayne Pl. G15 D10 6
Red Rd. G21 H19 23
Red Road Ct. G21 H19 23
Redan St. G40 L18 36
Redcastle Sq. G33 J23 39
Redford St. G33 K20 37
Redgate Pl. G14 H10 18
Redhill Rd., Cumb. B 1 70
Redlands La. G12 H14 20
Kirklee Rd.
Redlands Rd. G12 H14 20
Redlands Ter. G12 H14 20
Redlands Terrace La. H14 20
G12
Julian Av.
Redlawood Pl., G72 P25 68
Redlawood Rd.
Redlawood Rd. G72 P25 68
Redmoss Rd., Clyde. C 6 4
Redmoss St. G22 G16 21
Rednock St. G22 H17 22
Redpath Dr. G52 L10 32
Redwood Pl., Lenz. C22 12
Redwood Rd., Cumb. C 4 71
Reelick Av. G13 F 9 18
Reelick Quad. G13 F 9 18
Regent Moray St. G3 J14 34
Regent Park Sq. G41 N15 51

Regent Park Ter. G41 N15 51
Pollokshaws Rd.
Regent Pl., Dalm. D 6 4
Regent Sq., Lenz. D23 13
Regent St., Dalm. D 6 4
Regent St., Pais. L 7 31
Regents Gate, Both. Q27 69
Regwood St. G41 O14 50
Reid Av., Bear. C13 8
Reid Av., Linw. L 1 28
Reid Pl. G40 M18 52
Muslin St.
Reid St. G40 M18 52
Reid St. G73 O19 53
Reidhouse St. G21 H18 22
Muir St.
Reids Row, Bail. M26 56
Reidvale St. G31 L18 36
Renfield St. G2 K16 35
Renfield St., Renf. H 8 17
Renfrew Ct. G2 K16 35
Renfrew St.
Renfrew La. G2 K16 35
Renfield St.
Renfrew Rd. G51 J10 32
Renfrew Rd., Pais. L 6 30
Renfrew Rd., Renf. J10 32
Renfrew St. G3 J16 35
Rennies Rd., Renf. F 5 16
Renshaw Dr. G52 L10 32
Renshaw Rd., John. N 2 44
Renton St. G4 J17 36
Renwick St. G41 L15 35
Scotland St.
Residdl Rd. G33 G24 25
Reston Dr. G52 L10 32
Revoch Dr. G13 F10 18
Rhannan Rd. G44 P16 63
Rhannan Ter. G44 P16 63
Rhindmuir Av., Bail. L26 40
Rhindmuir Rd., Bail. L26 40
Rhinds St., Coat. M28 57
Rhinsdale Cres., Bail. L26 40
Rhumhor Gdns., John. N08 43
Rhymer St. G21 J18 36
Rhymie Rd. G32 M23 55
Rhynie Dr. G51 L13 34
Riccarton St. G42 N17 52
Riccartsbar Av., Pais. M 5 46
Richard St., Renf. H 8 17
Richmond Ct. G73 O20 53
Richmond Dr. G72 P21 66
Richmond Dr. G73 O20 53
Richmond Dr., Bish. G64 D19 11
Richmond Dr., Linw. K 1 28
Richmond Gdns., Chr. E25 14
Richmond Pl. G73 O20 53
Richmond St. G1 K17 36
Richmond St., Clyde. E 8 5
Riddell St., Clyde. D 8 5
Riddon Av. G13 F 9 18
Riddrie Cres. G33 K21 38
Riddrie Knowes G33 K21 38
Riddrie Ter. G33 H20 23
Provanmill Rd.
Riddrievale Ct. G33 J21 38
Riddrievale St. G33 J21 38
Rigby St. G32 L20 37
Rigg Pl. G33 K24 39
Rigghead Av., Cumb. A 3 71
Riggside Rd. G33 J23 39
Riggside St. G33 J23 39
Riglands Way, Renf. H 8 17
Riglaw Pl. G13 F10 18
Rigmuir Rd. G51 L11 33 ↘
Rimsdale St. G40 L19 37
Ringford St. G21 H18 22
Ripon Dr. G12 G13 20
Risk St. G40 L18 36
Risk St., Dalm. D 6 4
Ristol Rd. G13 G11 19
Anniesland Rd.
Ritchie Cres., John. M 2 44
Ritchie Pk., John. M 1 44
Ritchie St. G5 M16 51
River Rd. G32 O22 54
River Rd. Mansion- O15 51
house Rd. G41
Riverbank St. G43 O14 50
Riverford Rd. G43 O14 50

Riverford Rd. G73	N20	53
Riversdale Cotts G14	G 9	18
Dumbarton Rd.		
Riversdale La. G14	G 9	18
Dumbarton Rd.		
Riverside Ct. G44	R16	63
Riverside Pk. G44	R16	63
Linnpark Av.		
Riverside Pl. G72	P24	67
Riverside Rd. G43	O15	51
Riverview Av. G5	L16	35
West St.		
Riverview Dr. G5	L16	35
Riverview Gdns. G5	L16	35
Riverview Pl. G5	L16	35
Roaden Av., Pais.	O 3	45
Roaden Rd., Pais.	O 3	45
Roadside, Cumb.	A 3	71
Robb St. G21	H18	22
Robert Burns Av., Clyde.	D 8	5
Robert St. G51	K13	34
Robert Templeton Dr. G72	P23	67
Roberton Av. G41	N14	50
Roberts St., Dalm.	D 6	4
Robertson La. G2	K16	35
Robertson St.		
Robertson St. G2	K16	35
Robertson St., Barr.	Q 7	59
Robertson Ter., Bail.	L26	40
Edinburgh Rd.		
Robin Way G32	O23	55
Robroyston Av. G33	H21	24
Robroyston Rd. G33	G21	24
Robslee Cres., Thorn.	Q13	62
Robslee Dr., Giff.	Q13	62
Robslee Rd., Thorn.	R13	62
Robson Gro. G42	N16	51
Rock Dr. G78	N 7	42
Rock St. G4	H16	21
Rockall Dr. G44	Q17	64
Rockbank Pl. G40	L19	37
Broad St.		
Rockbank Pl., Clyde.	C 7	5
Glasgow Rd.		
Rockbank St. G40	L19	37
Rockburn Dr., Clark.	S14	62
Rockcliffe St. G40	M18	52
Rockfield Pl. G21	G20	23
Rockfield Rd. G21	G20	23
Rockmount Av., Barr.	R 8	59
Rockmount Av., Thorn.	Q13	62
Rockwell Av., Pais.	O 5	46
Rodger Dr. G73	P19	65
Rodger Pl., Ruth.	P19	65
Rodil Av. G44	Q17	64
Rodney St. G4	J16	35
Roebank Dr., Barr.	R 8	59
Roebank St. G31	K19	37
Roffey Park Rd., Pais.	L 8	31
Rogart St. G40	L18	36
Rogerfield Rd., Bail.	K26	40
Rokeby Ter. G12	H14	20
Great Western Rd.		
Roman Av. G15	E10	6
Roman Av., Bear.	C12	7
Roman Ct., Bear.	C12	7
Roman Dr., Bear.	C12	7
Roman Gdns., Bear.	C12	7
Roman Rd., Bear.	C12	7
Roman Rd., Clyde.	C 7	5
Romney Av. G44	P17	64
Rona St. G21	J19	37
Rona Ter. G72	Q21	66
Ronaldsay Dr., Bish.	E20	11
Ronaldsay Pl., Cumb.	D 1	70
Ronaldsay St. G22	F17	22
Ronay St. G22	F17	22
Rooksdell Av., Pais.	N 5	46
Rose Cotts. G13	G12	19
Crow Rd.		
Rose Dale, Bish.	F19	23
Rose Knowe G73	N18	52
Rose St. G3	K16	35
Rosebank Av., Blan.	R27	69
Rosebank Dr. G72	Q23	67
Rosebank Ter., Bail.	M27	57
Roseberg Pl., Clyde.	E 7	5
Kilbowie Rd.		

Rosebery Pl., Clyde.	E 7	5
Miller St.		
Rosebery St. G5	N18	52
Rosedale Av. G78	O 2	44
Rosedale Dr., Bail.	M25	56
Rosedale Gdns. G20	F14	20
Rosefield Gdns., Udd.	O27	57
Roselea Gdns. G13	F12	19
Roselea Pl., Blan.	R26	68
Rosemont Meadows, Both.	R27	69
Rosemount Cres. G21	J19	37
Rosemount St. G21	J18	36
Rosemount Ter. G51	L15	35
Paisley Rd. W.		
Rosemount, Cumb.	A 2	70
Rosevale Rd., Bear.	D12	7
Rosevale St. G11	J13	34
Rosewood Av., Pais.	N 4	45
Rosewood St. G13	F12	19
Roslea Dr. G31	K19	37
Roslyn Dr., Bail.	L27	41
Rosneath St. G51	K13	34
Ross Av., Renf.	J 7	31
Ross Hall Pl., Renf.	H 8	17
Ross St. G40	L17	36
Ross St., Pais.	M 7	47
Rossendale Rd. G43	O14	50
Rosshall Av., Pais.	M 8	47
Rosshill Av. G52	L 9	32
Rosshill Rd. G52	L 9	32
Rossie Cres., Bish.	F20	23
Rosslea Dr., Giff.	R14	62
Rosslyn Av. G73	O19	53
Rosslyn Rd., Bear.	C10	6
Rosslyn Ter. G12	H14	20
Horslethill Rd.		
Rostan Rd. G43	P14	62
Rosyth Rd. G5	N18	52
Rosyth St. G5	N18	52
Rotherwick Dr., Pais.	M 9	48
Rotherwood Av. G13	E11	7
Rotherwood Av., Pais.	O 3	45
Rotherwood La. G13	E11	7
Rotherwood Av.		
Rotherwood Pl. G13	F11	19
Rothes Dr. G23	E14	8
Rothes Pl. G23	E14	8
Rothlinn Av., Lenz.	B24	13
Rottenrow East G4	K17	36
Rottenrow G4	K17	36
Roual Ter., Pais.	L 7	31
Greenlaw Av.		
Rouken Glen Rd., Thorn. & Giff.	R12	61
Roukenburn St. G46	Q12	61
Roundhill Dr., John.	M 3	45
Rowallan Gdns. G11	H13	20
Rowallan La. E. G11	H13	20
Churchill Dr.		
Rowallan La. G11	H13	20
Churchill Dr.		
Rowallan Rd., Thorn.	R12	61
Rowallan Ter. G33	H22	24
Rowan Av., Renf.	H 8	17
Rowan Cres., Lenz.	C23	13
Rowan Dr., Dalm.	D 6	4
Rowan Gate, Pais.	N 6	46
Rowan Gdns. G41	M13	50
Rowan Gdns. G71	Q28	69
Rowan Pl. G72	P22	66
Allison Dr.		
Rowan Pl. G72	P23	67
Caledonian Circuit		
Rowan Pl., Blan.	S26	68
Rowan Rd. G41	M13	50
Rowan Rd., Cumb.	B 4	71
Rowan Rd., Linw.	K 1	28
Rowan St., Pais.	N 6	46
Rowand Av. Giff.	R14	62
Rowandale Av., Bail.	M25	56
Rowanlea Av. G78	O 3	45
Rowanlea Dr., Giff.	Q14	62
Rowanpark Dr., Barr.	P 7	59
Rowans Gdns., Both.	Q28	69
Rowans, The, Bish.	E18	10
Rowantree Av. G73	P19	65
Rowantree Gdns. G73	P19	65
Rowantree Rd., John.	N09	43
Rowchester St. G40	L19	37

Rowena Av. G13	E11	7
Roxburgh Dr., Bear.	B12	7
Roxburgh La. G12	H14	20
Saltoun St.		
Roxburgh Rd., Pais.	O 2	44
Roxburgh St. G12	H14	20
Roy St. G21	H17	22
Royal Bank Pl. G1	K17	36
Buchanan St.		
Royal Cres. G3	J15	35
Royal Cres. G42	N16	51
Royal Exchange Bldgs. G1	K17	36
Royal Exchange Sq.		
Royal Exchange Ct. G1	K17	36
Queen St.		
Royal Exchange Sq. G1	K17	36
Royal Inch Cres., Renf.	G 8	17
Campbell St.		
Royal Inch Ter., Renf.	G 8	17
Royal Ter. G3	J15	35
Royal Ter. G42	N16	51
Queens Dr.		
Royal Terrace La. G3	J15	35
North Claremont St.		
Royston Hill, G21	J18	36
Royston Rd. G21	J18	36
Royston Sq. G21	J18	36
Rozelle Av. G15	D10	6
Rubislaw Dr., Bear.	D12	7
Ruby St. G40	M19	53
Ruchazie Pl. G33	K21	38
Ruchazie Rd. G32	L21	38
Ruchill Pl. G20	G15	21
Ruchill St. G20	G15	21
Ruel St. G44	O16	51
Rufflees Av., Barr.	Q 8	59
Rugby Av. G13	F10	18
Rullion Pl. G33	K21	38
Rumford St. G40	M18	52
Rupert St. G4	J15	35
Rushyhill St. G21	H19	23
Cockmuir St.		
Ruskin La. G12	H15	21
Ruskin Pl. G12	H14	20
Great Western Rd.		
Ruskin Sq., Bish.	E19	11
Ruskin Ter. G12	H15	21
Ruskin Ter. G73	N19	53
Russel Pl., Linw.	L 1	28
Gilmerton Rd.		
Russell Cres. G81	B 6	4
Russell Cres., Bail.	M26	56
Russell Dr., Bear.	C12	7
Russell Rd., Clyde.	C 6	4
Russell St. G11	J13	34
Vine St.		
Russell St., John.	M 1	44
Russell St., Pais.	K 5	30
Rutaerford Av., Chr. & Waterside	C25	14
Chryston Rd.		
Rutherford La. G2	K16	35
Hope St.		
Rutherglen Rd. G5	L17	36
Ruthven Av., Giff.	R14	62
Ruthven La. G12	H14	20
Downside St.		
Ruthven Pl., Bish.	F20	23
Ruthven St. G12	H14	20
Rutland Cres. G51	L15	35
Rutland La. G51	L15	35
Govan Rd.		
Rutland Pl. G51	L15	35
Ryan Rd., Bish.	E19	11
Ryan Way G73	Q20	65
Rye Cres. G21	G20	23
Rye Rd. G21	G20	23
Rye Way, Pais.	N 3	45
Ryebank Rd. G21	G20	23
Ryecroft Dr., Bail.	L25	40
Ryedale Pl., G15	D10	6
Ryefield Av., John.	N08	43
Ryefield Pl., John.	N08	43
Ryefield Rd. G21	G19	23
Ryehill Gdns. G21	G20	23
Ryehill Pl. G21	G20	23
Ryehill Rd. G21	G20	23
Ryemount Rd. G21	G20	23
Ryeside Rd. G21	G19	23

Rylands Dr. G32   M24 55
Rylands Gdns. G32   M24 55
Rylees Cres. G52   K 9 32
Rylees Pl. G52   L 9 32
Rylees Rd. G52   L 9 32
Ryvra Rd. G13   G11 19

Sackville Av. G13   G12 19
Sackville La. G13   G12 19
  Sackville Av.
Saddell Rd. G15   D10 6
St. Abbs Dr., Pais.   N 4 45
St. Andrews Av., Bish.   E18 10
St. Andrews Av., Both.   R28 69
St. Andrews Cres. G41   M15 51
St. Andrews Cres., Pais.   J 5 30
St. Andrews Cross G41   M16 51
St. Andrews Dr., Pais.   J 6 30
St. Andrews Drive G41   N14 50
St. Andrews La. G1   L17 36
  Gallowgate
St. Andrews Rd. G41   M15 51
St. Andrews Rd., Renf.   J 8 31
St. Andrews Sq. G1   L17 36
St. Andrews St. G1   L17 36
St. Anns Dr., Giff.   R14 62
St. Blanes Dr. G73   P18 64
St. Boswells Cres., Pais.   N 4 45
St. Brides Av., Udd.   O29 57
St. Brides Rd. G43   O14 50
St. Brides Way, Both.   Q28 69
St. Catherines Rd.,   R14 62
  Giff.
St. Clair Av., Giff.   Q14 62
St. Clair St. G20   J15 35
  Woodside Rd.
St. Conval Pl. G43   O13 50
  Shawbridge St.
St. Cyrus Gdns., Bish.   E20 11
St. Cyrus Rd., Bish.   E19 11
St. Enoch Sq. G1   L16 35
St. Enoch Wynd G2   K16 35
  Argyle St.
St. Fillans Rd. G33   G23 25
St. Georges Cross G3   J16 35
St. Georges Pl. G2   J16 35
  St. Georges Rd.
St. Georges Rd. G3   J16 35
St. Germains, Bear.   D12 7
St. Helena Cres.,   C 8 5
  Clyde.
St. Ives Rd., Chr.   D27 15
St. James Av., Pais.   K 4 29
St. James Pl., Pais.   L 6 30
  Love St.
St. James Rd. G4   K17 36
St. James St., Pais.   L 6 30
St. Johns Ct. G41   M15 51
St. Johns Quad. G41   M15 51
St. Johns Rd. G41   M15 51
St. Johns Ter. G12   J15 35
  Southpark Av.
St. Jospehs Pl. G40   L18 36
  Abercromby St.
St. Kenneth Dr. G51   K12 33
St. Kilda Dr. G14   H12 19
St. Leonards Dr., Giff.   Q14 62
St. Margarets Pl. G1   L17 36
  Bridgegate
St. Mark St. G32   L21 38
St. Marnock St. G40   L19 37
St. Marys La. G2   K16 35
  West Nile St.
St. Marys Rd., Bish.   E18 10
St. Mirren St., Pais.   M 6 46
St. Monance St. G21   G18 22
St. Mungo Av. G4   K17 36
St. Mungo Pl. G4   K17 36
St. Mungo St., Bish.   F18 22
St. Mungos Rd. G67   C 2 70
St. Ninian St. G5   L17 36
St. Ninians Cres., Pais.   N 6 46
  Rowan St.
St. Ninians Rd., Pais.   N 6 46
St. Peters La. G2   K16 35
  Blythswood St.
St. Peters St. G4   J16 35
St. Ronans Dr. G41   N14 50
St. Ronans Dr. G73   P20 65
St. Stephens Av. G73   Q20 65

St. Stephens Cres. G73   Q21 66
St. Valleyfield St. G21   H18 22
  Ayr St.
St. Vincent Cres. G3   K14 34
St. Vincent Cres. La. G3   K15 35
  Corunna St.
St. Vincent La. G2   K16 35
  Hope St.
St. Vincent Pl. G1   K17 36
St. Vincent St. G2   K15 35
St. Vincent Ter. G3   K15 35
Salamanca St. G31   L20 37
Salen St. G52   L12 33
Salisbury Pl. G12   H14 20
  Great Western Rd.
Salisbury Pl., Dalm.   C 6 4
Salisbury St. G5   M16 51
Salkeld St. G5   M16 51
Salmona St. G22   H16 21
Saltaire Av., Udd.   P28 69
Salterland Rd. G53   P 9 60
Saltmarket G1   L17 36
Saltmarket Pl. G1   L17 36
  King St.
Saltoun Gdns. G12   H14 20
  Roxburgh St.
Saltoun La. G12   H14 20
  Ruthven St.
Saltoun St. G12   H14 20
Salvia St. G72   P21 66
Sanda St. G20   H15 21
Sandaig Rd. G33   L24 39
Sandbank Av. G20   G14 20
Sandbank Dr. G20   G14 20
Sandbank St. G20   G14 20
Sandbank Ter. G20   F14 20
Sandeman St. G11   J12 33
Sandend Rd. G53   O10 48
Sanderling Pl., John.   O08 43
Sandfield St. G20   G15 21
  Maryhill Rd.
Sandford Gdns., Bail.   L25 56
  Scott St.
Sandgate Av. G32   M23 55
Sandhaven Rd. G53   O10 48
Sandholes, Pais.   M 5 46
Sandholm Pl. G14   G 9 18
Sandholm Ter. G14   G 9 18
Sandiefauld St. G5   M17 52
Sandiefield Rd. G5   M17 52
Sandielands Av., Renf.   F 5 16
Sandilands St. G32   L22 38
Sandmill St. G21   J19 37
Sandra Rd., Bish.   E20 11
Sandringham Dr., John.   O 1 44
  Glamis Av.
Sandringham La. G12   H14 20
  Kersland St.
Sandwood Cres. G52   L10 32
  Sandwood Rd.
Sandwood Path G52   L10 32
Sandwood Rd. G52   L10 32
Sandy La. G11   J13 34
  Crawford St.
Sandy Rd. G11   J13 34
Sandy Rd., Renf.   J 8 31
Sandyford Pl. G3   K15 35
  Sauchiehall St.
Sandyford Place La. G3   J15 35
  Elderslie St.
Sandyford Rd., Renf.   K 7 31
Sandyford St. G3   K14 34
Sandyhills Cres. G32   M22 54
Sandyhills Dr. G32   M22 54
Sandyhills Gro. G32   N23 55
  Hamilton Rd.
Sandyhills Pl. G32   M22 54
Sandyhills Rd. G32   M22 54
Sandyknowes Rd.,   D 3 71
  Cumb.
Sanguhar Gdns., Blan.   R25 68
Sanilands St. G32   L22 38
  Annick St.
Sannox Gdns. G31   K19 37
Saracen Gdns. G22   G17 22
Saracen Head La. G1   L17 36
  Gallowgate
Saracen St. G22   H17 22
Sardinia La. G12   H14 20
  Great George St.

Sardinia Ter. G12   H14 20
  Cecil St.
Saucel Lonend, Pais.   M 6 46
Saucel St., Pais.   M 6 46
Saucelhill Ter., Pais.   M 6 46
Sauchenhall Rd., Chr.   C27 15
Sauchiehall St. G3   K15 35
Saughs Av. G33   G21 24
Saughs Dr. G33   G21 24
Saughs Gate G33   G21 24
Saughs Pl. G33   G21 24
Saughs Rd. G33   G21 24
Saughton St. G32   K21 38
Savoy Arcade G40   M18 52
  Main St.
Savoy St. G40   M18 52
Sawfield Pl. G4   J16 35
  Garscube Rd.
Sawmill Rd. G11   J12 33
  South St.
Sawmillfield St. G4   J16 35
Saxon Rd. G13   F11 19
Scadlock Rd., Pais.   L 4 29
Scalpay Pl. G22   F17 22
Scalpay St. G22   F17 22
Scapa St. G23   F15 21
Scapa St. G40   M19 53
  Springfield Rd.
Scaraway Dr. G22   F17 22
Scaraway Pl. G22   F17 22
Scaraway St. G22   F17 22
Scaraway Ter. G22   F17 22
Scarba Dr. G43   P13 62
Scarrell Dr. G45   Q19 65
Scarrell Rd. G45   Q19 65
Scarrell Ter. G45   Q19 65
Schaw Ct., Bear.   C11 7
Schaw Dr., Bear.   C12 7
Schaw Rd., Pais.   L 7 31
Schipka Pass. G1   L17 36
  Gallowgate
School Av. G72   P22 66
School Rd. G33   G24 25
School Rd., Pais.   L 9 32
School Wynd, Pais.   L 6 30
Schoolfield La., Bish.   E19 11
Scioncroft Av. G73   O20 53
Scone St. G21   H17 22
Sconser St. G23   E15 9
Scorton Gdns., Bail.   M24 55
Scotland St. G5   L15 35
Scotland St. W. G5   L14 34
Scotsblair Av., Lenz.   C23 13
Scotsburn Rd. G21   H20 23
Scotstoun Mill Rd. G11   J14 34
  Patrick Bridge St.
Scotstoun Pl. G14   H11 19
  Scotstoun St.
Scotstoun St. G14   H11 19
Scott Av., John.   O09 43
Scott Dr., Bear.   C11 7
Scott Rd. G52   K 9 32
Scott St. G3   J16 35
Scott St., Bail.   M25 56
Scott St., Dalm.   D 6 4
Scotts Rd., Pais.   M 8 47
Sea Path G53   P 9 60
Sea Pl. G53   P 9 60
Seafar Rd., Cumb.   D 2 70
Seafield Dr. G73   Q20 65
Seaforth Cres., Barr.   Q 7 59
Seaforth La., Chr.   E28 15
  Burnbrae Av.
Seaforth Rd. G52   K10 32
Seaforth Rd. N. G52   K10 32
Seaforth Rd. S. G52   K10 32
Seaforth Rd., Clyde.   E 7 5
Seagrove St. G32   L20 37
Seamill St. G53   P 9 60
Seamore St. G20   J15 35
Searfe Av., Linw.   L 1 28
  Killin Dr.
Seath Rd. G73   N19 53
Seath St. G42   N17 52
Seaward La. G41   L15 35
  Seaward St.
Seaward St. G41   L15 35
Second Av. G33   G22 24
Second Av. G44   P16 63
Second Av., Bear.   D13 8

Street	Ref	
Second Av., Clyde.	D 7	5
Second Av., Lenz.	E23	13
Second Av., Renf.	J 8	31
Second Av., Udd.	N27	57
Second Gdns. G41	M13	50
Second St., Udd.	O27	57
Seedhill Rd., Pais.	M 6	46
Seggielea La. G13	G11	19
Helenburgh Dr.		
Seggielea Rd. G13	G11	19
Seil Dr. G44	Q17	64
Selborne Pl. G13	G12	19
Selborne Rd.		
Selborne Place La. G13	G12	19
Selborne Rd.		
Selborne Rd. G13	G12	19
Selby Gdns. G32	L24	39
Selkirk Av. G52	M11	49
Selkirk Av., Pais.	N 4	45
Selkirk Dr. G73	O20	53
Sella Rd., Bish.	E20	11
Selvieland Rd. G52	L 9	32
Semple Pl., Linw.	K 1	28
Seres Rd., Clark.	S14	62
Sergeantlaw Rd., Pais.	P 4	45
Seton Ter. G31	K18	36
Settle Gdns., Bail.	M24	55
Seven Sisters, Lenz.	C24	13
Seventh Av., Udd.	O27	57
Seyton Av., Giff.	R14	62
Shaftesbury St., Dalm.	E 6	4
Shafton Pl. G13	F12	19
Shafton Rd. G13	F12	19
Shaftsbury St. G3	K15	35
Shakespeare Av., Clyde.	D 6	4
Shakespeare St. G20	G15	21
Shamrock Cotts. G13	G12	19
Crow Rd.		
Shamrock St. G4	J16	35
Shandon St. G51	K14	34
Govan Rd.		
Shandwick St. G34	K25	40
Shanks Av., Barr.	R 8	59
Shanks Cres., John.	N09	43
Shanks St. G20	G15	21
Shannon St. G20	G15	21
Shapinsay St. G22	F17	22
Sharp St. G51	K13	34
Sharrocks St. G51	L14	34
Clifford St.		
Shaw Pl., Linw.	L 1	28
Shaw St. G51	K13	34
Shawbridge St. G43	O14	50
Shawfield Dr. G5	N18	52
Shawfield Rd. G5	N18	52
Shawhill Rd. G43	O14	50
Shawholm Cres. G43	O13	50
Shawlands Arcade G41	O15	51
Shawlands Sq. G41	O15	51
Shawmoss Rd. G41	N14	50
Shawpark St. G20	G15	21
Shearer La. G5	L15	35
Shearer Rd. G5	L15	35
Sheepburn Rd., Udd.	O27	57
Sheila St. G33	H21	24
Sheldrake Pl., John.	O08	43
Shelley Ct. G12	G13	20
Shelley Rd.		
Shelley Dr., Clyde.	D 7	5
Shelley Rd. G12	G12	19
Shelly Dr., Udd.	Q28	69
Sheppard St. G21	H18	22
Cowlairs Rd.		
Sherbrooke Av. G41	M14	50
Sherbrooke Dr. G41	M14	50
Sherburn Gdns., Bail.	M24	55
Sheriff Park Av. G73	O19	53
Sherwood Av., Pais.	L 7	31
Sherwood Av., Udd.	P28	69
Sherwood Dr. G46	Q13	62
Sherwood Pl. G15	D10	6
Shetland Dr. G44	Q17	64
Shettleston Rd. G31	L20	37
Shettleston Sheddings G31	L21	38
Shiel Ct., Barr.	P 7	59
Shiel Rd., Bish.	E19	11
Shieldaig Dr. G73	Q19	65
Shieldaig Rd. G22	F16	21
Shieldburn Rd. G51	K11	33
Shieldhall Gdns. G51	K11	33
Shieldhall Rd. G51	K11	33
Shields Rd. G41	L15	35
Shilford Av. G13	F10	18
Shillay St. G22	F18	22
Shilton Dr. G53	P10	60
Shinwell Av., Clyde.	E 8	5
Shipbank La. G1	L17	36
Clyde St.		
Shiskine Dr. G20	F14	20
Shore St. G40	N18	52
Shortbridge St. G20	G15	21
Shanks St.		
Shortroods Av., Pais.	K 6	30
Shortroods Cres., Pais.	K 6	30
Shortroods Rd., Pais.	K 5	30
Shotts St. G33	K23	39
Shuna Pl. G20	G15	21
Shuna St. G20	G15	21
Shuttle La. G1	K17	36
George St.		
Shuttle St. G1	K17	36
Shuttle St., Kilb.	M07	42
Shuttle St., Pais.	M 6	46
Sidelaw Av., Barr.	R 8	59
Ochil Dr.		
Sidland Rd. G21	G20	23
Sidlaw Rd., Bear.	B10	6
Sielga Pl. G34	K25	40
Siemens Pl. G21	J19	37
Siemens St. G21	J19	37
Sievewright St. G73	N20	53
Hunter Rd.		
Silk St., Pais.	L 6	30
Silkin Av., Clyde.	E 8	5
Silverburn St. G33	K21	38
Silverdale St. G31	M20	53
Silverfir St. G5	M17	52
Silvergrove St. G40	L18	36
Silverwells Cres., Both.	R28	69
Silverwells, Both.	R28	69
Simons Cres., Renf.	G 8	17
Simpson Ct., Udd.	P27	69
Simpson St. G20	H15	21
Simshill Rd. G44	Q16	63
Sinclair Av., Bear.	C12	7
Sinclair Dr. G42	O15	51
Sinclair St., Clyde.	F 8	17
Singer Rd., Dalm. & Clyde.	D 6	4
Singer St., Clyde.	D 7	5
Sir Michael Pl., Pais.	M 5	46
Sixth Av., Renf.	J 8	31
Sixth St., Udd.	N27	57
Skaethorn Rd. G20	F13	20
Skaterig La. G13	G12	19
Skaterigg Rd. G13	G12	19
Crow Rd.		
Skelbo Path G34	J26	40
Auchengill Rd.		
Skelbo Pl. G34	J26	40
Skene Rd. G51	L13	34
Skerray Quad. G22	F17	22
Skerray St. G22	F17	22
Skerryvore Pl. G33	K22	38
Skerryvore Rd. G33	K22	38
Skibo Dr. G46	Q12	61
Skibo La. G46	Q12	61
Skipness Dr. G51	K12	33
Skirsa Ct. G23	F16	21
Skirsa Pl. G23	F15	21
Skirsa Sq. G23	F15	21
Skirsa St. G23	F15	21
Skirving St. G41	O15	51
Skye Av. G67	J 8	31
Skye Cres., Pais.	O 5	46
Skye Ct., Cumb.	D 1	70
Skye Dr., Cumb.	D 1	70
Skye Gdns., Bear.	C10	6
Skye Pl., Cumb.	D 1	70
Skye Rd. G73	Q20	65
Skye Rd., Cumb.	D 1	70
Skye St. G20	F14	20
Bantaskin St.		
Slakiewood Av., Gart.	F27	27
Slatefield St. G31	L19	37
Sleads St. G41	L15	35
Sloy St. G22	H17	22
Smeaton St. G20	G15	21
Smith Cres., Clyde.	C 7	5
Smith St. G14	J12	33
Smith Ter. G73	N19	53
Smithhills St., Pais.	L 6	30
Smiths La., Pais.	L 6	30
Smithy Ends, Cumb.	A 3	71
Smithycroft Rd. G33	J21	38
Snaefell Av. G73	Q20	65
Snaefell Cres. G73	P20	65
Society St. G31	L19	37
Soho St. G40	L19	37
Sollas Pl. G13	F 9	18
Solway Pl., Chr.	E26	14
Solway Rd., Bish.	E20	11
Solway St. G40	N18	52
Somerford Rd., Bear.	E12	7
Somerled Av., Renf.	J 7	31
Somerset Pl. G3	J15	35
Somerset Place Meuse G3	J15	35
Eldersie St.		
Somervell St. G72	P21	66
Somerville Dr. G42	O16	51
Somerville St., Clyde.	E 7	5
Sorby St. G31	L20	37
Sorn St. G40	M19	53
Souter La., Clyde.	D 8	5
South Annandale St. G42	N16	51
South Av., Clyde.	E 7	5
South Av., Pais.	O 6	46
South Av., Renf.	H 8	17
South Bank St., Clyde.	F 8	17
South Brook St., Clyde.	D 6	4
South Campbell St., Pais.	M 6	46
South Carbrain Rd., Cumb.	D 3	71
South Carmyle Av.	O22	54
South Chester St. G32	L22	38
South Cotts. G14	J12	33
Curle St.		
South Croft St., Pais.	L 6	30
Lawn St.		
South Crosshill Rd., Bish.	E19	11
South Deanpark Av., Udd.	R28	69
South Douglas St., Clyde.	F 8	17
South Dr., Linw.	L 1	28
South Elgin Pl., Clyde.	F 8	17
South Elgin St.		
South Elgin St., Clyde.	F 8	17
South Erskin Pk., Bear.	C11	7
South Exchange Ct. G1	K17	36
Queen St.		
South Frederick St. G1	K17	36
South Frederick St. G1	K17	36
Ingram St.		
South Hill Av. G73	P20	65
South Moraine La. G15	E11	7
Moraine Av.		
South Muirhead Rd., Cumb.	C 3	71
South Park Dr., Pais.	N 6	46
South Portland St. G5	L16	35
South Scott St., Bail.	M25	56
South Spiers Wf. G4	J16	35
South St. G14	H10	18
South Vesalius St. G32	L22	38
South Vw., Blan.	R26	68
South Vw., Dalm.	D 6	4
South Vw., Lenz.	E23	13
Gadloch Av.		
South Wardpark Ct., Cumb.	A 4	71
Wardpark Rd.		
South Wardpark Pl., Cumb.	A 4	71
South William St., John.	N09	43
South Woodside Rd. G4	J15	35
Southampton Dr. G12	G13	20
Southbank St. G31	L20	37
Sorby St.		
Southbar Av. G13	F10	18
Southbrae Dr. G13	G11	19
Southbrae La. G13	G12	19
Milner Rd.		
Southcroft Rd. G73	N18	52
Southcroft St. G51	K13	34

Street	Grid		Street	Grid		Street	Grid	
Strenabey Av. G73	Q20	65	Symington Dr., Clyde.	E 7	5	Telford Pl. G67	D 3	71
Striven Gdns. G20	H15	21	Syriam Pl. G21	H18	22	Telford Rd., Cumb.	D 3	71
Stroma St. G21	J19	37	*Syriam St.*			Templar Av. G13	E11	7
Stromness St. G5	M16	51	Syriam St. G21	H18	22	Temple Gdns. G13	F12	19
Strone Rd. G33	K22	38				Temple Pl. G13	F12	19
Stronend St. G22	G16	21	Tabard Pl. G13	F11	19	Temple Rd. G13	F13	20
Stronsay Pl., Bish.	E20	11	Tabard Pl. N. G13	F11	19	Templeland Av. G53	N11	49
Stronsay St. G21	J19	37	*Tabard Rd.*			Templeland Rd. G53	N11	49
Stronvar Dr. G14	H10	18	Tabard Pl. S. G13	F11	19	Templeton St. G40	L18	36
Stronvar La. G14	H10	18	*Tabard Rd.*			Tennant La., Pais.	L 4	29
Larchfield Av.			Tabard Rd. G13	F11	19	Tennant St., Renf.	G 8	17
Strowan Cres. G32	M22	54	Tabernacle La. G72	P22	66	*Campbell St.*		
Strowan St. G32	M22	54	Tabernacle St. G72	P22	66	Tennant St., Renf.	H 8	17
Struan Av., Giff.	Q13	62	Tain Pl. G34	K26	40	Tennyson Dr. G31	M21	54
Struan Gdns. G44	P16	63	Tait Av., Barr.	Q 8	59	Tern Pl., John.	O08	43
Struan Rd. G44	P16	63	Talbot Dr. G13	G10	18	Terrace Pl. G72	P24	67
Struie St. G34	K25	40	Talbot Pl. G13	G10	18	Terregles Av., G41	N14	50
Stuart Av. G73	P19	65	Talbot Ter., G13	G10	18	Terregles Cres. G41	N14	50
Stuart Dr., Bish.	F18	22	Talbot Ter., Udd.	O27	57	Terregles Dr. G41	N14	50
Succoth St. G13	F12	19	Talisman Rd. G13	G11	19	Teviot Av., Bish.	D19	11
Suffolk St. G40	L18	36	Talisman Rd., Pais.	O 3	45	Teviot Av., Pais.	O 3	45
Kent St.			Talla Rd. G52	L10	32	Teviot Cres., Bear.	E11	7
Sugworth Av., Bail.	L25	40	Tallant Rd. G15	D10	6	Teviot St. G3	K14	34
Sumburgh St. G33	K21	38	Tallant Ter. G15	D11	7	Teviot Ter. G20	H15	21
Summer St. G40	L18	36	Tallisman, Clyde.	E 8	5	*Sanda St.*		
Summerfield Cotts. G14	J12	33	*Onslow Rd.*			Teviot Ter., John.	O08	43
Smith St.			Tambowie St. G13	F12	19	Thane Rd. G13	G11	19
Summerfield Pl. G40	M19	53	Tamshill St. G20	G15	21	Tharsis St. G21	J18	36
Ardenlea St.			Tamworth St. G40	L19	37	Third Av. G33	G22	24
Summerfield St. G40	N19	53	*Rimsdale St.*			Third Av. G44	O16	51
Summerhill Rd. G15	D10	6	Tanar Av., Renf.	J 9	32	Third Av., Lenz.	E23	13
Summerlee Rd., Thorn.	Q12	61	Tanar Way, Renf.	J 9	32	Third Av., Renf.	J 8	31
Summerlee St. G33	K23	39	Tandlehill Rd., Kilb.	N07	42	Third Gdns. G41	M13	50
Summertown Rd. G51	K13	34	Tanera Av. G44	Q17	64	Third St., Udd.	O27	57
Sunart Av., Renf.	H 7	17	Tanfield Av. G32	K23	39	Thirdpart Cres. G13	F 9	18
Sunart Gdns., Bish.	E19	11	Tanfield Pl. G32	K23	39	Thistle Bank, Lenz.	D23	13
Sunart Rd. G52	L12	33	*Tanfield Av.*			Thistle Cotts. G13	G12	19
Sunart Rd., Bish.	E19	11	Tankerland Rd. G44	P16	63	*Crow Rd.*		
Sunningdale Rd. G23	F14	20	Tanna Dr. G52	M12	49	Thistle St. G5	L17	36
Sunningdale Wynd,	Q27	69	Tannadice Av. G52	M11	49	Thistle St., Pais.	N 5	46
Both.			Tannahall Rd., Pais.	L 4	29	Thomas Muir Av., Bish.	F19	23
Sunnybank St. G40	M19	53	Tannahall Ter., Pais.	L 4	29	Thomas St., Pais.	M 4	45
Sunnylaw Dr. G78	N 4	45	Tannahill Cres., John.	N09	43	Thompson Pl., Clyde.	C 8	5
Sunnylaw St. G22	H16	21	Tannahill Rd. G43	P15	63	Thomson Av., John.	M09	43
Sunnyside Av., Udd.	P27	69	Tannoch Dr. G67	D 3	71	Thomson Dr., Bear.	C12	7
Sunnyside Dr. G15	E10	6	Tannoch Pl. G67	D 3	71	Thomson St. G31	L19	37
Sunnyside Dr., Bail.	L27	41	Tannock St. G22	H16	21	Thomson St., John.	N09	43
Sunnyside Pl. G15	E10	6	Tantallon Dr., Pais.	N 4	45	Thomson St., Renf.	J 8	31
Sunnyside Dr.			Tantallon Rd. G41	O15	51	Thorn Brae, John.	M 1	44
Sunnyside Pl., Barr.	R 7	59	Tantallon Rd., Bail.	M25	56	Thorn Dr. G73	Q20	65
Sunnyside Rd., Pais.	N 5	46	Tanzieknowe Av. G72	Q22	66	Thorn Dr., Bear.	C11	7
Surrey La. G5	M16	51	Tanzieknowe Dr. G72	Q22	66	Thorn Rd. G46	P13	62
Pollokshaws Rd.			Tanzieknowe Pl. G72	Q22	66	Thorn Rd., Bear.	C11	7
Sussex St. G41	L15	35	Tanzieknowe Rd. G72	Q22	66	Thorn St. G11	J13	34
SutcliffeRd. G13	F12	19	Taransay St. G51	K13	34	*Dumbarton Rd.*		
Sutherland Av. G41	M14	50	Tarbert Av., Blan.	R26	68	Thornbank St. G3	J14	34
Sutherland Av., Bear.	B12	7	Tarbolton Dr., Clyde.	D 8	5	*Yorkhill Parade*		
Sutherland Dr., Giff.	R14	62	Tarbolton Rd. G43	P14	62	Thornbridge Av. G12	G14	20
Sutherland Rd., Clyde.	E 7	5	Tarbolton Rd., Cumb.	C 3	71	*Balcarres Av.*		
Sutherland St., Pais.	L 5	30	Tarbolton Sq., Clyde.	D 8	5	Thornbridge Av., Bail.	L25	40
Swan La. G4	J17	36	*Tarbolton Dr.*			*Bannercross Dr.*		
Swan Pl., John.	O08	43	Tarfside Av. G52	M11	49	Thornbridge Gdns., Bail.	L25	40
Swan St., Clyde.	D 6	4	Tarfside Gdns. G52	M11	49	Thornbridge Rd., Bail.	L25	40
Swanston St. G40	N19	53	Tarfside Oval G52	M11	49	Thorncliffe Gdns. G4	N15	51
Sween Dr. G44	Q16	63	Tarland St. G51	L12	33	Thorncliffe La. G41	M15	51
Sweethope Pl., Booth.	Q28	69	Tarras Dr., Renf.	J 9	32	Thorncroft Dr. G44	Q17	64
Swift Pl., John.	O08	43	Tarras Pl. G72	P23	67	Thornden Cotts. G14	G 9	18
Swindon St., Dalm.	D 6	4	Tassie St. G41	O14	50	*Dumbarton Rd.*		
Swinton Cres., Bail.	L26	40	Tattershall Rd. G33	J23	39	Thornden La. G14	G 9	18
Swinton Cres., Coat.	M28	57	Tavistock Dr. G43	P14	62	*Dumbarton Rd.*		
Swinton Dr. G52	L10	32	Tay Av., Pais.	N 3	45	Thorndene, John.	M 1	44
Swinton Pl. G52	L10	32	Tay Av., Renf.	H 9	18	Thornhill Av., Blan.	S26	68
Swinton Rd., Bail.	L25	40	Tay Cres. G33	J21	38	Thornhill Av., John.	N 1	44
Switchback Rd., Bear.	E12	7	Tay Cres., Bish.	E19	11	Thornhill Dr. G78	N 1	44
Sword St. G31	L18	36	Tay Pl., John.	O08	43	Thornhill Path G31	L20	37
Swordale Path G34	K25	40	Tay Rd., Bear.	E11	7	*Beattock St.*		
Swordale Pl.			Tay Rd., Bish.	E19	11	Thornhill Path G31	L20	37
Swordale Pl.	K25	40	Taylor Av. G78	M06	42	*Grier Path*		
Sycamore Av., John.	N 1	44	Taylor Pl. G4	K17	36	Thornhill, John.	N 1	44
Sycamore Av., Lenz.	C23	13	Taylor St. G4	K17	36	Thorniewood Gdns.,	O28	57
Sycamore Dr., Dalm.	D 7	5	Taylor St., Clyde.	F 8	17	Udd.		
Sydenham La. G12	H13	20	Taymouth St. G32	M22	54	Thorniewood Rd., Udd.	O27	57
Crown Rd. S.			Taynish Dr. G44	Q17	64	Thornlea Dr., Giff.	Q14	62
Sydenham Rd. G12	H14	20	Tealing Av. G52	M11	49	Thornley Av. G13	G10	18
Sydney Ct. G2	K16	35	Tealing Cres. G52	M11	49	Thornliebank Rd. G46	Q13	62
Argyle St.			Teasel Av. G53	Q10	60	Thornliebank Rd.,	R11	61
Sydney St. G31	L18	36	Teith Av., Renf.	J 9	32	Thorn., Giff.& G43		
Sydney St., Dalm.	D 5	4	Teith Dr., Bear.	D11	7	Thornly Park Av., Pais.	O 6	46
Sylvania Way S., Clyde.	E 7	5	Teith Pl. G72	P23	67	Thornly Park Dr., Pais.	O 6	46
Sylvania Way, Clyde.	E 7	5	Teith St. G33	J21	38	Thornly Park Rd., Pais.	O 6	46

Street	Grid	Page
Thornside Rd., John.	M 1	44
Thornton La. G20	F15	21
Thornton St. G20	F15	21
Thorntree Way, Udd.	Q28	69
Thornwood Av. G11	J13	34
Thornwood Av., Lenz.	C22	12
Thornwood Cres. G11	H11	19
Thornwood Dr.		
Thornwood Dr., G11	J12	33
Thornwood Dr., Pais.	N 4	45
Thornwood Gdns. G11	J13	34
Thornwood Pl. G11	H13	20
Thornwood Quadrant	H11	19
G11		
Thornwood Dr.		
Thornwood Rd. G11	J12	33
Thornwood Ter. G11	J12	33
Thornyburn Dr., Bail.	M26	56
Thornyburn Pla., Bail.	M26	56
Three Ell Rd. G51	K14	34
Govan Rd.		
Threestonehill Av. G32	L22	38
Thrums Av., Bish.	E20	11
Thrums Gdns., Bish.	E20	11
Thrush Pl., John.	O08	43
Thrushcraig Cres., Pais.	N 6	46
Thurso St. G11	J14	34
Dumbarton Rd.		
Thurston Rd. G52	L10	32
Tibbermore Rd. G11	H13	20
Tillet Oval, Pais.	K 5	30
Tillie St. G20	H15	21
Tillycairn Dr. G33	J23	39
Tilt St. G33	J21	38
Tintagel Gdns., Chr.	D27	15
Tinto Dr., Barr.	S 8	59
Tinto Rd. G43	P14	62
Tinto Rd., Bear.	C10	6
Tinto Rd., Bish.	E20	11
Fintry Cres.		
Tinto Sq., Renf.	J 7	31
Ochil Rd.		
Tinwald Av. G52	L 9	32
Tinwald Path G52	L10	32
Tiree Av., Pais.	O 5	46
Tiree Av., Renf.	J 8	31
Tiree Ct., Cumb.	D 1	70
Tiree Dr., Cumb.	D 1	70
Tiree Gdns., Bear.	C10	6
Tiree Rd., Cumb.	D 1	70
Tiree St. G21	J20	37
Tirry Way, Renf.	J 9	32
Morriston Cres.		
Titwood Rd. G41	N14	50
Tiverton Av. G32	M23	55
Tobago Pl. G40	L18	36
Tobago St. G40	L18	36
Tobermory Rd. G73	R20	65
Todburn Dr., Pais.	O 6	46
Todd St. G31	K20	37
Todholm Rd., Pais.	N 7	47
Todholm Ter., Pais.	N 7	47
Toll La. G51	L14	34
Paisley Rd. W.		
Tollcross Rd. G31	L20	37
Tolsta St. G23	E15	9
Tontine La. G1	L17	36
Bell St.		
Tontine Pl. G73	Q21	66
Toppersfield, John.	O08	43
Torbreck St. G52	L12	33
Torbrex Rd., Cumb.	C 3	71
Torburn Av., Giff.	Q13	62
Tordene Path, Cumb.	B 1	70
Torgyle St. G23	E14	8
Tormore St. G51	L11	33
Tormusk Dr. G45	Q19	65
Tormusk Rd. G45	Q19	65
Torness St. G11	J14	34
Torogay Pl. G22	F18	22
Torogay St. G22	F17	22
Torogay Ter. G22	F17	22
Toronto Wk. G32	O23	55
Torphin Cres. G32	L22	38
Torphin Wk. G32	L22	38
Torr Rd., Bish.	E20	11
Torr St. G22	H17	22
Torran Rd. G33	K24	39
Torrance Rd., Bish.	C20	11
Torrance St. G21	H18	22
Torridon Av. G41	M13	50
Torrin Rd. G23	E14	8
Torrington Av., Giff.	S13	62
Torrington Cres. G32	M23	55
Torrisdale St. G42	N15	51
Torryburn Rd. G21	H20	23
Torwood La., Chr.	E28	15
Burnbrae Av.		
Toryglen Rd. G73	O18	52
Toryglen St. G5	N17	52
Toward Rd. G33	K23	39
Tower Av., Barr.	Q 8	59
Tower Cres., Renf.	J 7	31
Tower Dr., Renf.	J 7	31
Tower Pl. G20	G14	20
Glenfinnan Dr.		
Tower Pl., John.	N 1	44
Tower Rd., John.	N09	43
Tower St. G41	L15	35
Tower Ter., Pais.	M 5	46
Towerhill Rd. G13	E11	7
Towerhill Ter. G21	H19	23
Broomfield Rd.		
Towerside Cres. G53	N10	48
Towerside Rd. G53	N10	48
Towie Pl., Udd.	P27	69
Townhead Rd., Gart.	J28	41
Townhead Ter., Pais.	M 5	46
Townmill Rd. G31	K18	36
Townsend St. G4	J17	36
Tradeston St. G5	L16	35
Trafalgar St. G40	M18	52
Trafalgar St., Dalm.	D 6	4
Trainard Av. G32	M21	54
Tranent Pl. G33	K21	38
Traquair Av. G78	O 3	45
Traquair Dr. G52	M10	48
Treeburn Av., Giff.	Q13	62
Trees Park Av., Barr.	Q 7	59
Trefoil Av. G41	O14	50
Tresta Rd. G23	F16	21
Trident Way, Renf.	J 8	31
Newmains Rd.		
Trinity Av. G52	M11	49
Trinity Dr. G72	Q23	67
Trinley Brae G13	E11	7
Trinley Rd. G13	E11	7
Tronda Pl. G33	K24	39
Tronda Rd. G33	K24	39
Trondra Path G33	K24	39
Trongate G1	L17	36
Troon St. G40	M19	53
Trossachs Rd. G73	R20	65
Trossachs St. G20	H16	21
Troubridge Av., John.	O07	42
Troubridge Cres. G78	N07	42
Troubridge Cres., John.	O07	42
Truce Rd. G13	F10	18
Truro Rd., Chr.	D27	15
Tryst Rd. G67	C 2	70
Tudor La. S. G14	H11	19
Orleans Av.		
Tudor Rd. G14	H12	19
Tudor St., Bail.	M24	55
Tufthill Av., Bish.	E18	10
Tufthill Gdns., Bish.	E18	10
Tullis Ct. G40	M18	52
Tullis St. G40	M18	52
Tulloch St. G44	P16	63
Tullochard Pl. G73	Q20	65
Tummel St. G33	J21	38
Tummel Way, Pais.	N 3	45
Tunnel St. G3	K15	35
Turnberry Av. G11	H13	20
Turnberry Dr. G72	P18	64
Turnberry Gdns., Cumb.	A 2	70
Turnberry Pl. G73	P18	64
Turnberry Rd., G11	H13	20
Turnberry Wynd, Both.	Q27	69
Turnbull St. G1	L17	36
Turnlaw Rd. G72	R22	66
Turnlaw St. G5	M17	52
Turret Cres. G13	F11	19
Turret Rd. G13	F11	19
Turriff St. G5	M16	51
Tweed Av., Pais.	N 3	45
Tweed Cres. G33	J21	38
Tweed Cres., Renf.	H 9	18
Tweed Dr., Bear.	D11	7
Tweed Pl., John.	O08	43
Tweedsmuir Cres., Bear.	B12	7
Tweedsmuir Rd. G52	M10	48
Tweedmuir, Bish.	E20	11
Tweedvale Av. G14	G 9	18
Tweedvale Pl. G14	G 9	18
Twinlaw St. G34	J26	40
Tylnley Rd., Pais.	L 8	31
Tyndrum Rd., Bear.	C13	8
Tyndrum St. G4	J17	36
Tyne St. G14	J11	33
Tynecastle Cres. G32	K22	38
Tynecastle Pl. G32	K22	38
Tynecastle St. G32	K22	38
Tynwald Av. G73	Q20	65
Uddingston Rd., Both.	Q28	69
Uig Pl. G33	L24	39
Uist Cres. G33	H24	25
Uist St. G51	K12	33
Ulundi Rd., John.	N09	43
Ulva St. G52	L12	33
Unden Pl. G13	F12	19
Underwood La., Pais.	L 5	30
Underwood Rd. G41	O15	51
Tantallon Rd.		
Underwood Rd. G73	P20	65
Underwood Rd., Pais.	L 5	30
Union Pl. G1	K16	35
Gordon St.		
Union St. G1	K16	35
Union St., Clyde.	F 8	17
Union St., Pais.	N 6	46
Unity Pl. G4	J16	35
St. Peters St.		
University Av. G12	J14	34
University Gdns. G12	J14	34
University Pl. G12	J14	34
Unsted Pl., Pais.	M 7	47
Uphall Pl. G33	K21	38
Upland Rd. G14	H11	19
Upper Bourtree Ct. G73	Q20	65
Upper Bourtree Dr.		
Upper Bourtree Dr. G73	Q19	65
Upper Glenburn Rd.,	C11	7
Bear.		
Ure Pl. G4	K17	36
Montrose St.		
Urquhart Cres., Renf.	J 8	31
Urrdale Rd. G41	L13	34
Usmore Pl. G33	L24	39
Vaila Pl. G23	F15	21
Vaila St.		
Vaila St. G23	F15	21
Vale Wk., Bish.	F20	23
Valetta Pl., Dalm.	D 5	4
Valeview Ter. G42	O16	51
Vallay St. G22	F17	22
Valley Vw. G72	P23	67
Caledonian Circuit		
Valleyfield St. G21	H18	22
Van St. G31	L20	37
Vancouver Pl., Dalm.	D 5	4
Vancouver Rd. G14	H11	19
Vanguard St., Clyde.	E 8	5
Vanguard Way, Renf.	J 8	31
Varna La. G14	H12	19
Varna Rd. G14	H12	19
Veitchs Ct., Clyde.	C 6	4
Dumbarton Rd.		
Vennacher Rd., Renf.	H 7	17
Vennard Gdns. G41	N15	51
Vere St. G22	H17	22
Vermont Av. G73	O19	53
Vermont St. G41	L15	35
Vernon Dr., Linw.	L 1	28
Verona Av. G14	H11	19
Vesalius St. G32	L22	38
Vicarfield Pl. G51	K13	34
Vicarfield St.		
Vicarfield St. G51	K13	34
Vicarland Pl. G72	Q22	66
Vicarland Rd. G72	P22	66
Vicars Wk. G72	P22	66
Victoria Circus G12	H14	20
Victoria Cres. G12	H14	20
Dowanside Rd.		
Victoria Cres. La. G12	H14	20
Victoria Crescent Rd.		
Victoria Cres. Rd. G12	H14	20

Street	Ref
Victoria Cross G42	N16 51
Victoria Rd.	
Victoria Dr. E., Renf.	J 8 31
Victoria Dr., Renf.	H 7 17
Victoria Park Corner G14	H11 19
Victoria Park Dr. N. G14	H12 19
Victoria Park Dr. S. G11	H11 19
Victoria Park Gdns. N. G11	H12 19
Victoria Park Gdns. S. G11	H12 19
Victoria Park La. N. G14	H11 19
Victoria Park La. S. G14	H11 19
Westland Dr.	
Victoria Park St. G14	H11 19
Victoria Rd. G33	G23 25
Victoria Rd. G42	N16 51
Victoria Rd. G73	P19 65
Victoria Rd., Barr.	Q 7 59
Victoria Rd., Lenz.	D23 13
Victoria Rd., Pais.	N 5 46
Victoria St. G73	O19 53
Victoria St., Clyde.	E 8 5
Victory Dr., Kilb.	M07 42
Glentyan Av.	
Viewbank, Thorn.	Q13 62
Viewfield Av., Bail.	L24 39
Viewfield Av., Bish.	F18 22
Viewfield Av., Blan.	R27 69
Viewfield Av., Lenz.	C23 13
Viewfield Dr., Bail.	L24 39
Viewfield Dr., Bish.	F18 22
Viewfield La., G12	J15 35
Gibson St.	
Viewfield Rd., Bish.	F18 22
Viewfield Rd., Coat.	M28 57
Viewfield Ter. G12	J15 35
Southpark Av.	
Viewmount Dr. G20	F14 20
Viewpark Av. G31	K19 37
Viewpark Dr. G73	P19 65
Viewpoint Pl. G21	G18 22
Viewpoint Rd. G21	G18 22
Viking Way, Renf.	J 8 31
Vanguard Way	
Villafield Av., Bish.	D19 11
Villafield Dr., Bish.	D19 11
Villafield Loan, Bish.	D19 11
Village Rd. G72	P24 67
Villiers Ct. G31	L18 36
Sword St.	
Vine St. G3	J13 34
Vinegarhill St. G31	L19 37
Vinicombe La. G12	H14 20
Vinicombe St.	
Vinicombe St. G12	H14 20
Vintner St. G4	J17 36
Violet St., Pais.	M 7 47
Virginia Bldgs. G1	K17 36
Virginia St.	
Virginia Ct. G1	K17 36
Virginia St.	
Virginia Pl. G1	K17 36
Virginia St. G1	K17 36
Viscount Av., Renf.	J 8 31
Voil Dr. G44	Q16 63
Vorlich Ct., Barr.	R 8 59
Vulcan St. G21	H18 22
Waddel Ct. G5	L17 36
Waddel St. G5	M17 52
Waldemar Rd. G13	F11 19
Waldo St. G13	F12 19
Walker Ct. G11	J13 34
Walker St.	
Walker Dr., John.	N 1 44
Walker Sq. G20	F14 20
Bantaskin St.	
Walker St. G11	J13 34
Walker St., Pais.	M 5 46
Walkerburn Rd. G52	M10 48
Walkinshaw Cres., Pais.	L 4 29
Ferguslie Park Av.	
Walkinshaw Rd., Renf.	H 5 16
Walkinshaw St. G40	M19 53
Walkinshaw St., John.	M09 43
Walkinshaw Way, Pais.	K 5 30
Broomdyke Way	
Wallace Av., John.	N 2 44
Wallace Pl., Blan.	R27 69
Wallace Rd., Renf.	J 7 31
Wallace St. G5	L16 35
Wallace St. G73	O19 53
Wallace St., Clyde.	F 7 17
Wallace St., Pais.	L 6 30
Wallacewell Cres. G21	G19 23
Wallacewell Pl. G21	G19 23
Wallacewell Quad. G21	G20 23
Wallacewell Rd. G21	G19 23
Wallbrae Rd., Cumb.	D 3 71
Wallneuk Rd., Pais.	L 6 30
Wallneuk, Pais.	L 6 30
Incle St.	
Walls St. G1	K17 36
Walmer Cres. G51	L14 34
Walmer Ter. G51	L14 34
Paisley Rd. W.	
Walnut Cres. G22	G17 22
Walnut Cres., John.	N 1 44
Walnut Dr., Lenz.	C22 12
Walnut Pl. G22	G17 22
Walnut Rd. G22	G17 22
Walter St. G31	K20 37
Walton St. G41	O15 51
Walton St., Barr.	Q 8 59
Wamba Av. G13	F12 19
Wamba Pl. G13	F12 19
Wandilla Av., Clyde.	E 8 5
Wanlock St. G51	K13 34
Warden Rd. G13	F11 19
Wardhill Rd. G21	G19 23
Wardhouse Rd., Pais.	O 5 46
Wardie Path G33	K24 39
Wardie Pl. G33	K25 40
Wardie Rd. G33	K25 40
Wardlaw Av. G73	O19 53
Wardlaw Dr. G73	O19 53
Wardlaw Rd., Bear.	E12 7
Wardpark Rd., Cumb.	A 4 71
Wardrop St. G51	K13 34
Wardrop St., Pais.	M 6 46
Ware Path G33	K25 40
Ware Rd. G33	K24 39
Warilda Av., Clyde.	E 8 5
Warp La. G3	K15 35
Argyle St.	
Warren St. G42	N16 51
Warrington St. G20	G15 21
Warriston Cres. G33	K20 37
Warriston Pl. G32	K22 38
Warriston St. G33	K20 37
Warroch St. G3	K15 35
Washington Rd., Renf.	K 6 30
Washington St. G3	K16 35
Water Brae, Pais.	L 6 30
Smithhills St.	
Water Brae, Pais.	M 6 46
Forbes Pl.	
Water Rd., Barr.	Q 8 59
Waterfoot Av. G53	O11 49
Waterford Rd., Giff.	Q13 62
Waterloo La. G2	K16 35
Waterloo St.	
Waterloo St. G2	K16 35
Watermill Av., Lenz.	D23 13
Waterside La., Kilb.	N08 43
Kilbarchan Rd.	
Waterside St. G5	M17 52
Waterside Ter., Kilb.	N08 43
Kilbarchan Rd.	
Watling St., Udd.	O27 57
Watson Av. G73	O18 52
Watson Av., Linw.	L 1 28
Watson St., G1	L17 36
Watson St., Udd.	P27 69
Watt Low Av. G73	P19 65
Watt Rd. G52	K 9 32
Watt St. G5	L15 35
Waukglen Dr. G53	Q10 60
Waukglen Path G53	Q10 60
Waulkmill Av., Barr.	Q 8 59
Waulkmill St., Thorn.	Q12 61
Waverley Cres., Cumb.	D 1 70
Waverley Ct., Udd.	R28 69
Waverley Dr. G73	O20 53
Waverley Gdns. G41	N15 51
Waverley Gdns., Pais.	N 2 44
Waverley Rd., Pais.	O 3 45
Waverley St. G41	N15 51
Waverley Ter. G31	L19 37
Whitevale St.	
Waverley Way, Pais.	O 3 45
Waverley Rd.	
Waverley, Clyde.	E 8 5
Onslow Rd.	
Weardale La. G33	K23 39
Weardale St. G33	K23 39
Weaver La., Kilb.	M07 42
Glentyan Av.	
Weaver St. G4	K17 36
Weaver Ter., Pais.	M 7 47
Weavers Av., Pais.	M 4 45
Weavers Rd., Pais.	M 4 45
Webster St. G40	M19 53
Webster St., Clyde.	F 9 18
Wedderlea Dr. G52	L10 32
Weensmoor Pl. G53	Q10 60
Weensmoor Rd. G53	P10 60
Weeple Dr., Linw.	L 1 28
Weighhouse Clo., Pais.	M 5 46
Weir Av., Barr.	R 8 59
Weir Rd., Linw.	K 1 28
Weir St. G5	L16 35
Weir St., Pais.	L 6 30
Weirwood Av., Bail.	M24 55
Weirwood Gdns., Bail.	M24 55
Welbeck Rd. G53	P10 60
Welfare Av. G72	Q23 67
Well Grn. G43	O14 50
Well Rd., Kilb.	M07 42
Well St. G40	L18 36
Well St., Pais.	L 5 30
Wellbank Pl., Udd.	P27 69
Church St.	
Wellbrae Ter., Chr.	E27 15
Wellcroft Pl. G5	M16 51
Wellfield Av., Giff.	Q13 62
Wellfield St. G21	H18 22
Wellhouse Cres. G33	K24 39
Wellhouse Path G33	K24 39
Wellhouse Rd. G33	K24 39
Wellington La. G2	K16 35
West Campbell St.	
Wellington Pl., Dalm.	D 5 4
Wellington Rd., Bish.	D20 11
Wellington St. E. G31	L20 37
Wellington St. G2	K16 35
Wellington St., Pais.	L 5 30
Calendonia St.	
Wellington Way, Renf.	J 8 31
Tiree Av.	
Wellmeadow Rd. G43	P13 62
Wellmeadow St., Pais.	M 5 46
Wellpark G31	K18 36
Wellpark St. G31	K18 36
Wells St., Clyde.	D 6 4
Wellshot Dr. G72	P21 66
Wellshot Rd. G32	M21 54
Wellside Dr. G72	Q23 67
Wemyss Gdns., Bail.	M25 56
Wendur Way, Pais.	K 5 30
Abbotsburn Way	
Wenloch Rd., Pais.	N 6 46
Wentworth Dr. G23	E15 9
West Av. G33	G23 25
West Av., Renf.	H 8 17
West Av., Udd.	P28 69
West Brae, Pais.	M 5 46
West Campbell St. G2	K16 35
West Campbell St., Pais.	M 4 45
West Chapelton Av., Bear.	D12 7
West Chapelton Cres., Bear.	D12 7
West Chapelton Dr., Bear.	D12 7
West Chapelton La., Bear.	D12 7
West Chapelton Av.	
West Coats Rd. G72	Q21 66
West Cotts., Gart.	H25 26
West Ct., Dalm.	D 6 4
Little Holm	
West Duntiblae Rd., Lenz.	B25 14
West George La. G2	K16 35
West George St.	
West George St. G32	K16 35
West Graham St. G4	J16 35

Street	Ref		Street	Ref		Street	Ref
West Greenhill Pl. G3	K15 35		Westmuir Pl. G73	O18 52		Wilkie Rd., Udd.	P28 69
West La., Pais.	M 4 45		Westmuir St. G31	L20 37		Wilkie St. G31	L19 37
West Lodge Rd., Renf.	H 7 17		Westpark Dr., Pais.	L 4 29		William St. G2	K16 35
West Nile St. G2	K16 35		Westray Circus G22	G17 22		William St., Clyde.	C 7 5
West Princes St. G4	J15 35		Westray Ct., Cumb.	D 2 70		William St., John.	M09 43
West Regent La. G2	K16 35		Westray Pl. G22	F17 22		William St., Pais.	M 5 46
Renfield St.			Westray Pl., Bish.	E20 11		Williamson Park W. G44	R15 63
West Regent St. G2	K16 35		*Ronaldsay Dr.*			Williamson Pl., John.	N 1 44
West St. G5	L16 35		Westray Rd., Cumb.	D 2 70		Williamson St. G31	M20 53
West St. G5	M16 51		Westray Sq. G22	F17 22		Williamson St., Clyde.	D 7 5
West St., Clyde.	F 9 18		Westray St. G22	F17 22		Williamwood Dr. G44	R15 63
West St., Kilb.	M07 42		Westwood Av., Giff.	Q13 62		Williamwood Pk. G44	R15 63
West St., Pais.	M 5 46		Westwood Quad., Clyde.	E 8 5		Willoughby Dr. G13	G12 19
West Thomson St.,	D 7 5		Westwood Rd. G43	P13 62		Willow Av., Bish.	F19 23
Clyde.			Weymouth Dr. G12	G13 20		Willow Av., John.	N 2 44
West Whitby St. G31	M20 53		Whamflet Av., Bail.	K26 40		*Hillview Rd.*	
Westbank La. G12	J15 35		Wheatfield Rd., Bear.	E11 7		Willow Av., Lenz.	C23 13
Gibson St.			Wheatlands Dr., Kilb.	M07 42		Willow Dr., Blan.	S26 68
Westbank Quad. G12	J15 35		Wheatlands Farm Rd.,	M07 42		Willow Dr., John.	N09 43
Gibson St.			Kilb.			Willow St. G13	F12 19
Westbank Ter. G12	J15 35		Whin Dr., Barr.	Q 7 59		Willowbank Cres. G3	J15 35
Gibson St.			Whin St., Clyde.	D 7 5		Willowbank St. G3	J15 35
Westbourne Cres., Bear.	C11 7		Whinfield Path G53	Q10 60		Willowdale Cres., Bail.	M25 56
Westbourne Dr., Bear.	C11 7		Whinfield Rd. G53	Q10 60		Willowdale Gdns., Bail.	M25 56
Westbourne Gdns. La.	H14 20		Whinfold Av. G72	O21 54		Willowford Rd. G53	Q 9 60
G12			Whinhill Rd. G53	M10 48		Wilmot Rd. G13	G11 19
Lorraine Rd.			Whinhill Rd., Pais.	N 7 47		Wilson Av., Linw.	L 1 28
Westbourne Gdns. N.	H14 20		Whins Rd. G41	N14 50		Wilson St. G1	K17 36
G12			Whirlow Gdns., Bail.	L25 40		Wilson St., Pais.	M 5 46
Westbourne Gdns. S.	H14 20		Whirlow Rd., Bail.	L25 40		*William St.*	
G12			Whistlefield, Bear.	D12 7		Wilson St., Renf.	H 8 17
Westbourne Gdns. W.	H14 20		Whitacres Path G53	Q10 60		Wilsons Pl., Pais.	M 6 46
G12			Whitacres Pl. G53	Q10 60		*Seedhill*	
Westbourne Rd. G12	H13 20		Whitacres Rd. G53	Q10 60		Wilton Cres. G20	H15 21
Westbourne Ter. La.	H13 20		Whitburn St. G32	K21 38		Wilton Crescent La. G20	H15 21
G12			White St. G11	J13 34		*Wilton Cres.*	
Westbourne Rd.			White St., Clyde.	F 8 17		Wilton Ct. G20	H15 21
Westbrae Dr. G14	H12 19		Whitecraigs Pl. G23	F15 21		Wilton Dr. G20	H15 21
Westburn	P24 67		Whitefield Av. G72	Q22 66		Wilton Gdns. G20	H15 21
Westburn Av. G72	P23 67		Whitefield Rd. G51	L14 34		Wilton Mansions G20	H15 21
Westburn Av., Pais.	L 4 29		Whiteford Rd., Pais.	N 7 47		*Wilton St.*	
Westburn Cres. G73	O18 52		Whitehall Ct. G3	K15 35		Wilton St. G20	H15 21
Westburn Dr. G72	P22 66		Whitehall St. G3	K15 35		Wiltonburn Path G53	Q10 60
Westburn Farm Rd. G72	P22 66		Whitehaugh Av., Pais.	L 7 31		Wiltonburn Rd. G53	Q10 60
Westburn Rd. G72	P25 68		Whitehaugh Cres. G53	Q10 60		Wilverton Rd. G13	F12 19
Westclyffe St. G41	N15 51		Whitehaugh Dr., Pais.	L 7 31		Winchester Dr. G12	G13 20
Westend Park St. G3	J15 35		Whitehaugh Path G53	Q10 60		Windhill Pl. G43	P14 62
Westend, Bear.	E13 8		Whitehaugh Rd. G53	Q10 60		*Windhill Rd.*	
Maryhill Rd.			Whitehill Av., Cumb.	C 1 70		Windhill Rd. G43	P13 62
Wester Cleddens Rd.,	E19 11		Whitehill Av., G33	G23 25		Windlaw Ct. G45	R17 64
Bish.			Whitehill Farm Rd. G33	G23 25		Windlaw Gdns. G44	Q15 63
Wester Common Dr.	H16 21		Whitehill Gdns. G31	K19 37		Windlaw Park Gdns.	Q15 63
G22			*Garthland Dr.*			G44	
Wester Common Rd.	H16 21		Whitehill La., Bear.	D11 7		Windmill Cres. G43	P13 62
G22			*Whitehill Rd.*			*Windhill Rd.*	
Wester Common Ter.	H16 21		Whitehill Rd. G33	F23 25		Windmill Pl. G43	P14 62
G22			Whitehill Rd., Bear.	C11 7		*Windhill Rd.*	
Wester Rd. G32	M23 55		Whitehill St. G31	K19 37		Windmillcroft Quay G5	L16 35
Westerburn St. G32	K21 38		Whitehurst, Bear.	C11 7		Windsor Cres., Clyde.	D 7 5
Carntynehall Rd.			Whitekirk Pl. G15	E10 6		Windsor Cres., John.	N 1 44
Westercraigs G31	K18 36		Whitelaw St. G20	F14 20		Windsor Cres., Pais.	L 7 31
Westergreens Av., Lenz.	C23 13		Whitelawburn Av. G72	Q21 66		Windsor Rd., Renf.	J 8 31
Parkburn Av.			Whitelawburn Rd. G72	Q21 66		Windsor St. G20	J16 35
Westerhill Rd., Bish.	D19 11		Whitelawburn Ter. G72	Q21 66		Windsor St. G32	L23 39
Westerhill St. G22	H17 22		Whitelaws Loan, Both.	Q28 69		Windsor Ter. G20	J16 35
Westerhouse Rd. G34	J25 40		Whiteloans, Udd.	Q28 69		Windsor Wk., Udd.	O28 57
Westerkirk Dr. G23	E15 9		*Wordsworth Way*			Windyedge Cres. G13	G11 19
Western Av. G73	O18 52		Whitemoss Av. G44	Q15 63		Windyedge Pl. G13	G11 19
Western Rd. G72	Q21 66		Whitestone Av., Cumb.	B 1 70		Wingfield Gdns., Both.	R28 69
Westerton Av., Bear.	F12 19		*Dungoil Av.*			*Blairston Av.*	
Westfield Av. G73	O18 52		Whitevale St. G31	L19 37		Winifred St. G33	H20 23
Westfield Cres., Bear.	E12 7		Whithope Rd. G53	Q 9 60		Winning Ct., Blan.	R27 69
Westfield Dr. G52	L10 32		Whithope Ter. G53	Q 9 60		*Ness Dr.*	
Westfield Dr., Bear.	E12 7		Whitriggs Rd. G53	P 9 60		Winning Row G31	L21 38
Westfield Rd., Thorn.	R12 61		Whitslade St. G34	J25 40		Winton Av., Giff.	R14 62
Westfield Villas G73	O18 52		Whittingehame Dr. G12	G12 19		Winton Dr. G12	G14 20
Westfields, Bish.	D18 10		Whittingehame Gdns.	G13 20		Winton Gdns., Udd.	O27 57
Westhouse Av. G73	O18 52		G12			Winton La. G12	G14 20
Westhouse Gdns. G73	O18 52		Whittliemuir Av. G44	Q15 63		Wirran Pl. G13	F 9 18
Westknowe Gdns. G73	P19 65		Whitton Dr., Giff.	Q14 62		Wishart St. G4	K18 36
Westland Dr. G14	H11 19		Whitton St. G20	F14 20		Wisner Ct., Thorn.	Q12 61
Westland Drive La. G14	H11 19		Whitworth Dr., Clyde.	E 7 5		Wiston St. G72	P24 67
Westland Dr.			Whitworth St. G20	G16 21		Woddrop St. G40	N19 53
Westlands Gdns., Pais.	N 5 46		Whyte Av. G72	P21 66		Wolseley St. G5	M17 52
Westlands, Bish.	D18 10		Wick St. G51	K13 34		Wood Farm Rd., Giff.	R13 62
Westminster Gdns. G12	H14 20		Wickets, The, Pais.	M 7 47		Wood La., Bish.	F19 23
Kersland St.			Wigton St. G4	H16 21		Wood Quad., Clyde.	F 9 18
Westminster Ter. G3	K15 35		Wigtoun Pl., Cumb.	B 3 71		Wood St. G31	K19 37
Claremont St.			Wilderness Brae, Cumb.	B 3 71		Wood St., Pais.	M 7 47
Westmoreland St. G42	N16 51		Wilfred Av. G13	F11 19		Woodbank Cres., John.	N09 43

Name	Grid	Page
Woodbank Ter. Gart.	G27	27
Woodburn Av., Blan.	S27	69
Woodburn Rd. G43	P14	62
Woodburn Rd., Cumb.	C 1	70
Woodcroft Av. G11	H12	19
Woodcroft Ter. G11	H12	19
Crow Rd.		
Woodend Ct. G32	N24	55
Woodend Dr. G13	G12	19
Woodend Dr., Pais.	M 8	47
Woodend Gdns. G32	N24	55
Woodend Pl., John.	N 1	44
Malloch Cres.		
Woodend Rd. G32	N23	55
Woodend Rd. G73	Q19	65
Woodend, Giff.	R13	62
Milverton Rd.		
Woodfield Av., Bish.	E19	11
Woodfoot Path G53	Q10	60
Woodfoot Pl. G53	Q10	60
Woodfoot Quad. G53	Q10	60
Woodford Pl. G53	Q10	60
Woodford Pl., Linw.	L 1	28
Woodford St. G41	O15	51
Woodgreen Av. G44	P17	64
Woodhall St. G40	N19	53
Woodhead Av. G71	R28	69
Old Bothwell Rd.		
Woodhead Cres., Both.	S28	69
Woodhead Cres., Udd.	O27	57
Woodhead Path G53	P10	60
Woodhead Rd. G53	P 9	60
Woodhead Rd., Chr.	G25	26
Woodhead Ter., Chr.	F25	26
Woodhill Rd. G21	G19	23
Woodhill Rd., Bish.	E19	11
Woodholm Av. G44	P17	64
Woodhouse St. G13	F12	19
Woodilee Cotts., Lenz.	C24	13
Woodilee Rd., Lenz.	C24	13
Woodland Av., Gart.	F27	27
Woodland Av., Pais.	O 6	46
Woodland Cres. G72	Q22	66
Woodland Vw., Cumb.	B 3	71
Braehead Rd.		
Woodland Way, Cumb.	B 3	71
Woodlands Av., Both.	Q28	69
Woodlands Cres., Both.	Q28	69
Woodlands Cres., Thorn.	Q12	61
Woodlands Dr. G4	J15	35
Woodlands Gate G3	J15	35
Woodlands Gate, Thorn.	Q12	61
Woodlands Gdns., Udd.	Q27	69
Woodlands Pk., Thorn.	R12	61
Woodlands Rd. G3	J15	35
Woodlands Rd., Thorn.	R12	61
Woodlands Ter. G3	J15	35
Woodlands Ter., Both.	Q28	69
Woodlea Dr., Giff.	Q14	62
Woodlinn Av. G44	P16	63
Woodneuk Av., Gart.	G28	27
Woodneuk Rd. G53	P10	60
Woodneuk Rd., Gart.	G27	27
Woodrow Circus G41	M14	50
Woodrow Pl. G41	M14	50
Maxwell Dr.		
Woodrow Rd. G41	M14	50
Woods La., Renf.	H 8	17
Woodside Av. G73	O20	53
Woodside Av., Lenz.	C23	13
Woodside Av., Thorn.	Q13	62
Woodside Cres. G3	J15	35
Woodside Cres., Barr.	R 8	59
Woodside Cres., Pais.	M 5	46
William St.		
Woodside Pl. G3	J15	35
Woodside Place La. G3	J15	35
Elderslie St.		
Woodside Rd. G20	H15	21
Woodside Ter. G3	J15	35
Woodside Ter., Bish.	D17	10
Woodside Terrace La. G3	J15	35
Woodlands Rd.		
Woodstock Av. G41	N14	50
Woodstock Av., Pais.	O 3	45
Woodvale Av., Bear.	E13	8
Woodvale Av., Giff.	S13	62
Woodvale Dr., Pais.	L 4	29
Woodville St. G5	L13	34
Wordsworth Way, Udd.	Q28	69
Works Av. G72	P24	67
Wraes Av., Barr.	Q 8	59
Wren Pl., John.	O08	43
Wright Av., Barr.	R 7	59
Wright St. G4	K18	36
Wright St., Renf.	J 7	31
Wrightlands Cres., Renf.	F 6	16
Wykeham Pl. G13	G11	19
Wykeham Rd. G13	G11	19
Wynd, The, Cumb.	A 3	71
Wyndford Dr. G20	G14	20
Wyndford Pl. G20	G14	20
Wyndford Rd.		
Wyndford Rd. G20	G14	20
Wyndham St. G12	H14	20
Wynford Ter., Udd.	O28	57
Wyper Pl. G40	L19	37
Gallowgate		
Wyvil Av. G13	E12	7
Wyvis Av. G13	F 9	18
Wyvis Pl. G13	F 9	18
Wyvis Quad. G13	F 9	18
Yair Dr. G52	L10	32
Yarrow Ct., Cumb.	P23	67
Yarrow Gdns. G20	H15	21
Yarrow Rd., Bish.	D19	11
Yate St. G31	L19	37
Yetholm St. G14	G 9	18
Yew Pl., John.	N 1	44
Yoker Ferry Rd. G14	G 9	18
Yoker Mill Gdns. G13	F 9	18
Yoker Mill Rd. G13	F 9	18
Yokerburn Ter., Clyde.	F 8	17
York Dr. G73	P20	65
York La. G2	K16	35
York St.		
York St. G2	L16	35
York St., Clyde.	E 8	5
York Way, Renf.	J 8	31
Yorkhill La. G3	K14	34
Yorkhill St.		
Yorkhill Par. G3	J14	34
Yorkhill St. G3	K14	34
Young St., Clyde.	D 7	5
Young Ter. G21	H19	23
Zambesi Dr., Blan.	R26	68
Zena Cres. G33	H20	23
Zena Pl. G33	H20	23
Zena St. G33	H20	23
Zetland Rd. G52	K 9	32

ADDENDUM The street names listed below should be added to the main index to street names:

Name	Grid	Page
Aird's La., G1	L17	36
Bridgegate		
Auchengreoch Av., John.	OO8	43
Auchengreoch Rd., John.	OO8	43
Bellshaugh Gdns. G12	G14	20
Bonawe St. G20	H15	21
Broom Path., Bail.	M24	55
Tudor St.		
Bute Rd., Pais.	J 5	30
Church Vw. G72	O22	54
Campsie Dr., Pais.	J 6	30
Cunningham Rd., G73	O18	53
Dalhouse Rd., Udd.	N25	56
Dover St. G3	K14	35
Drumclog Gdns. G33	G21	24
Drysdale St. G14	G 9	18
Duich Gdns. G23	E15	9
Dunalistair Dr. G33	G22	24
Edinburgh Rd. G33	K20	37
Edzell Ct. G14	J11	33
Edzell Pl. G14	J11	33
Foundary St. G21	H18	22
Gallowflat St. G73	O19	53
Reid St.		
Gartartan Rd., Pais.	L 9	32
Katrine Pl. G72	P22	66
Kelso Pl. G14	G 9	18
Kilkerran Dr. G33	G21	24
Kincaid Gdns. G72	P22	66
Lauder Dr. G73	P20	65
Laurieston Rd. G5	L17	36
Letterfearn Dr. G23	E15	9
Lloyd St. G73	N19	53
Lockerbie Av. G43	P15	63
Manse Av., Both.	R28	69
Marine Gdns. G51	L15	35
Mansionhouse Rd. G41	O15	51
Mavisbank Gdns. G51	L15	35
McDonald St. G73	O19	53
Greenhill Rd.		
Melrose Ct. G73	O19	53
Dunard Rd.		
Morriston Park Dr. G72	O22	54
Moss Path., Bail.	M24	55
Castle St.		
Mossvale Rd. G33	J23	39
Newpark Ct. G72	O22	54
Olifard Av., Both.	Q28	69
Orbiston Gdns. G32	L22	38
Balintore St.		
Orion Way G72	P22	66
Parsonage Row G1	K17	36
Parsonage Sq.G1	K17	36
Pinewood Sq. G15	D 9	6
Plantation Pk. Gdns. G51	L14	34
Reuther Av. G73	O19	53
Richmond Gro. G73	O20	53
St. Andrews Dr. W., Pais.	J 5	30
St. Bride's Way, Udd.	Q28	69
Sandyford Pl., G3	K15	35
Shieldbridge Gdns. G23	E15	9
Shiskine Pl. G20	F14	20
Shiskine Dr.		
Speirshall Clo. G14	G 9	18
Speirshall Ter. G14	G 9	18
Springfield Quay G51	L15	35
Thomson Gro. G72	O22	54
Trossachs Ct. G20	H16	21
Trossachs St.		
Victoria Pl. G73	O19	53
Greenbank St.		
Watt Low Av. G73	P18	64
William St. G3	K15	35
Yarrow Gdns. La. G20	H15	21
Yarrow Gdns		

ADDENDUM The street names listed below should be deleted from the main index to street names:

Name	Grid	Page
Auckengreoch Av.,John.	008	43
Auckengreoch Rd.,John.	008	43
Bonawe St. G20	H15	21
Kirkland St.		
Cartartan Rd., Pais.	L 9	32
Cunningham Rd. G73	020	53
Cambuslang Rd		
Drumclog Gdns. G33	G21	24
Auchinleck Av.		
Dunalistair Av. G33	G22	24
Edzell Pl. G14	J11	3
Edzell St.		
Ennerdale St. G32	L21	38
Gallowflat St G73	019	53
General Terminus Quay G51	L15	35
India St. G73	019	53
Langholm St. G14	G 9	18
Lauder Dr. G73	020	53
Locherbie Av. G43	P15	63
Mause Av., Both.	R28	69
Mossvale Rd. G33	H22	24
Olifard Av., Udd.	Q28	69
Peebles Dr. G73	P20	65
St. Bride's Way, Both.	Q28	69
Sandiefield Rd., G5	M17	52
Sandyford St. G3	K15	35
Sauchiehall St.		
Spiers Clo. G14	G 9	18
Spiers Ter. G14	G 9	18
Watt Low Av. G73	P19	65

Personal Information

Name	Address	Tel. No.	Notes
	Post Code		
	Post Code		
	Post Code		
	Post Code		
	Post Code		
	Post Code		
	Post Code		
	Post Code		
	Post Code		
	Post Code		

Personal Information

Name	Address	Tel. No.	Notes

| | Post Code | | |

| | Post Code | | |

| | Post Code | | |

| | Post Code | | |

| | Post Code | | |

| | Post Code | | |

| | Post Code | | |

| | Post Code | | |

| | Post Code | | |

| | Post Code | | |

Personal Information

Name	Address	Tel. No.	Notes
	Post Code		
	Post Code		
	Post Code		
	Post Code		
	Post Code		
	Post Code		
	Post Code		
	Post Code		
	Post Code		
	Post Code		